THE MISHNAH
RELIGIOUS PERSPECTIVES

THE MISHNAH

Religious Perspectives

BY

JACOB NEUSNER

BRILL ACADEMIC PUBLISHERS, INC.
BOSTON • LEIDEN
2002

Library of Congress Cataloging-in-Publication Data

Neusner, Jacob, 1932–
    The Mishnah : religious perspectives / by Jacob Neusner.
      p. cm.
    Originally published: Leiden : Boston : Brill, 1999. Handbuch der
  Orientalistik. Erste Abteilung, Der Nahe und Mittlere Osten ; 45. Bd.
    Includes bibliographical references and index.
    ISBN 0–391–04160–6
      1. Mishnah—Criticism, interpretation, etc. 2. Judaism—History—Talmudic
  period, 10–425. I. Title.

BM497.8 .N478384 2002
296.1'2306—dc21

                                                                2001056691

ISBN 0–391–04160–6

© Copyright 1999 by Koninklijke Brill NV, Leiden, The Netherlands

All rights reserved. No part of this publication may be reproduced, translated, stored in
a retrieval system, or transmitted in any form or by any means, electronic,
mechanical, photocopying, recording or otherwise, without prior written
permission from the publisher.

Authorization to photocopy items for internal or personal
use is granted by Brill provided that
the appropriate fees are paid directly to The Copyright
Clearance Center, 222 Rosewood Drive, Suite 910
Danvers MA 01923, USA.
Fees are subject to change.

PRINTED IN THE UNITED STATES OF AMERICA

TABLE OF CONTENTS

PREFACE

With its twin, *The Mishnah: Social Perspectives. Philosophy, Economics, Politics*, this book completes the condensation and recapitulation of large-scale research of mine. I now turn to research precipitated by questions of religion, encompassing the social history of ideas and the religious uses of language. The first question of religion concerns the relationship of the Mishnah to Scripture. The second takes up the relationship of the religious ideas people hold to the world in which they live. The third addresses the religious meaning of the formalization of language that characterizes the Mishnah in particular.

The religious perspectives on the Mishnah direct our attention to three questions. First, how does the Mishnah relate to Scripture, or, in the (later) mythic language of Rabbinic Judaism, "the oral Torah" to "the written Torah"? That question until now has elicited generalizations and episodic cases; here I provide a complete analysis, based on a systematic application of a single taxonomic program. Second, are we able to relate the stages in the unfolding of the Halakhah of the Mishnah to the principal events of the times, which delineate those stages? The question focuses on the pre-70 components of the Halakhah that later comes to the surface in the Mishnah, but extends to the periods from the destruction of the Temple in 70 to the Bar Kokhba War, concluded in ca. 135, then from the reconstruction, 135, to the closure of the Mishnah, 200 C.E. Third, how are we able to interpret the rhetorical forms of the Mishnah in the context of the social culture adumbrated by the documents sociolinguistics?

In these pages I provide a précis of parts of a number of completed pieces of research. The monographs summarized in the first chapter are these:

> *Scripture and the Generative Premises of the Halakhah. A Systematic Inquiry.* I.. *Halakhah Based Principally on Scripture and Halakhic Categories Autonomous of Scripture.* Atlanta, 1999: Scholars Press for South Florida Studies in the History of Judaism.

> *Scripture and the Generative Premises of the Halakhah. A Systematic Inquiry.* II. *Scripture's Topics Derivatively Amplified in the Halakhah.* Atlanta, 1999: Scholars Press for South Florida Studies in the History of Judaism.

Scripture and the Generative Premises of the Halakhah. A Systematic Inquiry. III. *Scripture's Topics Independently Developed in the Halakhah. From the Babas through Miqvaot.* Atlanta, 1999: Scholars Press for South Florida Studies in the History of Judaism.

Scripture and the Generative Premises of the Halakhah. A Systematic Inquiry. IV. *Scripture's Topics Independently Developed in the Halakhah. From Moed Qatan through Zebahim.* Atlanta, 1999: Scholars Press for South Florida Studies in the History of Judaism.

The Four Stages of Rabbinic Judaism. London, 2000: Routledge.

From Scripture to 70. The Pre-Rabbinic Beginnings of the Halakhah. Atlanta, 1999: Scholars Press for South Florida Studies in the History of Judaism.

What, Exactly, Did the Rabbinic Sages Mean by "the Oral Torah"? An Inductive Answer to the Question of Rabbinic Judaism. Atlanta, 2000: Scholars Press for South Florida Studies in the History of Judaism.

The second chapter abbreviates some of the findings of the following works:

A History of the Mishnaic Law of Purities. Leiden, 1974-1977: Brill. I-XXII.

I.	*Kelim. Chapters One through Eleven.* 1974.
II.	*Kelim. Chapters Twelve through Thirty.* 1974.
III.	*Kelim. Literary and Historical Problems.* 1974.
IV.	*Ohalot. Commentary.* 1975.
V.	*Ohalot. Literary and Historical Problems.* 1975.
VI.	*Negaim. Mishnah-Tosefta.* 1975.
VII.	*Negaim. Sifra.* 1975.
VIII.	*Negaim. Literary and Historical Problems.* 1975.
IX.	*Parah. Commentary.* 1976.
X.	*Parah. Literary and Historical Problems.* 1976.
XI.	*Tohorot. Commentary,* 1976.
XII.	*Tohorot. Literary and Historical Problems.* 1976.
XIII.	*Miqvaot. Commentary.* 1976.
XIV.	*Miqvaot. Literary and Historical Problems.* 1976.
XV.	*Niddah. Commentary.* 1976.
XVI.	*Niddah. Literary and Historical Problems.* 1976.
XVII.	*Makhshirin.* 1977.
XVIII.	*Zabim.* 1977.
XIX.	*Tebul Yom. Yadayim.* 1977.
XX.	*Uqsin. Cumulative Index, Parts I-XX.* 1977.

A History of the Mishnaic Law of Holy Things. Leiden, Brill: 1979. I-VI.

I.	*Zebahim. Translation and Explanation.*
II.	*Menahot. Translation and Explanation.*
III.	*Hullin, Bekhorot. Translation and Explanation.*
IV.	*Arakhin, Temurah. Translation and Explanation.*
V.	*Keritot, Meilah, Tamid, Middot, Qinnim. Translation and Explanation.*

A History of the Mishnaic Law of Women. Leiden, Brill: 1979-1980. I-V.
    I.   *Yebamot. Translation and Explanation.*
    II.   *Ketubot. Translation and Explanation.*
    III. *Nedarim, Nazir. Translation and Explanation.*
    IV. *Sotah, Gittin, Qiddushin. Translation and Explanation.*
A History of the Mishnaic Law of Appointed Times. Leiden, Brill: 1981-1983. I-V.
    I.   *Shabbat. Translation and Explanation.*
    II.   *Erubin, Pesahim. Translation and Explanation.*
    III. *Sheqalim, Yoma, Sukkah. Translation and Explanation.*
    IV. *Besah, Rosh Hashanah, Taanit, Megillah, Moed Qatan, Hagigah. Translation and Explanation.*
A History of the Mishnaic Law of Damages. Leiden, Brill: 1983-1985. I-V.
    I.   *Baba Qamma. Translation and Explanation.*
    II.   *Baba Mesia. Translation and Explanation.*
    III. *Baba Batra, Sanhedrin, Makkot. Translation and Explanation.*
    IV. *Shebuot, Eduyyot, Abodah Zarah, Abot, Horayyot. Translation and Explanation.*
A History of the Mishnaic Law of Purities. Leiden, 1977: Brill. XXII. *The Mishnaic System of Uncleanness. Its Context and History.*
The Mishnah before 70. Atlanta, 1987: Scholars Press for Brown Judaic Studies. [Reprise of pertinent results of *A History of the Mishnah Law of Purities* Vols. III, V, VIII, X, XII, XIV, XVI, XVII, and XVIII.]
A History of the Mishnaic Law of Holy Things. Leiden, 1979: Brill. VI. *The Mishnaic System of Sacrifice and Sanctuary.*
A History of the Mishnaic Law of Women. Leiden, 1980: Brill. V. *The Mishnaic System of Women.*
A History of the Mishnaic Law of Appointed Times. Leiden, 1981: Brill. V. *The Mishnaic System of Appointed Times.*
A History of the Mishnaic Law of Damages. Leiden, 1985: Brill. V. *The Mishnaic System of Damages*
Judaism. The Evidence of the Mishnah. Chicago, 1981: University of Chicago Press. Paperback edition: 1984. Second printing, 1985. Third printing, 1986. Second edition, augmented: Atlanta, 1987: Scholars Press for Brown Judaic Studies. = *Hayyahadut le'edut hammishnah.* Hebrew translation of *Judaism. The Evidence of the Mishnah.* Tel Aviv, 1987: Sifriat Poalim. = *Il Giudaismo nella testimonianza della Mishnah.* Italian translation by Giorgio Volpe. Bologna, 1995: Centro editoriale Dehoniane.

The third chapter revises the concluding chapter of the following item:

A History of the Mishnaic Law of Purities. Leiden, 1977: Brill. XXI. *The Redaction and Formulation of the Order of Purities in the Mishnah and Tosefta.*

Once more it is my pleasure to express thanks to my editor at Brill, Drs. Elisabeth Venekamp, who has encouraged me in this project; to the University of South Florida and to Bard College, who make possible my career in scholarship; and to those whom I consulted in executing this project, in particular Professor & Dean William Scott Green, University of Rochester.

Jacob Neusner
University of South Florida & Bard College

CHAPTER ONE

THE MISHNAH AND SCRIPTURE

The norm-setting or Halakhic part of Rabbinic Judaism's Oral Torah—the Mishnah to begin with—translates the Written Torah's—
the Pentateuch's—narratives into exemplary cases, turns the cases
into series—that is, rules—and transforms the rules into governing,
abstract principles. The formulation as abstractions of principles out
of rules, and rules out of cases turns the entire Halakhic corpus of the
Pentateuch from diverse, inert information into a working system.
The consequent "one whole Torah," oral and written, read as a
single, coherent statement, finds itself able to absorb and reconstitute
a nearly-unlimited variety of discrete and incongruous cases and
shape the social order anywhere Israel makes its life. These the system forms into a single set of coherent principles, an account of the
social order and its theological foundations. It follows that the Oral
Torah and the Written Torah form a single, coherent statement—
"one whole Torah," in the language of Rabbinic Judaism—each
stating the same message as the other, but the Written one in particu-
lars of stories and cases, the other in generalizations and rules. The
Oral Torah then identifies the moral of the stories of the Written
Torah and recasts that moral into social norms, and the Oral Torah
further translates Scripture's cases into governing rules yielding uniform procedures and regulations.

I. *Category-Formations of the Halakhah Wholly Framed by the Written Torah*

How are we to analyze the traits of the Oral Torah viewed as a
cogent phenomenon, without regard to the sequence or stages in its
unfolding? It is through a labor of comparison and contrast with the
correlative part of the Torah, the Written part. When we bring the
Halakhah into alignment with Scripture and identify those Halakhic
category-formations that simply recapitulate and refine, without con-
tributing more than mere amplification or extension, the Halakhic
statements of Scripture, we narrow the limits of what the Oral Torah
(in theory at least) can have contributed. In those recapitulative and

subordinate category-formations, we find ourselves wholly within the framework of the ideas systematically spelled out of the Written Torah and articulated within the theoretical, or theological, framework of the Written Torah's presentation thereof. Seven category-formations of the repertoire of the Halakhah find their definition, their generative problematic, their facts and their program of exposition wholly within Scripture's presentation of the same topics: Horayot, Negaim, Pesahim, Shebuot, Sotah, Sukkah, and Yoma. In these cases I find nothing in the Halakhah that contributes other than a derivative refinement of Scripture's own facts within Scripture's own hermeneutics for the topic at hand.[1] Stating matters more simply: Moses[2] identifies the topic in writing, and in accord with his own program for that topic Moses expounds the subject wholly in writing, and nothing in the record of the Oral Torah diverges or innovates in any way. As we shall see, an opposite set of category-formations simply possesses no counterpart in Scripture. Here whatever Moses wished to say about the subjects at hand he set forth solely within the framework of the Oral Torah. The former tells us nothing that is particular to the Oral Torah, the latter, only what is distinctive thereto.

I hasten to add, that a category-formation finds full articulation within the presentation in the Written Torah does not mean the sages of the Oral Torah made no contribution in their exposition of the category-formations defined and delineated by Moses in the Written Torah. At every point the way sages present the same topic encompasses important observations, formulations of not only clarification but original insight. The way in which sages combine subsets

---

[1] To Halakhic statements of the Mishnah and the Tosefta, the Tosefta and two Talmuds systematically supply proof-texts for Halakhic propositions of the Mishnah and (in lesser measure) the Tosefta itself. So too do the so-called Tannaite Midrashim, particularly Sifré to Numbers, Sifré to Deuteronomy, and Sifra. The implicit theory is, the Halakhah of the Oral Torah depends upon and requires the justification of the Written Torah. Were the Oral Torah to constitute principally an amplification and clarification of the Written one, as it is sometimes alleged to be, then the entire category-formation of the Halakhah of the Mishnah-Tosefta-Yerushalmi-Bavli, like that of the Tannaite Midrashim as they now are [!], would simply replicate that of the Written Torah. But, as we see in Chapter Three, that is simply not the case, and the problem of inductive inquiry into what the Oral Torah can have contained therefore becomes necessary.

[2] I frame the matter within the language of the religion under study, to which, in the phenomenological-analytical framework at hand, critical history is not relevant. I see nothing to be gained by speaking of "Moses" in quotation-marks, when I mean, the Pentateuch read whole and complete, start to finish, exactly as the framers of Rabbinic Judaism received and read (that part of) the Torah.

of a given category-formation, their introduction of an intersecting topic so as to shed light on the established one, their juxtapositions and points of reorganization and systematization—these all imprint the pattern of the sages' own intellect upon the heritage of the Written Torah. But while sages may and do say something new, in the present set of category-formations it is never fundamental and definitive. From what they say we learn a great deal about their powers of analysis, but let about their capacity for invention.

a. *Horayot*

Companion of tractate Shebuot, which centers on Leviticus Chapters Five and Six, Horayot, resting on Leviticus Chapter Four, deals with collective sin and its atonement. Cultic penalties for official instruction—that of the anointed priest—in error and the consequent sin are specified at Lev. 4:1-5; the entire congregation's doing so, Lev. 4:13-21; Lev. 4:22-26 move on to the ruler. Finally, at Num. 15:22-29, the unwitting sin of the entire community is addressed (the deliberate sin of the entire community, in the case of idolatry, already having been taken up elsewhere). So whether the ruler, the high priest, or the people, all are subject to the sanction invoked by the erroneous ruling of the court, which has caused this unwitting sin. Interstitial issues—did the court and the public act together, did the court issue the ruling while the public carried it out, and the like—are addressed in the Oral Torah's contribution to the Halakhah. The court, the ruler, and the high priest embody the community at large, the body of political institutions that, each in its own realm, bears responsibility for the whole. This tripartite division of political power dictates the organization of the Halakhic exposition before us.

The generative premises of the Halakhah of Horayot derive wholly from Scripture. What sages wished to say through the Halakhah of Horayot is, when it comes to deeds performed in good faith by the individual at the instance of the community and its authorities, the community, not the individual, bears collective guilt, and the individual is atoned for within the offerings of the community at large. That is precisely what Moses says. And to that statement, the Halakhah adds very little. Scripture stresses two facts, [1] unwitting violation of the Torah [2] by a person in a position of responsible authority precipitates the obligation for an offering. Types of offerings are differentiated, a point of no consequence to the

Halakhah. The offering expiates the unwitting sin of the entire community, encompassing individuals. The Halakhah adds to those facts only the logical complement: the error of instruction has to involve a detail of the law, not a principle. If a legal principle is at hand, all are responsible to know what the Torah states explicitly. The tertiary refinements—the community inadvertently, the court deliberately, and so on and so forth—represent standard exegetical initiatives, directed toward sorting out decisions for interstitial cases. Then the Halakhah as we have it rises in easy stages from Scripture, and what the Halakhah contributes to the law of Scripture is only the clarification of the obvious point that, error or no error, people are expected to know what the Torah says in so many words.

b. *Negaim*

The Halakhah of Negaim in the Oral Torah rests upon broad and deep foundations of that in the Written Torah: "Negaim has a vast Scriptural basis but few [orally-grounded] Halakhot...If you are in doubt about anything concerning Negaim, simply search the Torah" (B. Hag. 11a). The Halakhah of Negaim amplifies the law set forth at Leviticus 13. Leviticus 14 proceeds to spell out the purification rite for the person who has recovered from the affliction. The Halakhah is set forth by the Mishnah and the Tosefta in the order and in accord with the program of Leviticus:

Leviticus	*Mishnah-tractate Negaim*
	Colors of bright spots 1:1-4
	Change in the appearance of bright spots, 1:5-6
	Examination of bright spots 2:1-5
	General susceptibility to "plagues" 3:1-2
1. Swelling, eruption, spot Lev. 13:1-8	Skin of the flesh 3:3, 4:1-8:10
2. "Leprosy" Lev. 13:9-17	
3-4. Boil & Burning Lev. 13:18-28	Boil and burning 3:4, 9:1-3
5. Scall (itch) on head or beard Lev. 13:29-37	Scall 3:5, 10:1-9
6. Tetter	
7. Bald spot on forehead & temples Lev. 13:40-44	Bald spot on forehead and temples 3:6, 10:10
8. Leper dwells outside the camp Lev. 13:45-46	
9. Garments Lev. 13:47-59	Garments 3:7, 11:1-12

10. Leprosy on houses Lev. 14:33-53   Leprosy on houses 3:8, 12:1-7,
                                         13:1-12

11. Process of purification Lev. 14:1-32   Purification 14:1-13

The only point of difference in the logical unfolding of the subject comes at Nos. 10-11, where the Mishnah improves upon the Written Torah. It does so by moving leprosy on houses ahead of the process of purification, as a simply logical exposition of the topic—first the uncleanness, then its removal—requires.

The Halakhah contributes some important points of its own, while working over Scripture's rules. But one of the critical points turns out simply to state in Halakhic terms what Scripture says in an Aggadic framework. The single most important point concerns the definition of the nega'-mark that connotes uncleanness. It must be square-shaped. That brings the mark into alignment with the shape imputed to corpse-uncleanness at tractate Ohalot. It passes through a hand-breadth squared. Why must the spot be square-shaped? The answer presents itself when we invoke the analogy of corpse-uncleanness, which also passes through a square-shaped space. But here the space is much smaller, and it may well be diffused through the body. So too the raw flesh must be four sided. The decisive issue is the size and shape of the sign, and whether it grows or diminishes. If the raw flesh loses its four sided character, it ceases to signify uncleanness: the size and shape matter. That is the contribution of the Oral Torah.

So the key is the insistence of the Halakhah on the square shape of the indicator of uncleanness and whether, retaining its proportions, it grows or diminishes to nullity. The uncleanness of *nega'im* is as though the soul were leaking out of little square holes, rather than pouring forth from a large square hole affecting the entire corpse, such as takes place with the uncleanness of the soul that exudes at death. Two white hairs in the bright spot signify the same, and they must be equal in length. The signification of the raw flesh may derive from the decay that takes place after death; that is less certain in my view. What is clear is that the Torah insists that the markings endure for a period of time, a week, matching the week's uncleanness that the corpse causes, and the week of the purification-rite—all correlated with the seven days in which the world was created. Here is a mark that the created world is not functioning in accord with its nature.

Has Scripture contributed the analogy? Explicitly so. When Miriam contracts the ailment under discussion here (Num. 12:11),

Aaron asks Moses, "Let her not be as one dead" (Num. 12:12). The Halakhah then works out the logic of that analogy, and at no point do I discern the working of a system of thought about the topic that does not derive directly from Scripture. For a detailed demonstration of that fact, verse by verse, Halakhah by Halakhah, I refer the reader to Sifra's reading of Leviticus 13-14. Sages there demonstrate beyond any reasonable doubt that the native category, Negaim, simply states in concrete cases yielding abstract rules what Scripture sets forth in concrete cases. For the rest, the Halakhah adds clarifications, amplifications, extensions, and treatment of minor details. When Scripture dictates not only the subject but what is important about the subject, providing not only facts but the premises out of which further facts are generated, the result is Negaim.

c. *Pesahim*

The most important passage is at Ex. 12:1-28. Scripture deals with these topics in order: [1] setting aside and killing a lamb for the Passover (Ex. 12:1-13); [2] unleavened bread and the taboo against leaven and what is leavened, with the festival of unleavened bread (Ex. 12:14-20); and [3] the lamb again (Ex. 12:21-28). Deut. 16:1-8 is explicit that the sacrifice of the Passover lamb is to take place only in Jerusalem. Tractate Pesahim presents the topics in logical order, dealing in two sizable units, first with the prohibition of leaven and other preparations for the festival, and, second, offering the Passover-sacrifice, roasting and eating it. The Halakhah thus focuses upon the cult, even in connection with a rite that is carried out in the home; a third, rather perfunctory unit, Chapter Ten of the Mishnah-tractate, takes up the rite of the seder, the Passover-meal itself. The Halakhah in the present topic takes for granted knowledge of the existence of a Passover-ritual such as is contained in the *Haggadah*. The topical program of the Halakhah addresses only two subjects, leaven and its removal, and the Passover offering. It moves therefore from household to Temple, with the brief appendix of Chapter Ten reverting to the household. Removing leaven from the household aligns the household with the Temple, where baked products served to God do not contain leaven (or sweetening). Requiring the consumption of the Passover offering's meat at home introduces considerations of cultic cleanness. The upshot is, on Passover, the Israelite household, so far as is possible, is treated as analogous to the Temple. Scripture has supplied the facts, the Halakhah has expanded upon them and drawn out what is implicit in them.

The Halakhah of the Oral Torah takes as its program the laws of Scripture and does little more than amplify, extend, and clarify those laws. What makes Israel, and what defines its trait as Israel, so far as the Halakhah is concerned, is two matters: [1] the preparation of the home for the festival through the removal of leaven, which may not be consumed or seen at that time; and [2] the preparation and presentation of the Passover offering and the consumption of its meat in the household. These define the topics of Halakhic interest—and no others pertinent to the festival register. So the celebration of Israel's freedom turns into the transformation of Israel into a kingdom of priests and a holy people, celebrating its birth by recapitulating the blood-rite that marked the separation of Israel from Egypt and the redemption of Israel for life out of death, Israel's firstborn being saved from the judgment visited upon Egypt's. Just as in Scripture's account of matters, that defines the focus of the Halakhah: the act of sanctification unto life that marks, and re-marks every year, the advent of Israel out of the nations. The freedom that is celebrated is freedom from death, as the account of Exodus explicitly states. Passover marks the celebration of Israel's redemption, meaning, its separation from Egypt—the separation being marked off by blood rites on both sides—and its entry into the condition of cleanness so that a Temple offering may be eaten in the very household of the Israelite.

By treating the sacrifice in that intermediate realm—the sacrifice in the Temple, the meat eaten at home—the Halakhah takes account of the requirement of the Written Torah, which read as a harmonious statement dictates that the Passover take place in two locations, the home and the Temple. Dt. 16:1-8 places the rite in the Temple in Jerusalem. It is explicit that only in the Temple is the Passover offering to be sacrificed, and no where else. It is to be boiled and eaten in the same place, not at home, and in the morning the people are to go home. With that statement in hand, we should treat the Passover offering as a Temple rite, as much as the sacrifice for the Day of Atonement is a Temple rite. Then where is the altar in the home? Ex. 12:1-28 treats the offering as a rite for the home, with the blood tossed on the lintel of the house as a mark of an Israelite dwelling. The lintel then serves as the counterpart to the altar. That is where the blood rite takes place, where the blood of the sacrifice is tossed. Here we find as clear a statement as is possible that the Israelite

home compares to the Temple, the lintel to the altar, the abode of
Israel to the abode of God. Why the lintel? It is the gateway, marking
the household apart from the world beyond. Inside the walls of the
Israelite household conditions of genealogical and cultic cleanness
pertain, in a way comparable to the space inside the contained space
of the Temple courtyard. Scripture's presentation of the category of
Passover dictates the shape, structure, and proportions of the
Halakhic treatment of the same subject. Here is a fine example of a
category of the Halakhah that finds not only its topic but its problematic, not only its information but its generative premises, in Scripture.

d. *Shebuot*

In Shebuot, the very topical organization, characteristic of the
Mishnah-Tosefta-Yerushalmi-Bavli, gives way to the principles of
conglomeration that govern in the Written Torah. In Leviticus Moses organizes topics around classes of offerings associated with said
topics. The guilt offering governs at Leviticus 5-6, and the category-
formation, Shebuot, joins two distinct topics only because Shebuot
forms a response to the Written Torah's own topics and mode of
joining said topics. If Scripture dictated the category-formation of the
Halakhah of the Oral Torah, we should expect many more cases in
which topical principles of organization give way to other principles
of construction and composition altogether. A principal occasion for
a guilt-offering is the violation of an oath or transgression against a
bailment. Leviticus 5:1-6 set forth the oath of testimony, the case of
one who in the cult touches what is unclean, and the rash oath; all
bring a guilt-offering. Lev. 6:1-7 proceed to bailments in which a
false oath has been taken. The themes then are [1] oaths of adjura-
tion; [2] imparting uncleanness to the Temple and its Holy Things;
[3] the rash oath; [4] the false claim in connection with bailments.

The facts on which the Halakhah builds derive wholly from Scripture, and even the proportions of the category correspond with those
of the relevant passages of Scripture. The point that the Halakhah
investigates is the state of consciousness of uncleanness involved in
the contamination of the cult. The Halakhah explores the character
of the breach of faith toward God: knowingly, not knowingly—the
issue of intentionality lurks in the background. As to oaths, the
Halakhah finds its dynamic in the differentiation among spells of
awareness, comparable to the spells of knowing or unknown involved

in contaminating the cult. Here too we deal with the assessment of the mental state: the divisibility of a mental condition and the counts on which one is liable therefor. When it comes to the penalties for diverse types of oath, the point of interest derives from inadvertent as distinct from deliberate taking of a false oath. So far as the Halakhah forms more than a systematic presentation of facts but, rather, an inquiry into a problem instantiated by facts, the Halakhah takes as its problem the interplay of consciousness and activity: what did one know when, and with what result? Certainly that point of interest will not have astonished Moses, who formulates the law in such a way that the intentionality of the actor always comes to the fore: someone sins by swearing that he has not testimony to give when he does, and so throughout. Every case set forth by Moses involves a deliberate action, based on firm knowledge of facts and the consequences of one's own intentional deed. That is why someone, guilty in any of these, has the power to confess: he knew just what he was doing and did it anyhow—all the more so the breach of faith in regard to bailments! We may, therefore, conclude that the Halakhah has identified the animating consideration of Scripture's law, which is the deliberate act of deceit of one sort or another, and has recapitulated the character and the results of intended deceit.

e. *Sotah*

The ordeal imposed on the woman accused of unfaithfulness, spelled out in the Written Torah, elicits from the sages of the Oral Torah no searching inquiry. The Halakhah of the Mishnah narrates the rite, and the Tosefta and two Talmuds fill in some minor details. The tractate expands to cover other rites conducted in Hebrew or in other languages as well. The pertinent verses of Scripture are as follows (Num. 5:1-31. The Written Torah appears superficially to have set forth the program of the Oral Torah's Halakhah, but in fact, sages have redefined the entire program of the topic. First of all, the Halakhah takes the ordeal and encases it in juridical procedures, rules of evidence, guidelines meant to protect the woman from needless exposure to the ordeal to begin with. The Halakhah radically revises the entire transaction, when it says, if the husband expresses jealousy by instructing his wife not to speak with a specified person, and the wife spoke with the man, there is no juridical result: she still is permitted to have sexual relations with her husband and is permitted to eat heave-offering. But if she went with him to some private place and remained with him for sufficient time to become unclean, she is prohibited from having sexual relations with her husband and if the husband is a priest, she is prohibited from eating heave-offering. Before the ordeal is invoked, the Oral Torah wants some sort of solid evidence [1] of untoward sexual activity and also [2] of clear action on the part of the wife: at least the possibility, confirmed through a specific case, that adultery has taken place. Scripture leaves everything to the husband's whim, the "spirit of jealousy." So here if the husband gives his statement of jealousy and the wife responds by ignoring the statement, the ordeal does not apply. By her specific action the wife has to indicate the possibility that the husband is right. This is a far cry from Scripture's "spirit of jealousy." For the Written Torah, the ordeal settles all questions. For the Oral Torah, the ordeal takes effect only in carefully defined cases where [1] sufficient evidence exists to invoke the rite, but [2] insufficient evidence to make it unnecessary: well-established doubt, so to speak.

The Halakhah has taken as its problem the provision of justice for the woman accused of infidelity. Scripture's premise, that the ordeal accomplishes the same goal, certainly provides the foundations for the Halakhic structure. But the Halakhah has systematically recast the procedure to provide procedural protections that Scripture does not know. The Halakhah wants solid evidence of what the wife actually has done, specific cases. It further defines the status of marriage, so that if the marital bond is not absolutely beyond flaw, the rite is not pertinent. It also allows for the cancellation of the rite, until God's own involvement is irrevocable, his name having been blotted out. The Halakhah in sum transforms a case of doubt into one of near-certainty. The Aggadic reading of the topic introduces the proposition of divine justice, but the Halakhah, for its part, lays emphasis upon exactly the same matter. In providing for just procedures and a fair outcome, sages identify the principle of the just match of sin and punishment that, to begin with, Scripture clearly contemplates. So far as the Halakhah does more than recapitulate in generalizations the narrative of Numbers 5, it introduces the proposition that God acts justly, and that is the point emphasized at Numbers 5. So the category and its generative premise derive from Scripture.

f. *Sukkah*

Scripture supplies nearly all of the pertinent facts of the Halakhah's presentation of Sukkot, the feast of booths of tabernacles, so Lev. 23:33-43, though leaving to the Oral Torah the work of defining details; Numbers 29:12-38 specifies the offerings on the occasion of the festival of Sukkot, and Deuteronomy 16:13-15 specifies the use of the booth. Deuteronomy assigns the feast to Jerusalem, at the same time arranging for rejoicing in the towns elsewhere. Like Pesahim, Sukkah deals both with the household and with the Temple, in that order. The Halakhah takes as its task the presentation of three topics: [1] Temple rites, [2] home obligations, [3] special media for, and modes of, the celebration of the Festival. First comes the home rite: building the Sukkah; then we consider the media for the celebration, the lulab and etrog; finally we come to the Temple rites in their own terms and context. The highly analytical presentation comes at the beginning, with the matter of the Sukkah itself. There we find the more than merely routine, informative components of the Halakhah. The main point is, the Sukkah must resemble a dwelling, casting a shadow and affording protection from the sun. But it does not shelter from the rain, and a strong wind will knock it over. The upshot is that the Sukkah must derive from man's artifice and intent; it cannot be formed of what is attached to the ground, but must be made of what has grown from the ground, what is insusceptible to uncleanness, and what has been cut down. It must come about through the deliberate action of man, a natural Sukkah being an oxymoron, and it must represent an occasion, not a permanent arrangement, a permanent Sukkah being another oxymoron. The Sukkah-roofing must afford shelter by means of what derives from nature but has been detached from nature; human intervention then is required.

If the Halakhah invokes a single generative premise, one that produces significant rulings, it is the notion that the Sukkah must derive from man's plan and action taken to carry out that plan. The Sukkah cannot be formed of a natural bower, and it also must be made fresh for each year's observance (the sekhakh, or covering, is what counts). The covering must be insusceptible to uncleanness, therefore what is useless to man. All of these provisions invoke the consideration of man's attitude toward the project. Man's intent enters at another point as well: he must regard the sekhakh-material as inedible, serving no useful purpose. Since Moses instructs Israel, as a matter of commandment, to do thus and so, it is difficult to see the intrusion of issues of intentionality as other than a natural next step out of the program of Scripture: "Do this not at random, but as an act of fulfillment of the commandment that is set forth." Some may maintain that the imperative need not, and perhaps does not, contain the implication that the action in fulfillment must express an attitude of obedience, must represent a purposeful response to the commandment. But if that is not implicit in the language of Scripture, the sages who can have introduced that qualification surely have not asked us to take a long step beyond Scripture in coming to that conclusion. The Halakhah takes shape as a protracted meditation upon the centrality, in the relationship of Israel to God, of human intentionality and will. The rules before us, so far as they cohere, take shape around that very subject.

g. *Yoma*

Moses presents the offerings of the Day of Atonement as a narrative, mostly in Lev. 16:1-34, concluding with a reference to the requirement of affliction of soul in atonement for sin. In the Oral Torah, the Mishnah, Tosefta, Yerushalmi, and Bavli, the Halakhah of Yoma simply recapitulates that of the Written Torah. Of the eight chapters of the Mishnah (with their corresponding disquisitions in the Tosefta, Yerushalmi, and Bavli), the first seven provide a narrative, bearing interpolated materials, of the sacrificial rite of the Day of Atonement. The eighth does little more, taking up the rules of affliction of soul, that is, fasting. The two parts of the Torah (so sages saw matters) then deliver the message by their coordination. It is by repeating the Written Torah's narrative and then making a striking addition of a Halakhic character to that narrative that the Oral Torah accomplishes its goal. That is to focus upon the centrality of Israel's attitude—here, the power of the repentant spirit—in the very heart and center of the cult itself. If we compare the sequence of the Scripture's narrative to the presentation of the Halakhah, meaning in this case, the Halakhah of the Mishnah—there being nothing of weight or consequence in the posterior documents of the Halakhah—we see the following pattern:

Leviticus
16:3   He shall put on the holy linen coat

                                                          M. 3:6-7

16:6   Aaron shall offer the bull as a sin offering for himself and shall make atonement for himself and for his house

M. 3:8

16:7   Then he shall take the two goats and set them before the Lord...and Aaron shall cast lots upon the two goats, the lot for the Lord and the lot for Azazel

M. 3:9, 4:1

16:9   Aaron shall present the goat on which the lot fell for the Lord and offer it as a sin offering, but the goat on which the lot fell for Azazel is sent away into the wilderness

16:11   Aaron shall present the bull as a sin offering for himself and for his house

M. 4:2-3

16:12   He shall take a censer full of coals of fire from before the altar and two handfuls of sweet incense and shall bring it within the veil

M. 5:1-2

16:14   He shall take some of the blood of the bull and sprinkle it with his finger on the front of the mercy seat

M. 5:3

16:15   Then he shall kill the goat of the sin offering which is for the people

M. 5:4

16:18   Then he shall go out to the altar which is before the Lord and make atonement for it and shall take some of the blood of the bull and of the blood of the goat and put it on the horns of the altar

M. 5:5-6

16:20   And when he has made a end of atoning for the holy place and the tent of meeting and the altar, he shall present the live goat. And Aaron shall lay both his hands on the head of the live goat and confess over him all the iniquities of the people of Israel and all their transgressions and sins...and send him away into the wilderness

M. 6:2-6

16:23   Then Aaron shall come into the tent of meeting, bathe, and put on his garments and come forth and offer his burnt offering and the burnt offering of the people

M. 6:7-8

16:24   The high priest changes into golden garments and offers the ram and the ram of the people, so completing the offerings of the day

M. 7:3-4

16:31   You shall afflict yourselves

M. 8:1-7

Omitted are only the materials on Torah-reading, prayer, and atonement, M. 7:1-2. All that the Halakhah adds is the opening unit, the preparation of the high priest for the rite and the daily whole offering, and the closing materials on Torah-reading, prayer, and, above all, atonement. It is only when we reach the concluding statements of

the Halakhah—a single, stunning statement, at M. Yoma 8:6-7, that
we move beyond the Halakhic reprise of the Torah's narrative:

> M. 8:7 He who says, "I shall sin and repent, sin and repent"—they give
> him no chance to do repentance. "I will sin and the Day of Atonement
> will atone,"—the Day of Atonement does not atone. For transgressions
> done between man and the Omnipresent, the Day of Atonement
> atones. For transgressions between man and man, the Day of Atone-
> ment atones, only if the man will regain the good will of his friend. This
> exegesis did R. Eleazar b. Azariah state: "'From all your sins shall you
> be clean before the Lord' (Lev. 16:30)—for transgressions between man
> and the Omnipresent does the Day of Atonement atone. For transgres-
> sions between man and his fellow, the Day of Atonement atones, only if
> the man will regain the good will of his friend." Said R. Aqiba, "Happy
> are you, O Israel. Before whom are you made clean, and who makes
> you clean? It is your Father who is in heaven, as it says, 'And I will
> sprinkle clean water on you, and you will be clean' (Ezek. 36:25). And
> it says, 'O Lord, the hope [Miqweh = immersion pool] of Israel' (Jer.
> 17:13)—Just as the immersion pool cleans the unclean, so the Holy
> One, blessed be he, cleans Israel."

Here the presentation of the Halakhah tells us what is at stake, which
is the prophetic reading of the cult. Sages understood the prophets'
critique not as repudiation of the cult but as refinement of it, and in
the very context of their account of the blood-rite they therefore
invoke the prophets' norms alongside the Torah's. Jeremiah's call to
repentance, Isaiah's reflections on the role of death in the penitential
process, God's infinite mercy, Ezekiel's insistence on purity of spirit
—these flow into the exposition of the Halakhah. Above all, sages
underscore God's explicit promise to purify Israel, the promise set
forth in Ezekiel's and Jeremiah's prophecies. So the Halakhah recasts
the entire category of the Day of Atonement, taking the theme of
atonement to require an account of repentance, on the one side, and
God's power to forgive and purify from sin, on the other. The main
point is, the rites of atonement do not work *ex opere operato*, but only
conditionally. And it is the attitude and intention of the Israelite that
sets that condition.

II. *What the Oral Torah Did Not Contribute*

I stress that the question is, what of the categories themselves? And,
further, what of their articulation and amplification? Scripture has
provided the categories we have examined, and it has further dic-

tated the problematics or particular proposition that the Halakhah wishes to explore in connection with those categories. The Halakhah of the Oral Torah, subordinate at every point, both categorical and propositional, then amplifies, extends, refines, and clarifies the givens of Scripture's law. In its defense, it suffices to say, it presents nothing that is new but much that is true, truth being defined by the inner logic of the Written Torah and the Oral Torah's conformity thereto. In due course, we shall ask about the Oral Torah's taking over of Scripture's category-formations, since, it is self-evident, the Oral Torah, absorbing the factual trove that Scripture contributed, nonetheless did not adopt all of the received category-formations that Scripture offered—no division on the priesthood, for example, even while the Oral Torah recapitulated everything in the Pentateuchal legislation on the priesthood.

The issue that we settle with the facts adduced in these seven instances is, has the Halakhah defined categories and then turned to Scripture for data to realize, to actualize the category-formation? or has Scripture dictated the category-formations that it itself has also fleshed out with facts and rulings? What I have now proven beyond any reasonable doubt is that, for the seven category-formations at hand, it is Scripture that has defined the organizing category, supplying not only details but the main point conveyed by those building blocks, those structural components of the system as a whole. In their entirety, in nearly all details, the specified category-formations build upon generative premises dictated by explicit statements in Scripture. In the seven formations at hand, we find how not only the category-formations, but the generative premises of the Halakhah have been dictated wholly by Scripture. What about category-formations, the generative premises of which in no way call upon, relate to, or derive from, Scripture, either from what is explicit or even from what is implicit? To these we now turn.

What we do know now is that, at any point in its formative history, the Oral Torah can have set forth the category-formations, fully articulated, that Scripture defined; it did not have to invent the organizing problematic, let alone choose the topic; it had only to clarify details and recapitulate the whole within its own topical-logical principles of exposition, and this it did. So what we learn from the first category of category-formations concerns only a large conception of what is required to make sense of the whole, to state and hold the whole together in a single vast composite, the Halakhah in its divisions and topical tractates. Then, but only then, Scripture's legacy become the Oral Torah's heritage—a fact in the analysis of the final result of Halakhic organization, not a datum in the sequential, historical formation thereof.

III. *Category-Formations of the Halakhah Wholly Defined within the Oral Torah*

When we identify those category-formations of the Halakhah that have no foundations in the Written Torah (in line with the formulation of M. Hag. 1:9 cited earlier), we present the one component of the Halakhic structure that can have formed part only of the Oral Torah autonomous of the Written. These constructions by their basic traits assign themselves to origin in the Oral Torah—there alone. But that repertoire of category-formations need not have originated in Second Temple times. It suffices to say that merely because a category-formation is independent of Scripture's counterparts, and even though said construction finds in Scripture no match even for its factual repertoire, that does not mean the construction must be early, in Temple times, or even late, in the mid-second century; some of the category-formations identified as autonomous of Scripture in theme and in problematics and even in facts turn up only late in the process of forming the structure and system viewed whole and complete, that is, in the mid-second century. What the category-formations before us do bear in common is that while, in some cases, Scripture may have supplied facts that a given category-formation has encompassed and made its own, in none of them has Scripture set forth the coherent Halakhic category by the criterion operative in Chapter Two. Here we take up a cogent category of Halakhah lacking all Scriptural antecedent or even counterpart, a category-formation not touched upon anywhere in Scripture at all.

Now to elaborate on the type of category-formation analyzed in this setting, the Oral Torah's own constructions. What marks them as independent of Scripture? At stake is not whether or not Scripture contributes a singleton fact to the definition of a body of Halakhah, but whether Scripture has identified a cogent construction, a fully-executed formation, for systematic attention. For the Halakhah of the Oral Torah forms a large and cogent corpus of well-crafted compositions, each devoted to a topic, most—though by no means all—

engaged with a particular, provocative problem found urgent in the exposition of said topic. Halakhic categories therefore are classified as autonomous of Scripture because both traits characteristic of the ones dependant upon Scripture are lacking: [1] in no sustained and systematic manner does Scripture contribute the topic, and [2] what captures the interest of the Halakhah in the topic in no way derives from Scripture.

But three further criteria pertain. A free-standing category-formation, thus belonging to the Oral Torah at least in theory, then is a composition of Halakhah that is [1] coherent in itself and responsive to its own cogent concerns and that [2] addresses a topic not set forth in Scripture at all, or not set forth through Pentateuchal Halakhah in particular. Such is a category that [3] takes a position outside of the framework of the laws of the Pentateuch. Generative premises of the Halakhah of such a category-formation in no way derive from Scripture, any more than the topic itself is one that Moses expounds in Scripture.

To be sure, Scripture may provide episodic data, random information in one place or another, that in the Halakhic structure—but not in Scripture's—is folded into and forms part of a coherent category-formation. When in such instances Scripture alludes to a piece of information, it will do so haphazardly and make no point; the free-standing fact finds a place in no context whatever; and, on that account, Scripture's occasional facts bear no implicit premises whatever, offer no opportunity for investigation of problems that inhere but are not articulated. That is why it is futile in such instances to ask about generative premises defined by Scripture; the question is simply irrelevant to the data. Not only so, but the information that Scripture does supply may to begin with derive from other-than-Halakhic settings, consisting of narratives bearing theological implications that are realized not in Scripture's legal compositions and composites but solely in the normative rules of the Halakhah. So the Halakhah parts company with Scripture on several grounds. First, the Halakhah may address a topic that Scripture simply does not raise at all. Second, it may treat systematically what Scripture deals with in a haphazard and unorganized way. Later we take up the type of category-formation that takes a topic that Scripture does treat and investigates questions important in that topic that Scripture does not raise at all; the Halakhah may find important in a given subject matters that Scripture scarcely acknowledges.

IV. *Categories that Encompass in their System Facts Set forth in Scripture:*
[1] Berakhot

The principal theological category-formations of the Halakhah,
Berakhot and Taanit, in their basic construction stand wholly within
the framework of the Oral Torah. That judgment rests on a simple
fact. What here is treated Halakhically, as occasion for systematic
legislation, in the Written Torah never surfaces within the boundaries of Halakhic discourse. What originates in the Oral Torah, therefore, is not the contents of the Halakhah but the conviction that a
web of rules translates those fundamental theological affirmations
into an orderly and regular pattern of normative behavior. And that,
to state the point of it all, is the genius of the Oral Torah (if only part
of it). We begin with the fundamental statement of matters and proceed to a special problem.

The Halakhic category, Berakhot, provides rules governing [1] the
recitation of the *Shemaʿ*, [2] the pronouncement of the Prayer, [3]
conduct at meals with special attention to saying blessings before,
and grace after, eating; and [4] blessings to be recited in some other
connections. The legal structure of the Halakhah is systematic and
orderly, working its way through the everyday life, and registers important points in its own framework, e.g., rules of classifying food,
laws securing correct reverence at prayer, and the like. Referring to
passages of Scripture of a mainly-theological character, the Halakhah
in no way finds a model for its topical program, let alone for its
generative concerns, in Scripture. Scripture knows nothing of blessings before and Grace after meals, nor of blessings on other occasions, nor of the Prayer. It does supply the text of the *Shemaʿ*, in
Deuteronomy (and Numbers) but does not legislate concerning what
is now a liturgy in the way in which it does, e.g., for the Day of
Atonement, through narrative, or for the support of the Priesthood,
through laws. No legal passage of the Pentateuch presents rules for
systematization and development by Berakhot in a manner comparable to those that are taken up and amplified in the way, for example,
in which Yoma systematizes Leviticus 16, Negaim, Leviticus 13-14,
or Sotah, Numbers 5. But the category does call upon the Written
Torah for not only facts but, more important, for the theological
premises of belief that are embodied in its rules, as I shall spell out in
detail. So what the Oral Torah contributes is the systematization,
and, in context, the creedal theologization, of episodic verses of
Scripture.

Verses that figure in the Halakhah of Berakhot include the components of the *Shema'*, Dt. 6:4-9, Dt. 11;13, and reference to eating and saying a blessing, Dt. 8:10: "You will eat and be satisfied and bless the Lord your God for the good land that he has given to you." These verses pertain to details. But at much deeper layers of thought upon which the Halakhic construction rests we find adumbrated the theology of Israel's relationship to God that Scripture sets forth. Whether or not Scripture dictates the generative premises of the Halakhah stated by, not the substrate of beliefs embedded within, Berakhot is what defines our problem in the present instance. What we shall now see is that Scripture does not supply the generative premises that precipitate the articulation of the Halakhah: its rules, the actions it defines as normative. The comparison of the relationship between this category and Scripture and another may once again be expressed very simply: Horayot/Leviticus 4 ? Berakhot/Dt. 4:6-9. Here, then, is a case in which Scripture provides facts but no laws, and in which the theological but not the Halakhic premises of Scripture are taken over in the formulation of rules.

Because the written Torah contains no legislation about these practices, which are not even adumbrated in the Pentateuch, I maintain that the present body of Halakhah of the Oral Torah stands autonomous of Scripture. But when the Oral Torah identifies the creedal principles of the faith, it states what the Pentateuch says, no more, no less. These selected doctrines encompass God's unity and dominion, the Torah as God's plan, the categories, creation, revelation, redemption, as these organize holy Israel's existence, then bring about direct address to God conducted in the concrete presence of God, and finally, equally direct address to God when, in the center of Israel's ordinary life, Israel sustains itself with food. God's beneficence and benevolence are declared, and as Israel encounters evidences of God's intervention in the everyday, his activity is acknowledged with thanks. So the creed, prayers, and blessings that are encased in a web of rules and regulations recapitulate principal elements of the theology of the Torah, written as much as oral. When we ask, what premises concerning God's relationship with Israel pervade the Halakhah and come to concrete expression only in the Halakhah and not in the corresponding media of the Aggadah (here: inclusive of liturgy)? we find a body of Halakhah deeply dependent for its contents upon Scripture. By the Halakhah we are given the practical and concrete means by which those principles are made substantial, declared, acted out, imposed upon, discerned within, the everyday life of holy Israel, encompassing the ordinary Israelite. Within the details of the laws is embedded a major statement about what is between God and Israel. And while the law makes that statement in a prolix manner only through details, never stating the point in general terms, in fact its principles are few and accessible of economical formulation. It is a simple statement, and it is one that Moses surely would have approved for the Written Torah. But what are we to make of generative premises that the Halakhah takes for granted—but not one of which the Halakhah takes up and develops in its own terms and framework:

1.   God takes a constant and intense interest in the condition of Israelite attitudes and opinions. He cares that Israel affirm his unity and declare his dominion, through the recitation of the *Shema'* and related acts of prayer. He waits for the expression of love, he hears, he responds. That is why he pays close attention to the manner in which the obligation to do so is carried out, noting that it is done in a correct and respectful way. How else is a merely formal gesture to be distinguished from a truly sincere, intentional one? What is important is that when the correct words are spoken, they are spoken with the attitude of acknowledging God's dominion, as an explicit act of accepting the government of Heaven and the discipline ("yoke") of the commandments. That is what is meant in the laws covering reciting the blessings, for instance, *Blessed are you...who...,* or *Blessed are you, who has sanctified us by his commandments and commanded us to....* God values these words of acknowledgement and thanks. God further hears and responds to the praise, supplication, and thanks of Israel, as these are set forth in the Prayer. Reciting the Prayer while facing Jerusalem's Temple and the holy of holies, the Israelite directs the Prayer to the place in which God's Presence once came and one day will again come to rest. The attitude of the Israelite in reciting the Prayer acutely concerns God, and that must be an attitude of solemnity; the one who says the Prayer must conduct himself or herself as in the very presence of God, in the model of the rules of conduct before the emperor. How does God respond to Israel's acknowledgement, thanks, and above all, acceptance of his dominion? God sees to it that life is sustained, with special reference to food, and prayers that acknowledge the gift of life through food must respond with precision to the specificities of the gift: what particular class of food is involved? Finally, when Israel is embodied in a quorum of Israelites,

God's presence, not only his gifts, is to be noted properly in a call to attend upon the shared rite. Finally, God intervenes at all times, past, present, future, and in all circumstances, however humble and personal, and God's intervention is to be watched for and acknowledged. So when the Aggadah insists that all Israel—everyone who accepts the rule of the one and only God—will rise from the grave to eternal life, while the gentiles, defined by their idolatry and rejection of God, are destined to death, that point of insistence bears more than abstract interest. God is intimately involved in the on-going life of Israel, sustaining that life in the here and now, not only at judgment and in the world to come. At man's every act of breathing, on every occasion of nourishment, God renews the promise of the creation of life and confirms the promise of restoration at the end.

2. Through the life of prayer and fulfillment of commandments, Israel wraps itself before God in a cloak made up of the fabric of actions that sanctify—thread by thread. From Israel's perspective, all Israel and individual Israelites conduct life under the perpetual rule of that just and merciful God who made the world, and that rule is personal, immediate, and penetrating. If God immediately engages with Israel, for its part Israel, all together and one by one, seeks that engagement. That is because Israel lives and acts under God's perpetual gaze. In the morning the Israelite accepts God's dominion in an act of personal submission, then explicitly undertakes to carry out God's commandments, in all their concrete specificity. In exchange, the Israelite recognizes that whatever happens expresses a chapter in God's plan for creation a paragraph—perhaps only a sentence, a word, a mere letter—of God's intention for that particular person. That fact forms the premise of the Prayer, with its systematic, personal program of praise, supplication, and thanks. More broadly still, the very fact that the individual lives attests to God's will, by which every man lives or dies that very moment through the course of life. Life depends on food, the point of intersection, then, between man and God, the moment of special and appropriate acknowledgement of the gift of life: nourishment by this means provokes these words, by that means, those. Since God pays such close and continuing attention to what each person says and how he says it, what he does and why he does it, none need find surprising God's intervention or man's specific and appropriate response. That is why the correct formula of acknowledgement guides response, also, to all miracles, both the routine and the extraordinary, that embody God's interven-

tion. Throughout, there is no distinguishing Israel from the Israelite, what affects the whole obligates the one, what happens to the one forms the destiny of all.

V. *Categories that Encompass in their System Facts Set forth in Scripture:*
[2] Taanit

The category-formation, Taanit, joins two distinct topics, neither of them defined as categories, let alone legislated for, in the law of the Pentateuch: fasting in time of crisis, the rules governing conduct in the village when the priests of the place go up to serve in the Temple. The Halakhah's category-formation registers its own propositions in response to premises that the Halakhah itself has identified—a category completely autonomous of Scripture, with laws spun out of facts of Scripture and premises never framed in legal terms by Scripture. The first is how to respond to times of crisis, and that is through fasting. Drought and famine and war signal God's displeasure with Israel and occasion acts of repentance and atonement; these take the form of public fasting and prayer. In times of crisis Israel jointly and severally relates to God through acts of supplication joined to penitence for sin. The second, and quite unrelated, theme is how the community at home responds to the occasion on which the priestly component of the village goes up to Jerusalem to conduct the Temple rite for its assigned span of time. A delegation of Levites and lay-Israelites would accompany the priests, twenty-four of them through the year, and at home then the entirety of the community, meaning, non-priests, would participate at home through the recitation and study of verses of Scripture.

That prayer and fasting form the proper response to crisis is commonplace, e.g., 1 Kgs. 8:37-39: "If there is famine in the land, if there is pestilence or blight or mildew or locust or caterpillar, if their enemy besieges them in any of their cities; whatever plague, whatever sickness there is; whatever prayer, whatever supplication is made by any man or by all thy people Israel, each knowing the affliction of his own heart and stretching out his hands toward this house, then hear thou in heaven, thy dwelling place, and forgive and act and render to each whose heart thou knowest according to all his ways." So too Joel 1:14 is even more explicit: "Sanctify a fast, call a solemn assembly. Gather the elders and all the inhabitants of the land to the house of the Lord your God and cry to the Lord;" and Joel 2:15-17: "Blow the trumpet in Zion, sanctify a fast; call a solemn assembly, gather the people; sanctify the congregation, assemble the elders; gather the children," etc. These and other references (e.g., 1 Chr. 2:20:3-4, Zechariah 7:2-3, 8:19) to fasting contain no Halakhah, and on the basis of Scripture—Pentateuch, Prophets, Writings alike—we cannot have anticipated the formation of such a category. Nor does the institution of the *ma'amad*, which I translate as "delegation," rest upon a Halakhic composition in the Pentateuch.

The category-formation, as in the case of Berakhot, is both quite autonomous of Scripture and deeply engaged by Scripture's theology. The given of the Halakhah of Taanit in its two principal components places Israel into a plane of eternity in which the present participates in the reality of the past, the past plays its part in the quotidian moment too. That is in two ways, one with reference to history (fasting), the other, to nature (celebration of the priests at the altar). First, the lines of time are obscured, so that past and present form a continuum to which issues of chronology prove irrelevant. In the rite of fasting, therefore, the fearful community invokes the presence of Abraham, the precedent of the Sea, the pathos of Jonah, answering the question of why God should save Israel, how God saves Israel, and to what traits and acts of penitent Israel God ought respond in considering the condition of Israel. The boundaries of space are transcended. That is made explicit when Israel in the provinces takes up its position in the Temple, sending agents to represent the home-community when its priesthood takes its turn at the altar. What Israel celebrates, at home now in correspondence with the Temple, is the recapitulation of all creation, by definition an event the overspreads the entire world. So at the specified interval, Israel takes up its presence in the Temple and bears witness to the creation of the world that the cult celebrates: the Land to be sure, but only as culmination and triumph of all creation. The Halakhic statement of Taanit spells out how Israel relates to God through prayerful statements to him on both ordinary, natural and extraordinary, historical occasions. That is why regular prayers for rain, for example, are supplemented by penitential prayers and related activities, as the case requires. While Halakhic statements of the Pentateuch do not provide that premise, the entire corpus of theology that inheres in the Written Torah in general terms dictates that very point. The Oral Torah's Halakhah has embodied that conclusion not in general terms but in the concrete norms of public behavior. But knowing only the Pentateuchal law, we should never have imagined the construction of the category-formation, Taanit.

These two theological compositions animate the present category-formations (as they do implicitly for many others). And the two category-formations—Berakhot and Taanit—accomplish their tasks without at any point taking over and building upon the Halakhic corpus of Scripture. That is the main point at hand when we wish to know the relationship between Scripture and the generative premises of the Halakhah. The remainder of the cases before us present no comparable ambiguities. Each one of them stands wholly on its own foundations, never intersecting with Scripture's legal compositions or composites, though always infused with Scripture's theology of sanctification. The case before us tells us how the documents of the Oral Torah take up theological propositions of the Written Torah and present them within a Halakhic framework. Hence we gain here no insight into what the Oral part of the Torah can have contained, viewed in its own terms and framework; all we have is what the written record classified as "the Oral Torah" encompassed—a very different matter.

VI. *The Oral Torah Forms a Category out of Scripture's Topic: Tamid*

A second anomalous category-formation belonging to the Oral Torah but not representative of the character of that part of the Torah now comes to the fore. The Oral Torah, principally the Mishnah, selects the daily whole-offering to form a category-formation in its own terms and then finds nothing of interest in it.[3] The exposition—

---

[3] In the same class of category-formations of the Oral Torah is Middot, which describes the Temple buildings. Obviously, Scripture has defined the category. But the information collected and organized by Middot is difficult to correlate with either other information in Scripture, e.g., Ezekiel's Temple, or actualities. Archaeology has not established a close connection between the Halakhah of Middot and the actualities of the Temple architecture. I cannot explain the point of the tractate, any more than I can that of Tamid. But any account of the category-formations of the Halakhah set forth in the Pentateuch and in Mishnah-Tosefta-Yerushalmi-Bavli must take up all sixty one relevant, Halakhic tractates (excluding Eduyyot, which does not take shape as a category-formation, and Abot, which is not Halakhic and in no way conforms to the rhetorical plan and characteristic program of the Mishnah). As to Qinnim, it Halakhic in its focus but not in its character; it presents not laws but exercises in the application of legal principles of the types of sacrifice sorted out

a sustained narrative of how the rite is carried out—is utterly autonomous of Scripture. When we compare Yoma and Tamid, we see the
full state of affairs: the one depends entirely upon Scripture, builds
upon Scripture's own generative premise, and makes a statement of
enormous weight. The other does nothing of the sort.[4] The daily
whole offering, Tamid, is set forth at Numbers 28:3-8. Exodus 30:7-
8 adds the requirement of the incense offering. That is all that Scripture contributes: the fact of the daily whole offering. The Halakhah
frames its statement through a narrative of the procedures in the
Temple. As with Middot and Qinnim the exercise of the one and the
facts of the other illuminate. But in none of the three cases, inclusive
of Tamid, can I identify a message that the Halakhah wishes to
convey through its data.

But then there is a striking difference from Yoma. While Yoma
rests squarely on the Halakhic narrative of Leviticus 16, Tamid sets
forth an autonomous narrative. Sheqalim shows what can be done
with the same theme, the daily whole offering, that Scripture contributes with such slight amplification. So whether or not Scripture
dominates in the presentation of the category makes no difference.
The Halakhic narrative answers no questions that I can identify; it
simply says how things are done, and the account of matters contains
within itself no profound inquiry, no puzzling problem, that demands
attention. Here is a case in which free-standing Halakhah bears no

---

there. It follows that we find fifty-nine category-formations in Mishnah-Tosefta-
Yerushalmi-Bavli. How these category-formations correspond with those in the Pentateuch forms a separate problem, with which I do not deal. It suffices to say that the
Halakhah of the Oral Torah skips none of that of the Written Torah and responds
to all of it has been demonstrated in the so-called Tannaite Midrashim, Sifra, the
two Sifrés, and Mekhilta attributed to R. Ishmael. In a purely formal way, the same
fact is shown in the invaluable catalogue of Aharon Mordecai Hyman, *Torah
hakketubah vehammesurah 'al torah, nebi'im, uketubim* (Tel Aviv, 1938: Debir) I-III. Hyman
organizes the ancient and even medieval compilations of exegesis of each verse of
Scripture in the sequence of the verses of Scripture, so by consulting the verse, one
has a full account of where it is discussed in the Rabbinic corpus. No Halakhic verse
of the Pentateuch lacks a comment in the Oral Torah, a starting point for all else.
But since at issue here is the Halakhah of the Oral Torah, the native categories are
those of the Oral Torah, not the Written one: the organizing topics of the Halakhah,
not the verses of Scripture. It seems to me a topic of some interest to set forth the
Pentateuchal category-formations viewed whole, as the priests who received the Pentateuch surely saw matters.

[4] I did not treat Middot as a category-formation, having no comparable one to
justify doing so. But the fact that Yoma, parts of Menahot, parts of Parah, parts of
Negaim, and other Temple-tractates constitute free-standing category-formations
persuades me that Tamid should be placed in the same category.

message beyond its own information, answers no question through the provision of its data. Tamid represents a Halakhic category that does no more than amplify and clarify a topic introduced by Scripture. Scripture has offered a premise of considerable promise: the daily whole offering atones for all Israel. Sheqalim builds on that premise. Tamid ignores it, and finds no other issue of any interest. The one noteworthy point—the introduction of canonical prayer into the Temple rite—registers but leads nowhere. Here is another instance in which the overall plan of a composite of category-formations has precipitated the execution of a category-formation with no propositional content and only marginal Halakhic information (so far as Halakhah by its nature supplies information subject to generalization).

VII. *Categories beyond Scripture's Framework but Subordinate to Scripture's Own Categories: Demai*

Demai, the Halakhic category that encompasses produce concerning the tithing of which doubt exists, generates laws that dictate how a responsible person makes certain that what he purchases in the marketplace and eats or gives to another to eat will be properly tithed. So the topic is doubtfully-tithed produce, and the problematic that generates much of the Halakhah concerns public policy in dealing with cases of doubt: who is to be trusted by whom and for observance of what portion of the law (a problematic we meet again at Tohorot). All Israelites, the Halakhah takes for granted, separate heave-offering. But the other pertinent agricultural offerings, first tithe—a tenth of the crop remaining when heave-offering has been removed, given to the Levite, heave-offering of the tithe, that is to say, a tenth removed from the Levite's tithe and given to the priest, and second tithe or poorman's tithe (depending on the year of the Sabbatical cycle, first, second, fourth, and fifth, or third and sixth, respectively)—are designated only by those faithful to the rule. The specific problem that provokes the formation of the Halakhah before us concerns the heave-offering of the tithe given to the Levite, which heave-offering further goes to the priest. If not removed, the heave-offering of the tithe given to the Levite imparts the status of holiness to the produce in which it is mixed, even as would the heave-offering of the entire crop that everyone is assumed to designate and remove. The precipitating issue leads to a systematic discussion of large questions of social policy, with special reference to how the more observant negotiate life in the community of the less observant, all of them parties to the condition of Israel.

The generative issue is how those who properly separate tithes are to relate, commercially and commensally, to those that do not. The question addresses the issue, what is their responsibility for produce that they transfer to others, what is their obligation in regard to produce that they receive from others? The Halakhic problematic then defines the theological issue: how do Jews (using the term to refer to those deemed to belong to a common ethnic group) relate to Israel, meaning, the holy people whom God brought into being through the Torah at Sinai? And the answer that the Halakhah sets forth is, all Israel is Israel. What the Halakhah of Demai emphatically registers is that the Israelites who do not observe cultic cleanness in the household intermarry with, and will respect the convictions and conduct of, those that do. Other components of the Halakhah stress that those who do not observe cultic cleanness in the household will not wantonly or deliberately impart cultic uncleanness to the secular food of that component of Israel that does so. The premise of the Halakhah in both cases is one and the same: all Israel keeps some of the Halakhah, and some of Israel keeps it all—and all together, the two components form a single, holy Israel. That is why the Halakhah legislates for the situation that it treats here and in tractate Tohorot, which also stands autonomous of the Pentateuch. And viewed as a matter of social policy, that conviction underscores the wisdom of the Halakhah in requiring the observant to make provision for the unobservant, doing so, however, without intruding into their affairs in a haughty or hostile manner.

The Pentateuch contains nothing to lead us to anticipate so balanced and nuanced a corpus of Halakhah as Demai sets forth. In the Written Torah Moses does not legislate for a mixed society of observant, partly observant, and unobservant Israelites living side by side. On the contrary, when Israelites object to Moses's teaching, they are wiped out. Here, by contrast, even Samaritans, even less observant Israelites are assumed to exhibit integrity and good will, since they are held to keep the law correctly, as we noted: "He who leaves [his tithed] produce in the keeping of a Samaritan or an 'am ha'ares—[the produce remains] in its presumed status with regard to tithes and with regard to Seventh-Year produce." Where they err, where not,

not. The Halakhah sets forth no recriminations and pronounces no exclusions. If I had to select the relevant premises of Scripture, they would be those embodied in stories about Korach (Num. 16) or about Moab and Phineas's disposition of the Israelite and the Midianite woman (Num. 25)—not to mention Moses at the Golden Calf!—and they would not generate the Halakhah before us but a very different set of rules, such as we shall see in due course in the category, Abodah Zarah. Demai then stands at the opposite extreme from Shebuot, Horayot, Yoma, and the rest: a category utterly autonomous of Scripture, encompassing facts that Scripture has not supplied, spun out of premises and principles Scripture not only does not produce but can hardly be said to entertain on its own account.

But what does Demai teach about the Oral Torah—not about sages' profound grasp of sound public policy but about the revelation of category-formations and their principles distinct from those of Scripture? In Demai we deal with the ambiguities of the Israelite social order and with Halakhah framed to sort out those uncertain situations and guide the faithful in the right way. The category-formation at hand forms an essay in applied social policy, taking for granted a vast corpus of Halakhah—the Halakhah of tithing, for example, and of cultic cleanness—that derives from the Written Torah. In that way, we may best identify the counterpart to Demai in Qinnim, of all tractates—where a set of conundrums sharpen our capacity to reason about the classifications of offerings and the rules governing them, fully worked out in a sequence of illustrative problems. Here too, once we know the laws of Scripture and the possibilities of gray areas contained therein, we find illumination in problems and cases. That is why we take up in Demai a massive exercise in the study of interstitialities (in a logical, theoretical framework) and framing public policy in the real world (in the setting of actualities). So while the category-formation innovates, it is the character of the problems that its law takes up, not the very foundations of the law, that is expounded. So far as the Oral Torah serves as a free-standing, autonomous statement of category-formations and the laws that define them, we cannot discern the character of the Oral Torah from Demai.

Now we turn to the first of the four category-formations of the Oral Torah that characterize what belongs to the Oral Torah in particular and not to the Written one, by explicit declaration or by implication and secondary development.

VIII. *The Oral Torah's Own Categories: [1] Scripture's Imperatives without Scripture's Facts. Tohorot*

To the Halakhic category of Tohorot Scripture has contributed only one conception, but it is the one that, in context, has made all the difference: "You shall be holy, for I the Lord your God am holy" (Lev. 19:3). So far as the Oral Torah realizes and actualizes the Written, here is a fine case in point. But the category-formation before us in no way calls upon Scripture and finds in Scripture no puzzling, episodic data, certainly no generative premises worthy of even casual attention. Here is a category-formation, rich and dense in complex Halakhah, that Scripture in no way has brought into being, and to which Scripture makes remarkably slight contributions. And yet, even more than Demai, the Oral Torah has identified a principal concern of the Written Torah and realized that concern in a Halakhic structure and system. Called "Purities," generically, the Halakhic category of Tohorot covers four topics that correlate: [1] Fathers and Offspring of uncleanness; [2] removes of uncleanness, from the original source, and the affect of what is made unclean at one or more removes upon food in various degrees of sanctification; [3] matters of doubt in connection with the uncleanness of food and utensils and principles for their resolution; [4] relationships between those who keep the purity laws within the domestic household and those who do not, and how ambiguities are resolved in that connection. Of all of this Scripture knows details but not a fully-organized category-formation. Here sages have identified and classified data that, for reasons they discerned, cohered. The connections that, deeming them self-evident, they draw between four distinct categories of Halakhah having to do with purities therefore expose the rationality that animates their thinking throughout, that is, givens of the autonomous Oral Torah:

1. the relationship between sources of uncleanness and removes or successive levels of sanctification;
2. the relationship between Fathers and Offspring of uncleanness;
3. sorting out matters of doubt and determining probabilities;
4. the relationship of the *haber* and the *'am ha'ares*.

These four categories derive from the systematic presentation of the Halakhah by the Mishnah and the Tosefta, the only sustained statements on the matter that we have from antiquity, the Talmuds falling silent here. No one can doubt that the issue of removes can be

explored in discrete passages of Scripture, as the Talmuds to Mishnah-tractate Sotah Chapter Five (M. 5:2) demonstrate. And none can
miss the data in the Written Torah that, here and there, bear the
clear implication of differentiation between primary and secondary,
original and derivative, sources of uncleanness. Removes of uncleanness to the experienced Halakhic eye certainly inhere in all manner
of declarations by Scripture, so too, the points of differentiation between Fathers and Offspring of uncleanness. No one can imagine
that the Oral Torah has fabricated the entire corpus of Halakhah in
this critical, this key construction.

But the system as a system belongs to the category-formation,
Tohorot. For, as in the analysis of any category-formation, it is how
the four categories hold together that exposes the inner logic of the
framer of the system. The four main foci of Tohorot hold together
because to the sages they make a single statement, from logical beginning to necessary end, and the order is critical to the message that is
set forth. Specifically, sages contemplate an intangible world of confusion between classes of things and persons that are both alike and
not alike: things that may contract uncleanness but also attain sanctification; sources of uncleanness; things that may be unclean or
clean; persons who are Israelites all together, but who may or may
not keep certain laws of the Torah. What the Halakhah accomplishes
in each case is to identify things that are to begin with alike—that
stand along a single continuum, that bear traits in common—but
that also exhibit differentiating qualities. Viewed from another perspective, we deal with a variety of persons and objects that have had
each its own "history." Each must tell its own story, but the chapters
are the same: is the person or object, food or drink, to be classified as
unclean or clean? To answer that question, I need to know the following information:

1. the level of sanctification for which the cleanness is required
(how the person, object, food or drink has been subject to surveillance over time);

2. the character of the uncleanness to which the person or food
may or may not have been exposed, primary or secondary, and the
number of removes from exposure to that source at which the person
or food stands: immediate contact, once-removed, and so on out-
ward;

3. in what location (public, private domain), in what season (dry
or rainy), and within what sort of transaction, the exposure is supposed to have taken place or not taken place;

4. what sort of instructions, conditions, and rules were articulated to the parties who may or may not have imparted uncleanness by touching the food or drink or utensils that are subject to doubt

In reaching a decision on how to classify a person, object, food or drink, each of these questions requires an answer, and at every stage in the process of interrogation, we have to reconstruct the story of what has happened to this person, object, food or drink in the context established by the inquiry into the status that pertains. And having come this far, we realize what holds the whole together: the four principal parts of the Halakhah before us contribute to the single, sustained narrative that encompasses the person or object, the food or drink, and that determines the taxonomic outcome of the process. The narrative tells us what things the person or object has touched, what things those things have touched, and so on through a sequence of removes; and it further tells us the status imputed to the food or drink by the attitude and intentionality of the principal player in the drama, the person affected by the considerations at hand: uncleanness at the one side, sanctification at the other. All of this, amplified by the consideration of removes, forms a small narrative of a cosmic transaction.

In this unseen world the impalpable force of the attitude of responsible actors makes its impact everywhere. Uncleanness is relative to that which it affects, and the sensitivity to uncleanness of that which is affected by uncleanness depends upon the status imputed by man's will. Stated simply: if man assigns food or drink to the status of Holy Things and so acts as to preserve the cleanness of what is sanctified in that status, then the sources of uncleanness affect the food or drink through successive removes, as many as three (Parah will add yet another, as we shall see later on). If man's intentionality does not impart to the food or drink the standing of Holy Things but of ordinary, secular food or drink, then fewer removes from the source of uncleanness produce effects. It is the initial decision and attitude of man that makes the difference. If man is alert and capable of forming intentionality, if man can be interrogated in the assumption that he cares about contamination, then the rules of contamination are strictly enforced; if not, then they are null. A child cannot form an intention to preserve cleanness and, therefore, in a case of doubt, he also cannot be assumed to have imparted uncleanness. The 'am ha'ares is assumed to touch whatever he can reach—unless he is instructed not to. Then his intentionality, to respect the wishes of the

householder, is assumed to pertain and therefore to protect from
uncleanness what the *'am ha'ares* can have touched but probably did
not contaminate at all. At the critical turnings in the decision-making
process, the taxonomic question finds its answer in the relativities of
attitude and intention.

The Halakhah rests on the foundations of a single condition: Israel
is holy, wherever located; that is its natural condition. That is Scripture's generative contribution, and seen whole, the Oral Torah has
richly elaborated it. What removes Israel from its status as sanctified
is unnatural to Israel, but a given of the world. Sanctification is the
established condition for family and property (food, drink, clothing,
utensils). What removes the family, its food, drink, clothing and utensils, from the status of sanctification interferes with what ought to be
natural. Sources of uncleanness also come about by nature; sages
adhere rigidly to the definition of those sources that Scripture establishes and do not add a single new source or extend an existing
source in any consequential way. Holy Israel, then, confronts round
about the sources of contamination; its task is constantly to remain
alert and watchful, lest those contamination affect Israel. Israel must
watch not only what it eats and drinks and wears and where it stands
and sits and lies. Israel also must pay attention to what the food it
eats may have touched, who may have stood or sat upon the clothing
that it wears and the beds on which it takes a rest. To preserve the
condition it ought always to enjoy, which is, the state of sanctification, Israel has then to maintain a constant surveillance of the present
and past of the world in which it lives and the people among whom
it makes its life.

IX. *The Oral Torah's Own Categories: [2] Uqsin*

Dealing with fruit and vegetables, Uqsin concerns the status of parts
of produce connected with, but not integral to, the fruit that is eaten.
Do these connected parts of the produce share in the status as to
uncleanness of the principal components thereof? Like the category,
Tohorot, Uqsin invokes principles that pertain to food in general,
e.g., the volume of food that is required for susceptibility to affect a
given bit of edible material; whether or not intentionality is required
to classify edible material as food; issues of connection; and the like.
With special reference to fruit and vegetables, then, Uqsin systemati-

cally expounds matters of connection and intentionality. To Uqsin
Scripture makes no explicit contribution whatsoever, not the categorical topic, certainly not the problematic (the issue of connection
being absent from Scripture's repertoire of generative premises), and
the framers of the Halakhah in the Mishnah and the Tosefta do not
even pretend that it does. Scripture has no bearing in any direct way
on the generative premises of the Halakhah. The Halakhic category
at hand provides the occasion for sustained reflection on the interplay
between man's intentionality and the material world, and the message is, how man's sees things makes all the difference. The primacy
of intentionality over material actualities in the status of the components of produce—are they integral or extrinsic, connected or
deemed distinct—comes to expression not only in detail but also
explicitly.

Certainly the most fecund statement of intentionality comes at the
end. To understand the statement, we recall that what requires intention is food not usually consumed by human beings, and what does
not is food people naturally eat. Now, there are things which require
preparation to be made susceptible to uncleanness but do not require
intention, intention and preparation, intention and no preparation,
neither intention nor preparation. That familiar mode of schematiza-
tion of matters yields profound judgments. First comes the main one:
All edible foods which are designated for use by man require preparation but do not require intention. "Do not require intention"
means, these are foods that the generality of humanity deems edible.
They therefore fall into the class of food for purposes of contracting
uncleanness, whatever a given individual may have in mind. But they
have to be prepared as food for the generality of intentionality to take
effect. By contrast to what? Meat. To be classified as food, meat must
be prepared for eating. Not only so, but whatever its source, whatever its status, to be deemed food man must intend that it serve as
food; we do not take for granted that meat is food unless man means
to eat it (and then by deed confirms that intentionality). Placing
perfectly valid meat, from a beast or fowl, in the same class with meat
that Israelites cannot meat, e.g., carrion, fat that may be forbidden,
carrion and the like makes a striking statement. It is that eating meat
is not done by nature, in the way in which eating fruits and vegetables is—there, intentionality is not required, we recall!—but always
subject to a particular decision on man's part.

X. *The Oral Torah's Own Categories: [3] Ketubot*

Where the Oral Torah comes into its own, defining a category not composed by the Written Torah and dictating the corpus of law to embody that category, it is with respect to the position and status of women in Israelite society. Where Scripture says little or nothing, the Oral Torah frames large and capacious category-formations and articulates refined and fully-exposed laws therefor. Ketubot, which deals with the marriage-contract, invents an entirely new category, and Qiddushin, on the rite of betrothal, turns a casual fact of Scripture into a fully-spelled-out Halakhic category. Ketubot and Qiddushin systematically accord to a woman reciprocal and corresponding rights and obligations as the marriage as it unfolds. Ketubot in particular lays formidable emphasis upon reciprocal obligations and relationships encompassing not only the father of the woman but the woman herself, who has every right to decide freely upon relationships proposed to her and who is explicitly accorded the right of deliberation at every stage in the marital connection, beginning to end—both the right and the obligation, and, it goes without saying, responsibility as well. So, for the Halakhah, I cannot overstress, the generative premise posits reciprocity, according to the woman, as much as to the man both rights and responsibilities.

Such a mutuality of obligation between husband and wife (not the wife's father's family in general) finds no counterpart in the Halakhah of the Pentateuch, which, therefore, makes no provision for a marriage-agreement such as the ketubah. In the Written Torah Moses's system provides for special problems but no documentary protection for the wife, e.g., providing for restoration of dowry or alimony in the event of the husband's death or act of divorce, respectively. But we look in vain for systematic presentations, by Scripture, of laws concerning the Ketubah or the act of betrothal. So the topic systematically expounded in the Halakhah is treated by Scripture casually and episodically, and the generative premise of Scripture, when the topic is treated, contradicts that of the Halakhah. The marriage-contract defines the documentary locus for working out those rights and obligations; each party has an interest in the orderly formation of the social and economic fact of the marriage—and in its fair and orderly dissolution as well. Here the dissolution involves collecting the marriage-settlement from the husband's estate; as noted, elsewhere we deal with other aspects of the dissolution of the marriage (which may involve the dissolution of the household as well). That document and the arrangements it represents have no foundations in Scripture and constitute a contribution of the Oral part of the Torah alone. That is not to suggest the Written Torah makes no contribution at all, for Scripture figures. But that is only episodically, especially in two matters. And the novelty of the marriage-contract is underscored in them both. First comes the fine for rape, which is paid to the father, so Dt. 22:28-29, next comes Ex. 22:15-16 Another aspect of the Halakhah to which Scripture contributes concerns conflicting claims as to the virginity of the bride, so Dt. 22:13-21. The Written Torah makes provision for the claim of the father, but leaves a considerable gap when it comes to the woman herself. Accordingly, Scripture does not contribute the requirement of a marriage-agreement that provides for the woman's support in the event of divorce of death of the husband, that is left to the Oral Torah.

Ketubot does not owe its subject-matter to Scripture, though the category does encompass such information as Scripture supplies. Not does Scripture's treatment of the subject, so far as it occurs, in any way correspond at the level of premise with the Halakhic treatment of the same subject. In the present category-formation, therefore, the Oral Torah takes as its generative premise that reciprocal and corresponding rights and obligations devolve upon all parties to the marriage, at each point in the unfolding of the marriage. These parties are the girl, the boy, and the girl's family (father). The marriage-contract then defines the locus for the negotiation of the rights and obligations of each. All parties have an interest in the orderly formation of the social and economic fact of the marriage—the foundation, after all, of the household—and in its orderly dissolution as well. In the present context, that means, collecting the settlement from the husband's estate. Ketubot deals with the beginning, middle, and end of the marriage through human action, Yebamot, through supernatural action (death of the husband without children and disposition of the marital bond between the widow and the deceased's surviving brother). Scripture deals with the latter, but, so far as I am able to discern, not with the former transaction.

XI. *The Oral Torah's Original Categories: [4] Qiddushin*

Concerning the sanctification of a woman to a particular man, Scripture presents its slight data in a subordinate clause at Dt. 24:1, "When a man takes a wife and marries her." The act of "taking" involves "marries," the Hebrew word standing for, have sexual relations with. Effectively, therefore, nothing in Scripture prepares us for the topic, let alone the structure and system, of Qiddushin. But that is for a positive reason: the Halakhah insists upon the woman's concurrence in the transaction, of which for the woman in general the legal system of the written part of the Torah knows nothing. What we found in connection with Ketubot applies without qualification to Qiddushin. The topic and the generative premises that guide the formulation of the Halakhah on the topic—both are worked out in their own terms and framework, at no point in the setting of Scripture, which scarcely takes up the subject to begin with.

The problematic of the Halakhah of Qiddushin, the sanctification of a particular woman for a particular man, emerges in the intersection of the language of acquisition with the language of sanctification. A householder buys a cow, in acquiring it, he does not sanctify it. Unless he means to offer it on the altar in Jerusalem), a person who utilizes the same cow, e.g., milks it or uses it for ploughing, does not offend God. The issue of sanctification does not enter the transaction. But a householder acquires a woman thereby consecrates the woman as his wife. Another person who utilizes the same woman, e.g., has sexual relations with her and produces children by her, enormously outrages God (not to mention the husband). The category, sanctification and its opposite, applies. Yet in both instances the result is, acquiring title to, rights over the cow or the woman. Indeed, slaves, movables, and real estate prove analogous to the betrothal of a woman. The transaction by which a householder acquires a wife, slave, movables or real estate forms the genus, the language and categories and action-symbols proving constant.

But when it comes to the woman, an enormous point of difference renders the woman an active participant in the transfer of title. She has to consent, and when she does, her status as person, not merely as property, changes; and the change is called sanctification. So the opening exposition of the Halakhah serves to establish the genus—money, writ, usucaption for the slave, money, writ, act of sexual relations, comparable to usucaption, for the woman. These are compared and contrasted and firmly situated in a single classification: things that are acquired by the householder through a common repertoire of procedures of transfer of title from owner to owner.

The Written Torah speaks of "taking," the Oral Torah, of "sanctifying." The generative premise of the Halakhah of Qiddushin comes to expression in the very title of the category, and the operative language throughout, built on the root QDSh, sanctify. The language of sanctification encompasses the altar and its offerings, and, by extension, the table and the meat eaten upon it. But what generative symbol links the sanctity of the Temple to that of the bedroom, and what concrete model will govern the formulation of Halakhah within the theory of sanctification and sanctity that the Temple realizes? Here, that same language of sanctification is invoked in particular in the formulation of the Halakhah of family formation and dissolution, as much as in the setting of domestic meals in the model of food of Holy Things subject to protection from uncleanness. If Israel is to form a kingdom of priests and a holy people, and if belonging to the holy people comes about naturally, that is, by birth to a Jewish mother, as the Halakhah everywhere takes for granted, then genealogy will take its place beside theology as arbiter of the validity of acts of betrothal. Israel is formed by the householder with women who can be sanctified to the man at hand and who agree to enter into a sacred relationship with him, to maintain the domestic order of the householder and bear and raise children. When that relationship is characterized as holy and the result of an act of sanctification, the intent is not figurative or merely symbolic but material and concrete. Within the walls of the Israelite household through betrothal ("qiddushin") an act of sanctification takes place that bears as weighty consequences as does an act of sanctification of an animal for an offering to God in the Temple; the transaction at hand defines the locus at which Israel attains the sanctity that God proposes to bestow on it.

The difference between the consecrated offering for the altar and the consecrated woman for the marriage canopy, governing the entire process of sanctification of woman to man, lies in what distinguishes the human being, man or woman, from the beast: the freedom of will, the power of intentionality. The man may declare the woman sanctified, but if she objects, the act is null. If of age, she must accept the tokens of betrothal, directly or through her agent. If not of age, when she comes of age, she may reject an act of betrothal, even consummated, taken by others with control over her in her minority, her father if he is alive, her brothers if he is deceased. Then she simply ups and walks out, not requiring even a writ of divorce. No sanctification has ever taken place, the woman not having confirmed what has happened through the exercise of will of others with temporary jurisdiction over her. So the woman consecrated for her husband is like the beast sanctified for the altar, but with a formidable difference. The contribution of the Oral Torah is not only formidable in its dimensions but remarkably distinctive in its conception.

XII. *The Oral Torah's Original Categories*

Neither as to topic and expository program for said topic nor as to generative premises do Berakhot, Demai, Ketubot, Qiddushin, Taanit, Tamid, Tohorot, and Uqsin look to Scripture. The Hala-khah in those categories coalesces around its own topic, identifies the problematic of the topic, works out the concrete exegetical program, and identifies the implicit principles of cogency, all within a rationality and a logic that Scripture has not suggested. The question that is raised about the several topics, respectively, consequently does not derive from the Written Torah. None gains coherence by following the plan of Scripture on the same topic. That is not to suggest the autonomous constructions of the Halakhah utterly ignore the Pentateuch or raise questions unimagined within the Written Torah's narrative and legal repertoire. The Written Torah speaks of the cleanness of foods, though Tohorot and Uqsin, on domestic matters, stand on their own. The written Torah concerns itself with questions of marital relationships (we need go no further than Sotah to make that point!). But Qiddushin and Ketubot ask their own questions about relationships that Scripture for its part does not take up in juridical terms. The written Torah values piety outside of the Temple and its offerings, though Berakhot and Taanit pursue that of the individual and the village, never addressed in Scripture. The Written Torah defines the issues of tithing, and in that context, Demai's issue—doubtfully-tithed produce—finds a place for itself. And the daily whole offering is explicitly called for by Scripture, though the category-formation set forth by Tamid's narrative finds no counterpart therein.

The Oral part of the Torah pursues themes common to both parts of the Torah, identifies problems of its own, categories of its own invention, that the Written part of the Torah can accommodate. That is so, even if, in the documents before us, the Written part of the Torah has not precipitated the formation of said categories. With the entirety of the Pentateuchal Law in hand, we should have had little basis on which to fabricate category-formations corresponding to Qiddushin and Ketubot, Uqsin and Tohorot, Demai (for one set of reasons) and Taanit (for another set). And Tamid is a special case. Following the point of insistence of the Tosefta and two Talmuds in their provision of proof-texts where the Mishnah's formulation lacks them, we must conclude, the Written Torah can tell us why we have the Halakhic categories based on Scripture. But the Written Torah cannot tell us the reason we have the free-standing ones, certainly not Tohorot, Uqsin, Ketubot, and Qiddushin. In those category-formations, Moses set forth constructions and large conceptions that the Written Torah may accommodate but does not generate: Israel's holiness extends to the household and its table, women are possessed of rights of intentionality and sentience such that they form active players within Israel's polity. How these two quite distinct principles coalesce—the extension of sanctity beyond the limits of the Temple, the extension to women of the active intelligence yielding rights and responsibilities that pertain to man—defines a critical problem in the analysis of the Oral Torah as a coherent corpus. But before we can turn to the whole, we must identify the entire range of indicative traits of the Oral Torah's category-formation. So we continue our analysis of the parts. These are two. First come those category-formations that show the Oral Torah to depend upon, but to develop and amplify, components of the Written Torah. Then we consider those category-formations, the topic of which Scripture sets forth, but the entire problematics of which the Oral Torah has framed.

XIII. *The Oral Torah Systematizes the Written Torah's Category-Formations, Spirit and Letter Alike: The Four Interstitial Categories*

We have now addressed the extremes, first, category-formations dictated by the Written Torah and fully defined thereby, letter and spirit, second, category-formations original to the Oral Torah and entirely articulated therein, spirit and letter. In the former case the Written Torah has defined the topic and has set forth the main lines

of the law on that topic; the Oral Torah refines and polishes the
Written Torah's construction. In the latter case, the Oral Torah has
identified the topic on its own, and, it goes without saying, intuits the
generative tensions inherent therein and translates these into practical cases, exemplary of extensive principles. Of the fifty-nine pertinent category-formations of the Halakhah of the Mishnah-Tosefta-
Yerushalmi-Bavli, we have now taken up fifteen. The remaining
forty-four in the middle, we differentiate into distinct taxa by a simple
criterion: when in dialogue with the Written Torah, has the Oral
Torah made its own statement as well? And, if so, where do we find
its imprints? So we differentiate between spirit and letter, now in a
different way. The Written Torah refers to a subject, the Oral Torah
develops that subject. Would that, as we come close to the data,
matters remained so simple! But here we take up a wholly fresh
analytical program in the phenomenology of the Oral Torah: four
classes of interstitial tractates. The remaining forty-four do two
things: they [1] take up topics defined by the Written Torah and [2]
supply a quite fresh corpus of Halakhah.

a. *Subordinate but Not Concentric Expositions of the Same*
Category-Formations

First, we take up the Oral Torah's subordinated but still not completely concentric amplification of the Written Torah's category-formations. In simple terms, the Written Torah sets forth the letter and
the spirit, the Oral Torah extenuates the letter but does so entirely
within the spirit of the established topic. Here, some of the category-
formations carry forward Scripture's topic and remain within what is
implicit in Scripture's presentation of the topic, even while they
greatly augment Scripture's repertoire of laws. But the presentation
of Scripture's category-formation transcends the limits of Scripture's
detailed program; no comparison of the relationship of the Halakhah
of Horayot to Leviticus Four with the relationship of the Halakhah of
Abodah Zarah to, e.g., Ex. 23:13 or Dt. 7:5, can sustain the classification of both bodies of Halakhah within the same theme. If we
know what Scripture says about that theme, we can in general terms
predict the spirit of the Oral Torah's treatment of the theme, even
though we cannot outline the detailed program that will guide the
Oral Torah's articulation thereof. That is why the discussion focuses
upon areas in which the Oral Torah takes up a topic defined by the

Written Torah and develops it extensively, while, in my judgment, remaining well within the conceptual framework of the Written Torah. Here the spirit is the same but the letter gives substance to the spirit; the Written Torah has conveyed the spirit, the Oral Torah, the letter. If we wish to define what the Oral Torah contributes on its own to the fundamental corpus of principles of the Torah, however, we look elsewhere.

b. *Received Topics, Innovative Compositions of Category-Formations Thereof*

Second, we turn to category-formations of the Oral Torah that innovate, but do not wholly invent, new constructions. These encompass constructions that put together diverse topics, whether or not Scripture has defined said topics, into altogether new composites. Here Scripture contributes information but not a cogent presentation of information, refers to a subject casually or alludes to it unsystematically; then the Oral Torah gathers together diverse information and forms of it a single simple composition of its own. In these independent category-formations formed of data of Scripture together with data not originating there in any articulated way, we uncover part of the Oral Torah's contribution. It is that part of the Oral Torah's contribution that recasts received categories into new ones. A simple comparison of the bits and pieces of information utilized at Sanhedrin-Makkot, or, more strikingly still, at Miqvaot and the three Babas, suffices to make the point. Any account of the Oral Torah's share of the entire Torah will accommodate the enormously original reworkings of Scripture's fact into entirely fresh constructions bearing quite distinctive statements that are portrayed.

c. *Received Letter, New Spirit: The Asymmetrical Category-Formations of the Oral Torah*

Third, we deal with category-formations topically defined by the Written Torah but in precipitating concept vastly recast by the Oral Torah's treatment of the subject. In the former case the Oral Torah's category-formations are concentric with the Written Torah's, in the latter, they are quite asymmetrical. In the former case, the Oral Torah makes no independent contribution of its own, but explores the implications of that of the Written Torah in the spirit of the

Written Torah. In the present case the Oral Torah in an utterly original manner reworks the Written Torah's topic. Nothing in the Oral Torah's presentation of Shabbat-Erubin, to take the single most blatant case, could have hinted at the particular problematics worked out by that protean composition, nor should we have found it possible even to assess the proportions and the foci of the Oral Torah's presentation solely on the foundation of the Written Torah's equally fully-realized treatment of the topic of the Sabbath. Here is the Oral Torah at its most innovative: not when it invents a new category-formation or reconfigures received categories into new combinations, but where it presents something much more original than variations on a theme.

d. *A Fresh Statement out of a Familiar Topic and Routine Exposition Thereof*

Finally, we survey the most subtle set of all: the category-formations in which Scripture's topics are amplified along lines proposed by Scripture, but with unanticipated results, results that require a close reading of what is implicit in details of the Halakhah, not merely at the surface of its programmatic exposition, such as suffices in the first three sets. Here we move beyond questions of letter and spirit altogether. For on the surface the Oral Torah takes over the topic of Scripture and clarifies problems within the received framework. But beneath the surface, discrete details hither and yon coalesce to make points that quite reconstruct what is at stake. Out of the received category, amplified within Scripture's own program, the Oral Torah makes a statement of its own. And, I claim throughout, that statement simply brings to the surface what is embedded and implicit in Scripture, read within the correct hermeneutics. This the sages have discovered and we are able to reconstruct by picking out the critical details.

To clarify this category, a case facilitates the work. The Halakhic category-formation, Abodah Zarah, takes up Halakhic (and Aggadic) statements of Scripture and, in their spirit, works out a set of cognate topics; the topics as spelled out in the Oral Torah's Halakhah in every way register principles implicit in, indeed required by, those of the Written Torah. Circumstances (at least in theory) account for the topical amplifications of the Oral Torah, thus: new problems, established principles. By contrast, for the reconfiguration of Scripture's topic and facts into a profound, and theologically encompassing, statement, we turn to one of the case of Orlah. That case shows the Oral Torah engaged in a most subtle operation. On the surface the laws of Orlah appear simply to extend and clarify the corresponding rule of Scripture. But when we reflect upon the substance of those laws, penetrating into their implications guided by the sages' explicit reading of the pertinent verses of Scripture, now in the Tannaite Midrash-compilation Sifra, we find a surprising fact. The laws turn out to form a sustained and detailed commentary upon the topic, framed by appeal to a completely unanticipated hermeneutics. Specifically, Orlah is about not eating the produce of a fruit tree in its first three years and what to do with the yield of the fourth year. The Oral Torah turns that body of Halakhah into a systematic commentary, through rules of conduct, upon the narrative of the fruit-bearing tree in Genesis 1. Here, then, a remarkably original hermeneutics has shaped the laconic discourse of the Halakhah, and the details of the Halakhah upon which the Oral Torah focuses, on the surface dictated by the Written Torah, turn out to yield a message conveyed, and I think discovered, by the Oral Torah.

XIV. *Same Spirit, Same Letter—But Lots More Letters*

We turn to the entries of the first of my four categories, those in which the letter of the law of the Oral Torah gives life to the spirit of the Written Torah's declarations of category and principle alike.

a. *Abodah Zarah*

The topic of the category-formation, Abodah Zarah, derives from Scripture's Halakhic heritage: the disposition of idolatry. But the concrete problems that the Halakhah wishes to discuss in respect to that topic do not find definition in Scripture's presentation of the subject. On first glance, therefore, we might by inclined to classify the tractate among those that vastly overspread the limits of the Written Torah: same topic, fresh amplification. Nonetheless, the basic proposition implicit in Scripture's statement on the topic animates the Halakhic exposition, and on that basis, I classify the category, Abodah Zarah, among those in which Scripture's premises are derivatively amplified but not vastly augmented with fresh conceptions. On the other hand, the Halakhah raises so many questions not addressed in Scripture's law that the category in no way proves congruent with those entirely symmetrical with Scripture's counterparts, such as we examined earlier in this study. In the balance, by the criterion of derivative amplification I classify the category as I do, but with a measure of doubt. Readers will judge for themselves whether that classification proves compelling or shaky.

In its Land Israel is to wipe out idolatry, even as a memory. Scripture is clear that Israel is to obliterate all mention of idols (Ex. 23:13), not bow down to gentiles' gods or serve them but overthrow them and break them into pieces (Ex. 23:24): "You shall break down their altars and dash in pieces their pillars and hew down their Asherim and burn their graven images with fire" (Dt. 7:5). Israelites are commanded along these same lines at Dt. 12:2-3. Accordingly, so far as the Written Torah supplies the foundations for the treatment of the matter by the Oral Torah, the focus of discourse concerning the gentiles is idolatry. Scripture's Halakhah does not contemplate Israel's co-existing, in the land, with gentiles and their idolatry.

But what the Halakhic corpus addresses indicates that the Halakhah speaks to a world that is not so simple. The Halakhah takes for granted that, while the Land belongs to Israel, gentiles live there too—and run things. Israel no longer forms a coherent collectivity that engages in corporate action but a realm made up of individuals, with their distinctive circumstances and particular interests. The Halakhah of the Oral Torah commences its treatment of the same subject with the opposite premise from the one that animates Scripture: gentiles live side by side (whether or not in the Land of Israel) with Israelites, and Israelites have to sort out the complex problems of co-existence with idolatry. And that co-existence involves not whole communities, the People, Israel, and the peoples, whoever they may be, but individuals, this Israelite living side by side with that gentile. Not only so, but the Oral Torah uses the occasion of idolatry to contemplate a condition entirely beyond the imagination of Scripture, which is the hegemony of idolatrous nations and the subjugation of holy Israel. The Oral Torah makes of the discussion of idolatry the occasion for the discussion of Israel's place among the nations of the world and of Israel's relationships with gentiles. Furthermore, the Oral Torah's theory of who Israel is finds its context in the contrast with the gentiles.

The meeting point with the Written Torah is defined by the indicative trait of the gentiles, which is their idolatry; that is all that matters about them. But the Halakhah of the Oral Torah deals a more complex program of problems. It addresses, first, commercial relationships, second, matters pertaining to idols, and finally to the particular prohibition of wine part of which has served as a libation to an idol. The whole is regularized and ordered. There are relationships with gentiles that are absolutely prohibited, particularly occasions of idol-worship; as we shall see, the Halakhah recognizes that these are major commercial events. When it comes to commerce with idolaters Israelites may not sell or in any way benefit from certain things, may sell but may not utilize certain others, and may sell and utilize yet others. Here, we see immediately, the complex and systematic mode of thought that governs the Oral Torah's treatment of the topic vastly transcends the rather simple conception that animates Scripture's discussion of the same matter. There are these unstated premises within the Halakhah: [1] what a gentile is not likely to use for the worship of an idol is not prohibited; [2] what may serve not as part of an idol but as an appurtenance thereto is prohibited for Israelite use but permitted for Israelite commerce; [3] what serves idolatry is prohibited for use and for benefit. In reflecting upon relationships with the gentiles, meaning, idolaters, the Oral Torah moreover takes for granted a number of facts. These turn out to yield a single generalization: gentiles are assumed routinely to practice bestiality, murder, and fornication.

While the Halakhic development of Scripture's topic addresses circumstances not contemplated in Scripture, the Halakhah carries forward Scripture's perspectives and realizes Scripture's basic premises. The Halakhic program is independent, but its viewpoint wholly coincides with Scripture's. Here we may well characterize the Halakhah as secondary and derivative. The generative premise of the Halakhah is easily defined. The Halakhah distinguishes Israel from the gentiles, and it does so strictly within the limits of Scripture's law. By both parts of the Torah, gentiles by definition are idolaters, and Israelites by definition are those that worship the one, true God, who has made himself known in the Torah. In the Oral Torah, that is the difference—the only consequential distinction—between Israel and the gentiles. The Halakhah takes as its problem the concretization of that distinction, the demonstration of where and how the distinction in theory makes a huge difference in the practice, the conduct, of everyday affairs. What is at stake is that Israel stands for life, the gentiles like their idols for death. An asherah-tree, like a corpse,

conveys uncleanness to those who pass underneath it, as we noted at
M. 3:8: "And he should not pass underneath it, but if he passed
underneath it, he is unclean." Before proceeding, let us consider a
clear statement of why idolatry defines the boundary between Israel
and everybody else. The reason is that idolatry—rebellious arrogance
against God—encompasses the entire Torah. The religious duty to
avoid idolatry is primary; if one violates the religious duties, he breaks
the yoke of commandments, and if he violates that single religious
duty, he violates the entire Torah. Violating the prohibition against
idolatry is equivalent to transgressing all Ten Commandments. While
Moses in the Written Torah does not frame matters in that way,
everything that he does say points to that conclusion. We may say,
therefore, that while Scripture has contributed the topic, treated by
the Halakhah in its own way, Scripture has also dictated the principles that animate the amplification of that topic.

b. *Arakhin*

Principally as a matter of personal initiative individuals consecrate
something of value. Such supererogatory acts of sanctification may
pertain either to persons or to real estate, and both are covered
within the Halakhic category of Arakhin, Valuations. A person may
sanctify himself or his property, or he may sanctify the worth of
another party, and in either case is obligated to pay to the Temple
the value of what he has declared sacred. That represents the process
of "redemption," that is, redeeming with a payment of money what
has been sanctified for the purposes of the Temple. The process of
redemption regularizes the matter. The pertinent statement of Scripture is at Lev. 27:1-8. The Halakhah treats as part of the same
category the dedication of real estate, not only one's personal Valuation, to the Temple. Scripture treats the subject at Lev. 27:16-25. At
Lev. 27:28-9 the Halakhah takes up the disposition of things that are
declared herem. The final topic is the sale and redemption of a field
that has been received as an inheritance and of a dwelling place in a
walled city, Lev. 25:13-17, 25-34. Both personal valuations and dedi-
cations of real property—fields and houses under specified circumstances—represent donations to God through the Temple and the
priesthood. The Halakhah systematically expounds the program set
forth by the cited passages of Scripture, remaining wholly within the
bounds of the principles therein set down. Scripture stresses the vari-

ations in the value of persons. The Halakhah defines who may make such a pledge, how we sort out variables of ability to pay, and then takes up the vow of personal worth, distinct from the vow of valuation that Scripture defines but certainly congruent with its principle. The Halakhah defines the process for paying Valuations to the Temple. It further joins to the topic of pledges of personalty the matter of pledges of realty, clarifying the way in which we evaluate donated real estate that returns to the person who acquired the property by inheritance. The matter of herem is worked out in detail. Finally, we address the sale and redemption of inherited property and dwelling places in walled cities, a topic that invokes the same principles as pertain to the dedication of realty. Here, therefore, the Halakhah has treated as a single category four cognate categories of donations that Scripture presents separately and has supplied each with a set of regulations for actually applying the law of Scripture. The Halakhah receives the topic from Scripture and takes as its task the provision of rules for applying the law. However complex the details, though, the Halakhic statement of the Oral Torah proves simple: Israel has the power to effect the sanctification of what is subject to Israel's own will. Individually, not only jointly, Israel engages with God as God wishes to be engaged with. I do not see any point at which Scripture's laws would differ on these points.

c. *Bekhorot*

Like all Holy Things, the firstlings under certain conditions may be "redeemed," that is, may be transferred to a secular status in exchange for replacement of the value of what has been consecrated. The firstborn of man is redeemed for five shekels (Num. 18:16). The firstborn of a clean beast, of the flock or herd, is deemed holy and is given to the priest whether or not it is blemished. If it is not blemished, it is offered up on the altar, and the priests eat the meat; it is Lesser Holy Things. If it is blemished, it is the property of the priest, not of the altar of God, and is slaughtered as an unconsecrated animal and eaten without restrictions. If we know what Scripture says, we can outline in advance the program of the Halakhah. The pertinent verses of the Written Torah begin with the most general, covering firstborn whether of man or beast, at Ex. 13:2. The firstborn of man and of unclean beasts are redeemed, the proceeds assigned to the priests; the firstborn of clean beasts is slaughtered in the Temple

court, the meat then going to the priest, so Num. 18:15-18). If the
firstborn of a clean beast was blemished, it is given to the priest; he
may eat it anywhere or sell it or give it away, as his own property (Dt.
15:21-22). One must sanctify the firstling of an ox and declare it holy
(Dt. 15:10). Firstlings may not be brought to the Land from outside
(Dt. 14:23). A firstling must be eaten during its first year, whether
blemished or otherwise (Dt. 15:20-22). What renders a firstborn animal unfit for the altar renders a priest unfit for service, a signal of the
comparability of the firstborn and the priesthood (Lev. 21:18-20).
The Halakhah encompasses, also, the tithe of the herds and the
flocks (Lev. 27:32-33). The Halakhah has chosen, out of the topic of
firstlings, a diverse program of inquiry, not so well focussed as elsewhere. But out of the details, a few striking generalizations do
emerge, and these pertain to the critical tensions and generative concerns of the Halakhah overall: Land of Israel, people (genealogy) of
Israel, and how the sanctification of each dictates their respective
obligations to God. The Halakhah answers questions of clarification
and extension, undertaking inquiries natural to the topic: who is
obliged to set aside the firstborn, the distinction between the firstborn
of an unclean and of a clean beast, the status of gentiles, application
of Scripture's rules, the matter of blemishes. When we come to the
firstborn of man, the Halakhic program follows suit. The exposition
of tithe of cattle raises similarly routine questions.

d. *Bikkurim*

Firstfruits are presented on Pentecost, when the required declaration
is made in conformity with Dt. 26:1ff.; firstfruits are carried in a
basket that is waved by the priest before the altar. Animals are
brought as peace- and whole-offerings. The Halakhah rests upon
Scripture at three passages. The first treats the act of separating
firstfruits as acknowledgement of God's keeping his promise to give
his people the Land. The second encompasses the first harvest of
wheat within the calendar of the cult., so Deut. 26:1-11, Lev. 23:9-
21, and Numbers 28:26. Deuteronomy wants firstfruits from all produce to be presented to the priests of the central sanctuary, with two
declarations; no particular time is indicated, no sacrifices required.
The priestly code requires offerings but knows no declaration. But it
does specify that the firstfruits are presented at Pentecost. The
Priestly Code then involves a sheaf of barley from the first harvest,

presented to the priest on the day after the Sabbath of the feast of unleavened bread; the priest waves it with appropriate rites. That permits grain of the new harvest to be eaten. Seven weeks later is the day of firstfruits, two loaves and various other offerings waved by the priest as a wave-offering. Reading the Torah whole, the sages formed the Halakhah of Bikkurim out of the pertinent passages and framed the whole into a coherent statement. They required a single, annual presentation at the Temple of selections of all produce native to the Land, presented on Pentecost, with the required recitation. They are carried in a basket; the priest waves it before the altar. In addition oxen and pigeons are brought as peace- and whole-offerings, respectively. Scripture has set forth the main lines of inquiry into the present topic. The particular species of produce that serve, the particular classification of Israelite that presents the offering and defines it—these convey the entire message. The Oral Torah simply identifies the main points implicit in Scripture and elaborates upon them by expounding their practical implications. The entire statement responds to two questions: what is required, who is obligated? The answer is, what is required is firstfruits of those species in which the Land specializes, and who is obligated is, the Israelite who not only possesses a share in the Land but also derives from the Israel to whom the Land was initially handed over. The Halakhah amplifies Scripture's presentation of the subject, stressing this and that, but in no way moves far beyond the limits of Scripture's own account.

e. *Keritot*

Man bears responsibility for what he does, and the Written Torah explicitly imputes guilt even for actions committed inadvertently and not with the intention of violating the Torah. It follows that the Halakhah has to provide for penalties to expiate sin or crime, whether deliberate or otherwise. Here making its statement concerning the taxonomic power of intentionality, the Halakhah distinguishes deliberate from inadvertent sin or crime. A sin-offering is required in the case of an action, the deliberate commission of which is penalized by extirpation (early death, before the age of 60), and a suspensive guilt offering in the case of doubt. The principal interest then is in animal-offerings that expiate sin. The Written Torah contributes to the topic the following statement, at Lev. 5:17-19; I underline the key-language:

"If any one sins, <u>doing any of the things that the Lord has commanded not to be done, though he does not know it, yet he is guilty and shall bear his iniquity</u>. He shall bring to the priest a ram without blemish out of the flock, valued by you at the price for a guilt offering, and the priest shall make atonement for him for the error that he committed unwittingly, and he shall be forgiven. It is a guilt offering; he is guilty before the Lord"

Since the generative premise of the Halakhah is the distinction between deliberate and inadvertent sin or crime, with extirpation the penalty for the former, the guilt offering expiating the latter, Scripture has defined the foundations for the articulation and exegesis of the Halakhah. That is clear when we examine the principal statement of the Halakhah of Keritot, at M. Ker. 1:2:

For those [thirty-six classes of transgressions] are people liable, <u>for deliberately doing them</u>, to the punishment of extirpation, <u>and for accidentally doing them</u>, to the bringing of a sin offering, and for not being certain of whether or not one has done them, to a suspensive guilt offering.

The governing distinction set forth by the Halakhah simply builds upon Scripture's law. Three divisions make up the topical presentation, occasions on which the sin-offering or extirpation, as the case may be, is required, a single sin-offering and multiple sins, and the suspensive guilt-offering, required where one inadvertently may or may not have committed a sin. The order is logically necessary, since the suspensive guilt-offering cannot come before the sin- or guilt-offering for what one is certain he has done. In its principal divisions—the sin-offering as against extirpation, the suspensive guilt-offering as against the unconditional guilt-offering—the Halakhah treats in concrete terms the distinction between deliberate, intentional sin and unintentional law-violation. Nowhere else in the Halakhah do we find so sharp a line distinguishing the unintentional sin, penalized by an offering, and the intentional one, penalized by extirpation. The reason that that critical distinction concerns us in the particular Halakhah at hand is self-evident. Here is where God intervenes, and it is God above all who knows what is in man's heart and can differentiate intentional from unintentional actions. And it also is God who has the heaviest stake in the matter of intentional sin, for intentional sin represents rebellion against the Torah and God's rule through the Torah.

f. *Maaser Sheni*

Second tithe is comprised by ten percent of the net yield of the crop after other tithes have been removed; in the first and second, fourth and fifth years of the Sabbatical cycle, second tithe is to be designated as sanctified, then bodily transported to and eaten in Jerusalem. If that is not feasible, the sanctity inhering in the produce is to be converted into value in the form of coins for transport and expenditure there. The rules governing the handling of the produce pertain, where appropriate, to the disposition of the coins. The same rules apply to the fruit of an orchard in the fourth year after the orchard is planted. That matter is worked out in the laws of 'Orlah. Lev. 19:23ff. declares that the produce of a tree in the fourth year after planting must be "set aside for jubilation before the Lord." This is taken to mean, fourth year fruit, like Second Tithe, has to be eaten in Jerusalem. So the two classes of produce are subject to the laws set forth at Dt. 14:22-26. If the Written Torah calls Israel to Jerusalem for a meal with God as host, the Oral Torah explores its own issues, concerning the food for the meal in particular. But the exegesis treats the cases of Scripture as exemplary. This it does by treating in general terms the very specific conception of the Written Torah. That is why I classify the development of the topic as derivative and not independently developed.

The governing principle deriving from Scripture's case is that the sanctified food may be secularized, its value transferred into cash, then the coins, bearing the value of sanctified food, are brought to Jerusalem and converted back into food. What, exactly, does it mean to transfer "sanctity" to coins from food, then to food from coins? How do sages conceive such a transaction between Israel and God to take place? The Halakhah of the Oral Torah in practical terms takes up the important problems inhering in the conception of holiness: what exactly does "holiness" entail, that is, is it a matter of substance or of status? and when the one, when the other? The present case, involving the transfer of holiness or the status of sanctification to and from produce, to and from coins, requires sages to translate into concrete rules whatever conception of "the sacred" they maintained. For the sages may think about abstract questions, but they set forth their results in practical and concrete cases, certain that their disciples will grasp the rule inhering in the case. So the Halakhah engages sages in deep thought about what something's being "sanctified" actually means: what difference does it make when produce or coins are sanctified, as against when they are not sanctified? Then again, the affect upon what is designated as holy that is exerted at the moment of entry into a place that is holy—the interplay of status and location—has to be explored. A second concern, the final disposition of God's share of the crop ("the law of removal"), so that, by a given point in the year, the householder will have handed over what is owing to God's designated surrogates receives systematic attention as well at Dt. 26:12-19. The law of removal assures that the crops designated as holy will not accumulated in a hoard but will be distributed to those for whom God has assigned them, the priests, Levites, poor, the holy city, and the like. The exposition by the Halakhah of that topic likewise remains well within the borders of Scripture's presentation of the same. The way in which things become holy and cease to be holy forms the problem for sages, because in their view the sanctification is a status that is conferred or removed, not a condition that is intrinsic to things. Scripture itself dictates the conception that the produce designated as second tithe and so sanctified may be turned into money and carried in that form to Jerusalem, there to be converted back into (other) produce for consumption in Jerusalem. The details of the rules then yield a variety of governing principles.

g. *Meilah*

From the moment that an animal is designated as an offering ("sanctified"), the sacrifier may make no use of the beast. What happens when Holy Things unintentionally are used for ordinary purposes, God's property for the common Israelite's benefit? To state that the sacrilege was not deliberate, the value received must be returned, along with a penalty of a fifth more. But in the case of inadvertent sacrilege, no further penalty is imposed. Lev. 5:15-16 states, "If anyone commit a trespass of sacrilege and sin through error in the Holy Things of the Lord, then he shall bring his forfeit to the Lord, a ram without blemish for a guilt offering, and he shall make restitution for that which he has done amiss in the holy thing and add the fifth part thereto." We must lay stress on the phrase, "through error." The Halakhah rests upon the principle that people do not deliberately steal from God. Sacrilege involves any use of Holy Things for private purposes. What is involved, however, is limited. Once any party, for any reason, has legitimate access to Holy Things, then sacrilege no longer pertains, even though the individual Israelite who has unintentionally carried out the act has no right to make use of the Holy Things. The simple law of Scripture suffices to generate a sizable secondary expansion here. Scripture lays down that Israel's relationship with God requires clear lines of distinction between what belongs to God and what belongs to the Israelite. But the distinction between secular and sacred proves complex, the gradations are several, and the nuances such that Scripture's admonitions against trespassing on the territory of the sacred are considerably complicated.

The governing theory is, if we punish a person for inadvertently committing sacrilege, we treat as secular what has been subjected to sacrilege. That principle places narrow limits on the matter of sacrilege. For, the Halakhah holds, once anyone may legitimately use what is God's, then the status of sanctification—what belongs uniquely to God—is suspended. The premise of the Halakhah then rests on a reading of Israel's proper intentionality. Israelites are assumed not to wish to appropriate for their own use what belongs to God and will not do so. If they do so and realize it, they make amends. At stake in sacrilege is the minimum protection of Holy Things from inadvertent misuse, on the one side, and the maximum instantiation of the conditional, not absolute, status of sanctification, on the other. Then, balancing sacrilege against sanctification, the Halakhah weighs what is done by inadvertence against what is done with full deliberation. The act of sanctification vastly outweighs the act of sacrilege. That is because by the Written Torah's definition, sacrilege subject to an atoning offering—and that is what is at stake here—takes place by inadvertence, not by an act of will. Sanctification, by contrast, comes about by an act of praiseworthy will. The Halakhah has not only recapitulated the familiar notion of sanctification as a matter that is relative to circumstance, it has also made an eloquent statement indeed that in the cult Israel relates to God in full sincerity. The occasion of unintended sacrilege, its discovery and atonement, match the moment of sanctification: the Halakhah's disposition of both transactions underscore what the Halakhah finds important in the meeting of God and Israel at the altar: Israel's exemplary love and loyalty to God. While the Halakhah before us proves rich and dense, the lines of development from the category defined by Scripture prove straight and true.

h. *Menahot*

The Torah specifies numerous offerings of grain, wheat or barley, and these serve diverse occasions. The Oral Torah homogenizes these. It affords recognition only to two distinct grain offerings—the offering of the first barley of the new agricultural season, from the advent of the full moon of Nisan through Pentecost, called the 'omer, and the two loaves and show bread placed on the altar at Pentecost. All of the other diverse meal-offerings are encompassed within a common set of rules. These impose their own modes of differentiation, in place of Scripture's. Five classes of votive cereal offerings are specified: [1] a meal offering of fine flour, a meal offering baked in the oven in two forms, [2] cakes and [3] wafers, [4] a meal offering made in a griddle and [5] a meal offering made in a pan. All are subject to the same governing regulations: a tenth ephah of fine flour and a log of oil. The principal pertinent verses are Leviticus 2:1-13, Leviticus 6:7-11/14-18, and Leviticus 7:9-10. Obligatory meal offerings, in addition, include these: the meal offering of a poor sinner by reason of the sins specified at Lev. 5:11-13, the meal offering of jealousy, presented by the woman accused of adultery (Num. 5:15), the meal offering of the anointed priest or the cakes of the high priest presented every day (Lev. 6:13-16), and the meal offering brought with drink offerings along with whole offerings of peace-offerings brought by reason of vows or as votive offerings (Num. 15:2-16), with daily whole offerings and additional offerings (Num. 28:5ff.), with the whole offering of a bullock (Num.. 15:24), with the offerings of a Nazirite (Num. 6:15), with the offerings of the 'omer (first barley) and with the two loaves of show-bread (Lev. 23:13, 18), with the offerings of the person healed of the skin ailment (Lev. 14:10), with the two loaves and the show bread (Lev. 23:15-17, 24:5-9) and so on.

For its part, the Halakhah proceeds from the general to the differentiated. First of all, the Halakhah of the Oral Torah sets forth rules for meal-offerings of all categories and classifications, however prepared, for whatever purpose. Then it turns to general rules for the presentation of meal-offerings, e.g., the source for the grain, oil, and wine, the character of the measuring cups that are used for them all, and the like. It turns, third, to the special public offerings, the 'omer and the counterparts for Pentecost. At the end, the Halakhah reviews the language that is used for vows for votive offerings, and how that language is to be interpreted. The Oral Torah insists upon the systematic character of the cult, underscoring the ways in which the various, diverse offerings conform to a single pattern. But that well-crafted argument draws upon facts supplied by Scripture and simply forms them into a viable pattern. The Oral Torah cannot impose uniformities that do not exist. It can and does organize and systematize what Scripture leaves disparate. This it does by listing a rule and then exceptions thereto.

i. *Nedarim-Nazir*

The man or woman thereby adopts certain restrictions or prohibitions, whether, as in Nedarim, not to eat certain foods of any sort or to derive benefit from a given person, or, as in Nazir, not to eat grapes in particular, cut hair, or attend funerals (something the husband cannot ever prevent the wife from doing, but the Nazirite vow prevents the Nazirite from doing). These restrictions, that language, serve to provoke Heaven's interest in, and intervention into, the conduct of the man or the woman. Scripture presents the matter vowing as a dimension of the life of wives with their husbands or daughters with their fathers. That fact emerges from the pertinent verses of Scripture, which are Numbers 30:1-16 for Nedarim and Numbers 6:10-21 for Nazir. Building on Scripture's facts, the Halakhah of Nedarim-Nazir investigates the power of a person through invoking the name of Heaven to affect the classification in which he or she is situated and so his or her concrete and material relationships with other people. Scripture's facts make possible the formation of the sizable construction on vows, in which sages present their own, derivative reflections on the topic. But sages have not reshaped the topic into a medium for the presentation of an essentially fresh program of reflection and speculation. Rather, what they have done is to develop the main lines of thought implicit in Scripture itself, which takes exactly the view of the power of language that the Halakhah amplifies.

j. *Peah*

For tractate Peah Scripture forms the starting point of the Halakhah of the oral Torah for all topics but the soup-kitchen and the dole: the pe'ah-portion—a part of a field left unharvested, being specified at Lev. 19:9, gleanings at the same verse, forgotten produce at Dt.

24:19-20, the separated grapes at Lev. 19:10, defective clusters at Lev. 19:10, poorman's tithe at Dt. 26:12-13, and the definition of the poor at Lev. 19:10, Dt. 24:19, 21. Only the provision of the soup kitchen and the permanent dole, treated as an essentially secular procedure here, stand outside of Scripture. The main rules express a theory of what it means for Israelite householders to possess the Land. Support for the poor, like support for the priesthood and Levites, underscores God's ownership and reinforces the provisional character of the householder's possession. For the landless—the priesthood, the Levites, and the poor—God sets aside what is coming to him from the produce of the Land. That equalizes Israel in relationship to the Land. Some possess, others do not, portions of the Land, but all gain what they need from its produce; the householders then hold what they have on sufferance, covenantally. In that way those either not enlandised with Israel to begin with or dispossessed of their portion of the Land later on gain a position within that holy community that is nourished—and given definition—by the Land. The poor, the priests, and the Levites rely upon God. That reliance takes the form of their dependence on divine ownership of the Land for their share in its yield. Unlike the householder, they own nothing and possess nothing in the Land. But among the sacerdotal castes, the poor reach the pinnacle: they not only do not possess a portion in the Land, but the very food that the Land yields to them itself bears no marks of individual ownership. They do not own even what they eat—and they also do not worry. God provides—just as Scripture says.

k. *Rosh Hashanah*

The celebration of the appearance of the new moon defines the program of the Halakhic category, Rosh Hashanah, with its special interest in four of the sequence of new months, each signifying the beginning of a new year for one purpose or another. But among these, the most important is the new moon of Tishré, marking Rosh Hashanah, the new year, and the Halakhah of the Oral Torah focuses upon the occasion as marked in synagogue, not in Temple rites. Scripture's presentation of the themes pertinent to the Halakhic category, Rosh Hashanah, commence with the identification of the new moon of Nisan, Ex. 12:1-2, Ex. 23:16 and Ex. 34:22. The New Year par excellence, the one marked by the new moon of Tishré, is covered in Lev. 23:23-25. The same matter is presented in the more elaborate statement of Num. 29:1-6. Scripture has defined the key concerns of Rosh Hashanah, which are, first, celebration of the first of Tishré, and, second, the sounding of the Shofar. The Halakhah then builds on each topic. The Halakhah stresses the matter of the Shofar and the occasion for its utilization in line with Gen. 22. It follows that the Oral Torah, both its Halakhah and its Aggadah, takes up a position entirely symmetrical with the Written Torah. That is why I classify the category as a derivative amplification of Scripture, if not solely of Scripture's law.

1. Shebi῾it

Tractate Shebi῾it elaborates the Torah's commandment, at Lev. 25:1-8. The language of Scripture, assigning a Sabbath to the Land, dictates the topic and the way in which the Halakhah will actualize the topic, start to finish. But in the secondary amplification of matters, the Halakhah's prevailing issues and concerns will make their mark as well. A second, correlative commandment, at Dt. 15:1-3, is treated as well. The entire Halakhic structure rests squarely upon the foundations of Scripture and systematically amplifies the principles set forth there. The Halakhah outlines where and how man participates in establishing the sanctity of the Sabbatical year, expanding the span of the year to accommodate man's intentionality in working the land now for advantage then. It insists that man's perceptions of the facts, not the facts themselves, govern: what looks like a law violation is a law violation. In these and other ways the Halakhah of Shebi῾it works out the problematics of man's participation in the sanctification of the Land in the Sabbatical year. The topic of the law, restoring the perfection of creation, then joins with the generative problematics of the Halakhah to make the point that Israel has in its power the restoration of the perfection of creation, the ordering of all things to accord with the condition that prevailed when God declared creation God, therefore sanctified creation and declared the Sabbath. Scripture not only defines the topic and its generative premises. Scripture also dictates the blatant affirmation that God pays the closest attention to Israel's attitudes and intentions pervades the tractate. Otherwise there is no way to explain the priority accorded to Israelite perception of whether or not the law is kept, Israelite intention in cultivating the fields in the sixth year, and other critical components of the governing, generative problematic.

m. *Sheqalim*

Scripture describes the half-sheqel at Ex. 30:11-16. The collection of
the half-sheqel as a ransom "that there be no plague...when you
number them" plays no role in the Halakhah of the Oral Torah. The
conception that through the half-sheqel, everyone acquires a share in
the atonement offering predominates. And the stress on the public
offerings as atonement offerings, which the Halakhah of the Oral
Torah picks up, clearly begins in the Written Torah. Like Scripture,
the Oral Torah clearly understands the half-sheqel as a tax in support of the Temple and its atonement-offerings in behalf of Israel.
What the Halakhah of the Oral Torah contributes is the articulation
of the analogous relationship of the half-sheqel to tithes and heave-
offering. It is through this particular medium that all Israel, not only
the enlandised components of Israel, relate directly and concretely to
God. Here is a fine case in which Scripture supplies not only the
topic but the indicative facts that are amplified by the Halakhah.
Scripture's point, developed by the Mishnah, is that Israel relates to
God not only one by one, but all together. What is at issue? The
Tosefta makes explicit what is at stake in the matter: They exact
pledges from Israelites for their shekels, so that the public offerings
might be made of their funds. This is like a man who got a sore on
his foot, and the doctor had to force it and cut off his flesh so as to
heal him. Thus did the Holy One, blessed be he, exact a pledge from
Israelites for the payment of their shekels, so that the public offerings
might be made of their funds. For public offerings appease and effect
atonement between Israel and their father in heaven. Likewise we
find of the heave-offering of shekels which the Israelites paid in the
wilderness, as it is said, "And you shall take the atonement money
from the people of Israel land shall appoint it for the service of the
tent of meeting; that it may bring the people of Israel to remem-
brance before the Lord, so as to make atonement for yourselves" (Ex.
30:16). So what the sheqel accomplishes is to form of all Israel a
single entity before God: all have sinned, all atone, all together—just
as Scripture says.

n. *Yebamot*

While the Halakhah devotes one of its most elaborate and beautifully
articulated disquisitions to the topic of the status of the deceased
childless man's widow in respect to his family, in fact, the Halakhah

simply amplifies the explicit view of the Written Torah, which frames matters in terms of maintaining the deceased's "name" in Israel. That means, the deceased's widow is to produce a child with a surviving brother, so carrying forward the purpose of the original union, if not as originally contemplated. The pertinent verse of Scripture, Dt. 25:5-10. The match of the penalty—the deceased's brother is called a name—to the failure—not preserving the deceased's name—rests on the premise that the original act of consecration of this woman to this man meant to bring a new generation into being. The most important datum of the Halakhah is that the levirate marriage, brought about by Heaven's intervention—death without offspring—is fully comparable to the marriage brought about by a man with a woman of his choice. The counterpart of the act of betrothal of a secular union is the act of "bespeaking" (my translation for the Hebrew word, *ma'amar,* act of speech) by which a surviving brother indicates his intention of entering into levirate marriage. Just as the act of sanctification effects acquisition in the case of a woman only when both of them are agreed, so a statement of bespeaking effects acquisition of a sister-in-law only when both of them are agreed. The act of bespeaking sustains the original act of sanctification. The surviving brother confirms the intentionality of the deceased brother and quite properly proposes to realize the deceased's original act of will in consecrating that particular woman: to produce children. The upshot may be stated very simply. The bed is sanctified by the man's intention, together with the woman's acquiescence, ratified by a deed. It is desanctified by [1] the man's intention, communicated to a fully-sentient woman, ratified by the deed of drawing up and delivering the properly witnessed document of divorce. It also is desanctified [2] by the death of the husband, his intention having been realized in offspring. So intentionality may be nullified by contradictory intentionality or by the full accomplishment of the original intention—the one or the other. In laying out matters in this way, sages have taken the facts of Scripture and penetrated into what is implicit in them.

XV. *Where the Letter Gives Life to the Spirit*

In these fifteen category-formations of the Oral Torah we see how the Oral Torah identifies the spirit of the Written Torah and finds

ways of translating the spirit into the life of the social order of holy
Israel. Here the Written Torah may be compared to desert flowers,
the Oral Torah, the rare rainfall. The rain brings life to the sleeping
bud, which blooms. The spirit without the letter is null. The letter
comes about solely by reason of the spirit (to violate the limits of the
metaphor), for without the spirit, there is no letter.

The letter of the law the Oral Torah renders choate and concrete
precisely the intent—the spirit—of the Written Torah's topics and
presentation of those topics. In the Written Torah Moses declares
idolatry abhorrent to Israel. In the Oral Torah that principle animates detailed laws for a situation not contemplated in the Written
Torah, a Land of Israel in which Israel is domiciled but not in control. The Written Torah sets forth a variety of distinct rules on firstfruits. At Bikkurim the Oral Torah frames them into a coherent
statement, diverse, distinct rules being made to work together in that
one statement. The Written Torah explicitly differentiates intended
from unintended violations of the law of the Torah. At Keritot the
Oral Torah systematizes and organizes the cases of the working of
that distinction. The Written Torah provides a variety of cases illustrative of the donation and disposition of second tithe. As I characterize matters in general, so here too, the Oral Torah turns cases into
rules.

The Written Torah creates the category of theft from God, sacrilege. The Oral Torah adds, people do not deliberately steal from
God, so the Halakhah has to work out the implications of the inadvertence of sacrilege. The Written Torah defines a formidable array
of meal-offerings, and at Menahot the Oral Torah systematizes that
information, identifying principles of classification that encompass
the whole. The Written Torah identifies language as a medium of
power embodied in the vow and the special vow of the Nazirite. The
Oral Torah sets forth the working of that power. The Written Torah
lays out rules for providing a share of the crops for the poor. The
Oral Torah introduces, at Peah, into that process considerations it
deems implicit and works them out in detail. At Rosh Hashanah we
see how the Oral Torah joins two distinct formulations of matters by
the Written Torah, the Halakhic and the Aggadic, translating what is
implicit in lore into the currency of law. Hermeneutics that generate
Halakhic exegesis at Peah animate Shebi'it as well, and the Oral
Torah's formulation of that topic, fully exposed in the Written Torah, makes concrete and articulate as law what is implicit in the

theology of the Sabbath that underpins the Halakhah of the Seventh Year in Scripture itself. Scripture's letter as to the half-sheqel-tax is taken up, generalized into a governing conception, and recast as detailed law at Sheqalim. At Yebamot the written Torah presents rules and the Oral Torah brings to the surface what is implicit in those rules—issues of intentionality and the exclusion thereof—and frames a further set of rules by consequence. The remaining items follow a single pattern. The Written Torah defines the possibility of pledging personal valuations. The Oral Torah realizes that possibility in full detail. The same pattern accounts for the character of Bekhorot.

Any account of the Oral Torah seen on its own and not as a secondary amplification and dependant extension of the Written Torah will consider the cases set forth here—but only for insight into the method of the Oral Torah. How, within its logic and rationality, does the Oral Torah read the Written Torah. What we do not gain here is access to the Oral Torah's substantive program. If the Oral Torah conveys a fresh way of establishing the categorical structure and functioning system of God's plan for Israel, we shall have to find that way elsewhere. What follows shows us the way: new categories, renewal of received categories, both of them reliable signals of the workings of an autonomous intellect.

XVI. *Types of Independent Exposition of Received Category-Formations. When the Oral Torah Reorganizes the Written Torah's Category-Formation*

The Oral Torah set forth its own compositions, that is, subjects of its own devising, realized in laws of its own making. In some instances, Scripture contains references to activities not amplified by laws, e.g., Scripture knows about fasting but not about laws on the conduct of the rite; it refers to blessings and prayers but does not set forth rules for reciting blessings and regulations on how prayers are to be said (let alone what prayers are to be said). The upshot is, Scripture treats as episodic—even as idiosyncratic—what the Oral Torah subjects to public regulation and systematization. And then there are the Oral Torah's utterly original category-formations, topics upon which Scripture bears ever so lightly, articulated in accord with a problematic that in no way animates the Halakhic corpus of Scripture. But the Oral Torah contributes category-formations of another class as

well. Here the Written Torah supplies information, sometimes extensive in articulation, that the Oral Torah puts together in its own,
distinctive way. The Written Torah cannot be said to have defined a
category-formation to impart coherence to diverse bits of information, and the Oral Torah does exactly that. Or the Written Torah
spells out compositions of Halakhah that the Oral Torah combines
into composites, bearing an altogether fresh message. Or—in between—the Written Torah defines a category, the Oral Torah, a
distinct category, which is forthwith juxtaposed with that of the Written Torah.

The Halakhah as portrayed in the Mishnah (therefore also the
Tosefta-Yerushalmi-Bavli, thus, the Oral Torah) sets forth a number
of category-formations of one or another of these three types, and, in
each case, the Oral Torah turns out to have made a statement
through its juxtapositions of topics, deriving either wholly or partially
from Scripture. The same mode of innovation through recombina-
tion of topics then characterizes the two Talmuds, particularly the
second of the two. Juxtapositions—the making of connections—that
jar and disrupt both in the fundamental exposition of the Halakhah
and in the formulation of the Talmuds' amplifications thereof turn
out to bear an entirely pertinent, even urgent, message for the larger
discourse in which they take their place. Indeed, these topical composites themselves commonly constitute a comment through the juxtaposition of established categories in the formation of a new one.
Properly understood, the topical miscellanies do not jar and do not
violate the document's prevailing rationality. Such jarring juxtapositions turn out to bear an entirely pertinent, even urgent, message for
the larger discourse in which they take their place. That message is
taken for granted, not demonstrated but rather insinuated as a given.
Properly understood, the Oral Torah's composite-category-forma-
tions, like the Talmuds' later topical miscellanies, do not jar and do
not violate the Rabbinic system's prevailing rationality: what it takes
for granted as self-evident recombinations of initially-distinct categories. In each case taken up here, the exposition of the recombinant
category-formation requires a close reading of the topics that are
juxtaposed and the rationality that makes them cohere.

a. *Baba Qamma-Baba-Mesia-Baba Batra*

The three tractates of the Civil Law, Baba Qamma, the first gate,

Baba Mesia, the middle gate, and Baba Batra, the last gate, form a single, continuous statement. The Babas aim at the preservation of the just social order, the preservation of the established wholeness, balance, proportion, and stability of the social economy realized at the moment of perfection This idea is powerfully expressed in the organization of the three tractates that comprise the civil law, which treat first abnormal and then normal transactions:

i. *Illicit Transactions; Restoring Order*
   Baba Qamma
      i.   Damage by Chattels 1:1-6:6
      ii. Damages Done by Persons 7:1-10:10
   Baba Mesia
      iii. The Disposition of Other Peoples' Possessions; Bailments 1:1—3:12
      iv. Illicit Commercial Transactions. Overcharge, misrepresentation, usury 4:1-5:11
ii. *Licit Transactions; Preserving Order*
      v.   Hiring Workers. Rentals and Bailments 6:1-8:3
   Baba Mesia, Baba Batra
      vi. Real Estate B.M. 8:4-10:6, B.B. 1:1-5:5
   Baba Batra
      vii. Licit Commercial Transactions 5:6-7:4
      viii. Inheritances and Wills. Other Commercial and Legal Documents 8:1-10-8

The framers deal with damages done by chattels and by human beings, thefts and other sorts of malfeasance against the persons and the property of others. The civil law in both aspects pays closest attention to how the property and person of the injured party so far as possible are restored to their prior condition, that is, the state of normality disrupted by the damage done to property or injury done to a person. So attention to torts focuses upon penalties paid by the malefactor to the victim, rather than upon penalties inflicted by the court on the malefactor for what he has done. The pertinent verses of Scripture figure only within the framework of the exposition of the law. That is because while the triple-tractate draws heavily upon Scripture where Scripture pertains to its program, the tractate sets forth its own program, following the problematic defined in terms of the triple-tractate's own goals. Here Scripture contributes some topics, not others, and the generative premises of the entire statement vastly overspread the limits of Scripture's presentation of those topics that to begin with originate there. The Halakhic category-formation intersects with Scripture's discrete categories, but it is asymmetrical and only partly concentric. The first half of the tractates, which break in the middle of Baba Mesia, focuses upon repairing damage that is done to the social order, the second half, upon preserving the balance and perfection of that same social order. Israel on its own, in its interior relationships, is governed by Halakhah that establishes and maintains stasis, which signifies perfection, all things in their place, all persons possessing appropriate value in property, security in person. That goal the Halakhah accomplishes by righting imbalances and preserving them.

The successive components of the category-formation followed in the Mishnah-Tosefta-Yerushalmi-Bavli move from abnormal to normal events, I-IV, then V-VIII. The whole begins with damages done by chattels or by persons, thefts and other sorts of conversion of the property of others, with special attention to how we restore to a state of normality the property and person of the injured party. Numbers I-IV run through the whole of Baba Qamma and half way through Baba Mesia, to M. B.M. 5:11. The second half of the three tractates then shifts to normal transactions, not those involving torts and damages: labor relationships, rentals and bailments, real estate transactions, inheritances and estates, units V-VIII. Then the whole produces two complementary constructions, first abnormal or illicit, then normal or licit transactions. That is shown by the correspondence of unit IV, illicit commercial transactions (overcharge and usury) and unit VII, licit commercial transactions, the legal transfer of goods, unstipulated conditions and how they are enforced. This plan furthermore explains why we treat bailments twice, at III.C, damages to bailments, and then at V.C, E, responsibilities of the bailee. The former fits into the larger structure of law on the restoration of the balance of the social order (here, the value possessed by parties to the transaction at the outset, equitably distributed at the end), the latter, that on the preservation of the same order. If we look again at the picture of the whole given at the outset, we see a clear picture. The whole of Baba Qamma takes up the results of wicked intentionality, an act of will that takes the form of malice, on the one side, or flagrant neglect of one's duties, on the other. The rules of Baba Mesia address the situations in which intentionality plays a role, is excluded as irrelevant, and may or may not enter into the adjudication of a situation of conflict. And, as we have seen, the topics treated in Baba Batra in common take account of the idiosyncrasy of intentionality and exclude private interest from intervening in customary arrangements.

The entire repertoire of topics lays itself out as a huge essay on the role of man's intentionality and consequent responsibility—his will, his private plans—in the ordering of Israel's inner life. All topics grouped as illicit transactions involve righting the wrongs done by people on their own account. When free will is taken into account, encompassing negligence and malice, the social order requires forceful intervention to right the balance upset by individual aggression. Some licit transactions permit individual intentionality to register, specifically, those freely entered into and fairly balanced among contracting parties. And some licit transactions leave no space for the will of the participants and their idiosyncratic plans. Considerations of fairness take over and exclude any engagement with the private and the personal. So Israel's social order takes account of intentionality, especially controlling for the damage that ill will brings about.

The first fifteen chapters then treat intentionality in the form of negligence as a critical factor in assessing damages. But normal licit transactions are carried forward in accord with those rules of balance, proportion, and coherence that yield a society that is stable and enduring, fair and trustworthy. In the second fifteen chapters, intentionality forms only one consideration in the process of preserving the status, as to value, of parties to transactions and exchanges; it may make all the difference, no difference, some difference; it may not enter into consideration at all. That underscores the judgment of the Halakhah that, when it comes to righting wrongs against chattels and persons, the malefactor has acted willfully and has therefore to be penalized in an equitable manner. By his act of will, he has diminished the property or person of the victim; he must then restore the property or person to its prior value, so far as this is possible, and may not benefit from what he has done.

What Scripture presents episodically, the Halakhah portrays systematically. That is certainly so in Baba Qamma. But the purpose of the tractates in no way comes to realization in the articulation of the law of Scripture on the topics at hand. That is proved by the simple fact that most of Baba Mesia and Baba Batra pursues problems to which Scripture in no way devotes itself. So where Scripture provides topics of the Halakhah, the Oral Torah faithfully attends to that Halakhah; but the Oral Torah in no way limits itself to Scripture's repertoire of topics. More to the point, the Oral Torah organizes the Halakhah systematically, but in accord with its own system and its problematics, not in accord with the system—the order, the program—of the Written Torah. We have, therefore, to look elsewhere for the religious program that animates the Halakhah of the Babas.

Through their exposition of Scripture's laws of injury and misappropriation and through their formulation of their own, much more elaborate topical program for the civil order and the resolution of conflict at home, sages expose the rationality and order that inheres in the episodic rules of Scripture. Since, in their intellectual context, consistency, immutability, coherence mark perfection, sages affirm that in its details the Torah's design for dealing with conflict within holy Israel promises to perfect Israel's workaday world in the model set forth at Sinai. The Written Torah makes clear God's intense interest in the justice and equity of the Israelites' ordinary transactions among themselves. They are to form the kingdom of priests and the holy people. Their conduct with one another—the Written Torah's civil law insists in every line—shapes God's judgment of them and therefore dictates their fate. So sages here demonstrate what a man can do actively to participate in the perfection of the social order through the results of his own and his chattels' conduct. Here the consideration of man's free will proves paramount: what man by an act of will has upset, man by an act of will must restore.

In accord with the Halakhah of Baba Qamma man undertakes to assume responsibility for what he does, always in just proportion to causation. Within Israel's social order what God wants a man to do is take responsibility for his own actions, for the results of what he or his chattel has done—no more, no less. A man can and must take responsibility for not only what he does but also—and especially— what he brings about, the things he may not do but does cause to happen. Viewed in this way, the laws of Baba Qamma form a massive essay upon the interplay of causation and responsibility: what one can have prevented but through negligence (in varying measure depending on context) has allowed to take place, he is deemed in that same measure to have caused. And for that, he is held in that same measure to make amends. Responsibility begins in right attitude. Man must form the intentionality of taking responsibility for his actions; this he must do by an act of will. That is why the whole of Baba Qamma plays itself out as an exercise in the definition of the valid intentionality in transactions involving damage and conflict. Where one has diminished another, he must willingly take responsibility for his deed of omission or commission (as the tractate unfolds).

Baba Mesia and Baba Batra complete the picture. Here the issue is sustaining the social order; attitude and intentionality come into play, but in a different way from before. Sin, crime, torts and damages—these carry forward bad attitudes; differentiating types and degrees of intentionality when addressing how the social order is disrupted yields nothing of interest. By contrast, in treating ordinary exchanges and transactions, the Halakhah turns out to form an essay on when intentionality matters and when it does not. When it comes to restoring the perfection of society, specifically, where do we take account of intentionality and where not? Intentionality or attitude matters in situations of conflict. Then the attitude of both parties makes all the difference, since to resolve conflicting claims, we have in the end to conciliate all parties to a common outcome; there, intentionality or attitude forms the critical medium for restoring and sustaining balance and order. Parties to an exchange are now responsible to one another, and they must intend the outcome to be a proportionate and equal exchange of value. Both parties must accept the outcome, that is, form at the end the same attitude toward the transaction. A claim of ownership ends in an act of despair. Responsibility is proportionate to the attitude of the bailee, that is, to the degree of accountability that he has accepted to begin with. So much for the uses of intentionality in the restoration and maintenance of the social order.

Social order restored, the status quo as to value regained, what forces hold the whole together? Where responsibility prevails, man's own will and intentionality, God's will in the Torah, and the customary arrangements of a stable, just society—all these variables come into play and are to be sorted out. That is why, while single message addresses the abnormal and the illicit, the realm of torts and damages: take responsibility, a much more complex message states the requirements of maintaining matters. That message responds to the realities of the ideal society that the Halakhah makes possible. Specifically, Israel in its interior arrangements is to hold in the balance [1] personal will, [2] the Torah's law, and [3] the long-standing customary requirements of enduring order. In the Babas, as this survey of the Halakhah has shown, these distinct and inter-related forces —man's will, God's law, and accepted public practice—are far from abstractions. In the interplay of individual will, God's absolute law, and ancient, enduring custom, comes about the realization of Israel in the here and now. It is self-evident that the messages conveyed by the Halakhah of the Babas originate not in the law of Scripture, which does not coalesce into a single coherent statement in any

event. Rather the strikingly coherent structure before us arises out of
the deep layers of rationality that infuse the formation of the principles and then the details of the Halakhah of the Oral Torah: the
program and its articulation and exegesis.

b. *Hagigah*

Hagigah forms an original category-formation out of two closely related topics on a single theme, the occasions on which common folk
come to the Temple, that is, the pilgrim festivals, and that Halakhah
is devoted to two matters: the festival-offerings and the conditions of
cultic cleanness that pertain and govern the right to consume part of
the meat of those offerings. Three pilgrim festivals then draw to the
Temple the ordinary people. The pilgrims' three offerings called for
by the pilgrimage: an appearance-offering involve a burnt offering,
which yields no food for the sacrifier [the one who benefits, achieving
atonement through the offering] or sacrificer [the one who carries
out the rite, e.g., the priest]; a festal offering (Hagigah), which falls
under the rules of peace-offerings and does yield meat for the
sacrifier; and peace-offerings of rejoicing, subject to the same law as
the festal-offering. Since the ordinary folk are going to eat sacrificial
meat, they have to make themselves ready to consume food in the
status of Holy Things. The Halakhah then encompasses not only the
pertinent offerings but the rules of cleanness that govern on the occasion of the festivals. The act of rejoicing encompasses the eating of
meat. The three requirements—appearing before God, keeping a
feast to the Lord, and rejoicing—are made explicit in Scripture, Ex.
23:17, Dt. 16:15, and Dt. 16:14, respectively. The Halakhah takes up
the pilgrims' complementary obligations of sacrifice and cultic purity.
The Israelite is to be seen in the Temple court on the feast with a
whole-offering (birds or cattle) and that is obligatory: "None shall
appear before me empty-handed" (Ex. 23:15). Keeping the feast furthermore means presenting a peace-offering when one makes his
appearance on the first festival day of the feast. The duty of rejoicing
involves a peace-offering in addition to the festal peace offering: "the
peace-offering of rejoicing in the feast," in line with Dt. 27:7: "And
you shall sacrifice peace offerings and shall eat there and you shall
rejoice before the Lord your God." As to the offerings themselves, on
Passover, Pentecost, and Tabernacles, families present the appearance offering and the festal offering, an obligatory burnt offering and

peace-offerings, respectively. The obligatory appearance-offering is located by sages at Dt. 16:14-17.

The Halakhah concerning the pilgrimage goes over the ground of Scripture and clarifies details. Were we to consider that part of the topic on its own, we should assign it to the classification of topics devised by Scripture and fully worked out within the framework of Scripture. But the pilgrimage bears in its wake a concern for cultic cleanness in the Temple, a status to be achieved by ordinary folk, not only priests and Levites or Jerusalemites. When we come to the rules of cleanness as these pertain to the cult, we find a topic taken for granted in Scripture but independently amplified by the Halakhah of the Mishnah-Tosefta-Yerushalmi-Bavli. The main point of the Halakhah of Hagigah is, whatever is done at home serves in the household, but the cult is clearly differentiated from the household, with special reference for those that preserve cultic cleanness even within the household. That is expressed in connection with persons and utensils alike. One may immerse a utensil for purposes of cultic cleanness, but, when it comes to use in the cult, a utensil has to be processed to begin with in a state of insusceptibility to uncleanness and so must be cultically clean when it becomes susceptible, and still it must be immersed for use in the cult, that is, in connection with Holy Things. So too, for the cult one must wash hands even if the food that the hands will touch is insusceptible to uncleanness, which is not the case with heave offering. The attitude of the pilgrim governs. The effect of his act of purification through immersion is dictated by the attitude with which he immerses. If one was unclean and immersed with the intention of becoming clean, that serves. He who immerses in order to rise up from uncleanness to cleanness, lo, this person is clean for all purposes. He who immerses—if he had the intention of becoming clean, he becomes clean. And if not, he remains unclean. If he immersed for eating food in the status of Holy Things and is thereby confirmed as suitable for eating food in the status of Holy Things, he is prohibited from engaging in the preparation of purification water. If, however, one immersed for the matter requiring the more stringent rule, he is permitted to engage in the matter requiring the less stringent rule. If he immersed but was not confirmed, it is as though he did not immerse.

But there are realms to which the attitude of the Israelite gains no access. The area within the veil excludes all but the priesthood, so the intentionality of Israelites is null therein. It is in connection with the pilgrimage for which Hagigah provides that these matters become urgent. And, we note, on that occasion, the limits of intentionality and its power are reached. The intentionality to attain cleanness in the domestic household now does not suffice, nor do the rules and regulations that pertain when ordinary folk in their homes eat their food as though they were in the Temple in Jerusalem. The Halakhah embodies the difference between imagination and intention, on the one side, and actuality, on the other. What suffices in the pretense that one's table forms the altar, the members of the household, the priesthood and its ménage, the home, the Temple, now does not serve. Actuality intervenes: the real Temple imposes its own, very strict rules, and all of the proper intentions in the world will not serve now. The table compares to the Temple, the household to the priesthood, the boundaries of the home to the Temple—but in a hierarchical structure, encompassing rules of both sanctification and uncleanness.

c. *Kelim*

No where does Scripture legislate concerning the definition of objects that are or are not susceptible to uncleanness, which is the topic of the category-formation of Kelim. Nearly the entire corpus of laws of the Oral Torah that we shall examine stands autonomous of the Written part. The Written Torah tells us a great deal about sources of uncleanness (Lev. 11-15, Num. 19) and a fair amount about modes of purification, but not a great deal about the nature of utensils to be purified: "an article of wood or a garment or a skin or a sack, any vessel that is used for any purpose." Several passages of the Written Torah pertain. The most important is Lev. 11:29-35: utensils are made unclean by dead creeping things, and purification is accomplished through breaking the object. Scripture further contributes facts important in the consideration of objects that are subject to cultic contamination at Lev. 15:4-7. Lev. 15: 9-12 turns from the bench, bed, or chair to the saddle, subject to merkab-uncleanness, to be differentiated from midras-uncleanness. Lev. 15:19-27 give the counterpart rules for women afflicted with discharge outside of the menstrual period. The uncleanness that a corpse exudes, Num. 19:1ff., affects utensils in one important detail, specified at Num. 19:14-15. Num. 31:19-24 deals with utensils of leather and of metal in the context of corpse-uncleanness.

The program of the Halakhah is set forth in the following outline of the Mishnah's and the Tosefta's treatment of the topic:

I. Proem for Purities: Hierarchies of Uncleanness and Corresponding Hierarchies of Sanctification
    A. The Hierarchy of Sources of Uncleanness: From Least to Most Virulent
    B. The Hierarchy of Sources of Uncleanness: Those That Pertain to Man
    C. The Hierarchy of Loci of Sanctification: From Least to Most Holy

II. The Susceptibility to Uncleanness of Clay Utensils
    A. Wood, Leather, Bone, Glass, and Clay (Earthenware)
    B. Damage That Renders Clay Utensils Useless and Therefore Insusceptible to Uncleanness
    C. The Point, in the Process of Manufacturing Clay Utensils, at Which the Utensils Become Susceptible to Uncleanness; and, When Broken Down, The Point at Which They cease to Be Susceptible to Uncleanness. Ovens
    D. The Insusceptibility to Uncleanness of the Insides of Tightly-Sealed Clay Utensils

III. Susceptibility to Uncleanness of Metal Utensils
    A. When Objects Made of Metal Become Susceptible, and When They Lose Susceptibility
    B. Specific Metal Objects and their Status
    C. The Point, When a Metal Object Is Broken Down, at which the Object Ceases to be Susceptible to Uncleanness
    D. Further Metal Objects and their Status

IV. Utensils of Wood, Leather, Bone, and Glass
    A. When Objects Made of Wood, Leather, Bone, and Glass Become Susceptible, and When They Lose Susceptibility
    B. Specific Objects Made of Wood, Leather, Bone, and Glass and their Status
    C. The Point, in the Process of Manufacturing Utensils of Wood, at which the Utensils Become Susceptible to Uncleanness; and, When Broken Down, the Point at which They Cease to Be Susceptible to Uncleanness
    D. The Point, in the Process of Manufacturing Utensils of Leather, at which the Utensils Become Susceptible to Uncleanness; and, When Broken Down, the Point at which They Cease to Be Susceptible to Uncleanness
    E. The Status as to Uncleanness of Specific Leather Objects

V. The Measure of Breakage that Renders an Object Useless, Not Longer Fit to Serve as a Receptacle, and therefore Insusceptible to Uncleanness. General Rules
    A. Specific Objects and the Measure of a Whole That Renders Them No Longer Serviceable as a Receptacle
    B. Taking the Measure of Specified Objects to Assess their Status

The mass of detail yields the handful of principles that govern throughout. Considerations of form and function, mediated by the variable of man's intentionality in respect to objects and their usefulness, dictate the status of utensils. A single point holds the whole together: what man deems useful for his purposes is susceptible to uncleanness, and what man disregards and deems useless is insusceptible. That is where intentionality governs. That is to say, that of which man is unlikely to take account—a shard, a remnant—but to treat as null will not form an object to which man is going to be alert, about which he will take care, of which he will take note. Such a useless lump of material cannot enter the status of sanctification, because sanctification takes effect for that of which man is cognizant—that concerning which he forms an intentionality (in this instance: of sanctity). What man treats as null he also cannot sanctify, the possibility of subjecting to intentionality that to which one is to begin with indifferent. Sanctification stands for the highest level of consideration, and the status of uncleanness pertains in most intense degree to what is accorded that highest measure of alert concern.

The Mishnah's theory of matters contrasts uncleanness and sanctification, each hierarchized on its own and (in theory at least) in synopsis with the other. That is what dictates the specification of the religious principles operative in the Halakhah of Kelim. So at stake in the contrast of uncleanness and sanctification, in the Halakhic formulation, is where one can go, and cleanness involves access to ever holier places, uncleanness, exclusion therefrom. Certainly the Written Torah will have found the matter of the spatial consequence of sanctification and uncleanness familiar, since one principal result of contracting uncleanness throughout Leviticus is that one may not enter the camp or tabernacle or holy place. The juxtaposition and contrast of the hierarchization of status as to uncleanness, framed in terms of persons and the effects of their uncleanness, against the loci of sanctification, framed in enlandised terms, accordingly makes its own point. Uncleanness removes a person from what is most holy to what is less holy, that is, from the focus of sanctification, step by step, point by point, ultimately from the Holy of Holies. The Halakhah of the Oral Torah bears a second message, one for which the Written Torah prepares us only in part. Leviticus is explicit that when priests eat their rations ("heave-offering"), they must be in a state of cultic cleanness, comparable to, though less stringent than, the cultic cleanness they must attain to consume their share of the Holy Things of the altar. Scripture knows that priests should not contract corpse-uncleanness except under limited circumstances, must marry in accord with the restrictions, as to the sexual status of their wives, and must be in body unflawed (Lev. Chapter Twenty-One). The Halakhah further takes for granted that (some) Israelites will not eat ordinary food that is in a state of cultic uncleanness, and they also will not, in a state of cultic uncleanness, eat ordinary food that is cultically clean. Once we have established that the opposite of uncleanness is sanctification, we realize what is at stake. Israelites, not priests, are to eat ordinary food, not Holy Things or priestly rations, at home and not in the Temple courtyard or in Jerusalem, as though they were priests, as though the food were Holy Things or priestly rations, and as though they were located in the Temple.

Scripture treats sanctification as a process that works *ex opere operato*. I cannot, furthermore, point to a single passage in which, in so many words or anything close, Scripture makes the status of unclean-

ness depend upon matters of circumstance, relation, and attitude.
Just as sanctification in a concrete case takes place without regard to
circumstance or will, so uncleanness is a process that is inexorable.
What is susceptible to uncleanness is what is useful, and what is
broken, no longer useful, is no longer unclean, hence, no longer
susceptible to become unclean. But that is not how the Halakhah of
the Oral Torah sees matters. Whether or not sanctity inheres, uncleanness is relative, contextual, dependant upon matters of will and
attitude. Perhaps matters begin with the principle of Scripture that
what is useless is insusceptible or clean (as the case may be), which
the Oral Torah then amplifies: who defines usefulness, and how do
we know? And from that humble question a path is opened for the
entry of the entire matter of intentionality: how does one propose to
use an object? whether the attitude of one is the same as that of the
other, or whether we take account only of individual preference? how
the form of a utensil governs its usefulness, without respect to the
plans of the user of the vessel? and on and on. In any event, whether
pursuing a line of thought opened by the Written Torah or formulating matters in an independent and fresh way, the Oral Torah in its
Halakhah explicitly and repeatedly insists that uncleanness does not
inhere in things and is not an absolute and intrinsic, material trait,
but rather, a matter of status imputed by man himself.

The status of utensils as to whether or not they can receive uncleanness is relative to the form of materials imparted by man and
the use of materials decided by man: the attitude and intentionality
of man, confirmed by his actions. Time and again masses of details
make a single point: what man finds useful, what serves man's principal purpose and carries out his generative initiative, marks the materials, that is, the object that they form, as susceptible to uncleanness. So if the materials are located in a tent of a corpse, they can
receive and retain the uncleanness exuding from the corpse. And
what man deems negligible and of no account is useless and insusceptible. Materials located in a tent of a corpse that man has not formed
into something of which he takes not do not receive uncleanness. So
it is man who decides whether the entire system of cultic cleanness
pertains or does not pertain, and that represents a considerable shift
from the conception of uncleanness that Scripture puts forth. The
lesson of Kelim is clear. What man values can be sanctified and
therefore also can be made unclean by sources of contamination that
otherwise affect only the cult. It is by an act of will that holy Israel,

living in the Land of Israel, transforms itself into a kingdom of priests and a holy people, and its food into priestly rations. All that ordinary Israel has to undertake to sanctify the household and its table is to pay attention to those matters that, to begin with, God has identified as matters of cultic concern. The Halakhah in so stating has independently developed the topic that Scripture has rather casually contributed.

d. *Megillah*

Inventing its own category-formation, the Halakhah transforms the presentation of the holiday of Purim into the occasion for legislating about the declamation of the Torah in the synagogue; along the way, the Halakhah provides some further rules for the synagogue. What marks the presentation of the category as fresh and independent is the transformation of the case, declaiming the Esther-scroll in public, into the rule for declaiming the Torah in the synagogue. Esther 9:16-32 forms the basis for a corpus of rules on reading the Torah in the synagogue. The Halakhah begins with the laws covering the declamation of the scroll of Esther, then proceeds to the more general topics of synagogue governance and the declamation of the Torah therein.

By the juxtaposition of what is explicitly required in Scripture—the reading of the Scroll of Esther—with synagogue-rules, sages establish that the declamation of Scripture takes place most suitably in the congregation gathered in a particular building erected and set aside for that purpose—not for prayer, not for sacrifice, not for study, but for Torah-declamation. What then defines the synagogue? It is not contained space of a particular character but the presence of the quorum of male Israelites assembled for the conduct of certain specific activities. The Halakhah does not specify the traits that a building must exhibit to qualify for use as a synagogue, though it does recognize that a building certainly may be consecrated for synagogue-activities alone. But the Halakhah does indicate what is necessary for the conduct of the activities particular to a synagogue, and that is in terms of the presence of holy Israel, embodied in ten males. By contrast, the Temple cannot be defined as the place where ten Israelites come together to kill a cow. The enlandised household cannot be set forth as a location where ten Israelites produce crops, only a plot of ground owned by an Israelite in the Land of Israel that produces crops.

In the Oral Torah's Halakhic vision of where God and Israel
intersect, the synagogue finds a merely subordinated place. First, the
Halakhic requirements for the synagogue scarcely specify much of
interest. The Halakhah differentiates categories that it values, and by
that criterion, the synagogue enjoys a low priority. True, the location
is to be treated with respect. But while acutely detailed laws define
appropriate use of space for burying the dead, no counter-part rules
of weight and substance, comparable to the ones on burial grounds,
set forth the delineation of space for the synagogue. We know how
large a burial plot must be, and how much space is allocated to
individual kokhs; the Halakhah of the Oral Torah does not tell us
how large the ark that contains the Torah must be, or how much
space is allocated to individual scrolls. The Halakhah devotes to the
Temple, not only its activities but its space, a corpus of minute regulations with no counterpart for the synagogue. Nothing comparable
to the tractate Middot, on the layout of the Temple, attends to syna-
gogue-organization and construction. The Halakhah, finally, in
minute detail defines the priest, his responsibilities and rewards. But
no comparable native-category devotes discussion to the sage and
what he is to do. Second, the Halakhah assigns to the provenience of
the synagogue as consecrated space few critical activities of the life
with God. The rhetoric of the Halakhah takes for granted that study
of the Torah *may* take place anywhere, but *does* take place in the beth
hammidrash or house of study. The synagogue is not identified with
the house of study or with the activity of study in sages' sense; declaiming the Torah and reciting prayers in public do not compare.
Third, when it comes to public prayer, the Halakhah of the Mishnah
assigns that activity to the venue of the Temple in the context of the
Daily Whole Offering, so insists the Halakhah of Tamid. The upshot
is, prayer—public or personal—in no way is linked by the Halakhah
of the Oral Torah to the synagogue in particular, and the synagogue
enjoys only a subordinate role in the everyday meeting with God that
Israel undertakes. Its primary purpose then finds its definition in
sages' choice of topical companions for the synagogue: those having
to do with declaiming the Torah. The Halakhah, as always, states the
main point best. In its scale of priorities, the synagogue ranks low,
well below a Torah-scroll. Nothing in Scripture has precipitated the
union of topics, let alone systematic discussion of the synagogue, set
forth by the Halakhah of Megillah.

e. *Miqvaot*

The paradox of water is that it both contracts and also removes uncleanness. It imparts susceptibility to uncleanness, when deliberately put onto seed for example, and among other liquids water also receives uncleanness when touched by a source of uncleanness. But under some conditions, in correct volume, deriving from the appropriate source, water also has the power to diminish or even remove uncleanness, still water the former, flowing water the latter. So, it is clear, we shall deal with diverse classifications of water, on the one side, and with rules governing those classifications of water that bear the power to remove uncleanness but then do not themselves receive uncleanness, on the other. Of all this Scripture knows nothing, though to such a taxonomy of types of water, Scripture makes its contribution. When Scripture speaks of putting into water—immersing—an unclean person or garment, it further specifies, "and it shall be unclean until evening, then it will be clean." So immersion does not purify, but in a measure removes uncleanness. Scripture proves remarkably reticent to deal with questions involving how the "putting into water" is carried out, not defining the sort of water that works, as is shown by Lev. 11:31-32, Lev. 15:13, Lev. 11:40, Lev. 14:8:, Lev. 15:5, Lev. 15:16, Lev. 15:21, Lev. 15:27, Lev. 16:28, Lev.17:15, Lev. 22:6-7, Num. 10:7, Num. 17:17, and Dt. 23:11:12. Scripture supplies no information about the character of the water into which the unclean object is to be put, how such water is collected, how much is required, and the like.

Of the six kinds of water that the Halakhah differentiates for purposes of removing uncleanness, these two take priority, still water that in the requisite volume has collected from rain-drippings, which is to say, water that accumulates naturally from heaven, and living or spring or flowing water, from deep in the earth, which removes corpse-uncleanness and that of the Zab and of *nega*ʿ-uncleanness. The former defines the problematic of the Halakhah, in these aspects: [1] it must not be subjected to human intervention or intentionality, [2] it must not be collected in utensils; [3] but it must flow naturally (with the flow permissibly directed by man) to its collection-point in the pool. And, conversely, drawn water imparts uncleanness and if poured into a collection of rain-water of a volume insufficient to constitute a valid immersion pool spoils the water into which it is poured. What is it that turns water from a source of uncleanness (if drawn) or a facilitator for the transmission of uncleanness (if poured upon seed through an act of will) to the medium for removing uncleanness is then obvious. The matter may be expressed positively and negatively. It is the negative fact that water has not served human purposes or been subjected to human activity. Water left in its natural condition, in sufficient volume, pouring down from heaven in the form of rain and collecting on its own upon the earth—that is Heaven's medium for removing uncleanness. Required to preserve passivity, man may only dig a hole into which rain-water will naturally flow. But that is how uncleanness takes place, by nature, rarely by an act of human intentionality.

And that match underscores the positive message of the Halakhah. Just as uncleanness comes about by nature not by human activity or intentionality, so nature serves to remove uncleanness and naturally to restore the normal condition of persons and objects, which is cleanness. Nature restores what nature has disrupted, the celestial removing the chthonic, so to speak. That is in two stages, still water marks the cessation of uncleanness, sunset the beginning of the new cycle of Israel in conformity with the purposive character of nature. Now then we come to interpret the opposed rules of water for immersion pools and water for the purification of corpse-uncleanness. The question is, why does still water unaffected by human agency restore the natural condition disrupted by uncleanness other than that of the corpse and its analogues, while by contrast purification-water systematically subjected to human intervention—constant attention, deliberate action, start to finish—alone removes corpse-uncleanness? We have then to account for the exclusion of man from the one process, the radical insistence upon his inclusion, in full deliberation, within the other. The reason is, we deal with two essentially distinct types of uncleanness, one ordinary and natural, the other extraordinary and in violation of nature.

Uncleanness that comes about by reason of any cause but death and its analogues is removed by the Heaven's own dispensation, not by man's intervention: rain-fall, sunset suffice. Ordinary purification is done by nature, resulting from natural processes. Water that falls from heaven and, unimpeded by man, collects in sufficient volume restores the natural condition of persons and objects that have contracted uncleanness at second hand or by reason of minor sources of contamination. Still water serves for the moment, until sun set marks the new now-clean spell in the story of the person or the object. But as to persons and objects that have contracted uncleanness from death, nature on its own cannot produce the kind of water that bears the power to remove that uncleanness and restore the condition of nature. Only man can. And man can do this only by the highest level of concentration, the most deliberate and focussed action. The water is not still, but flowing water: living water overcoming death. And the water is kept alive, in constant motion until it is stirred with the ash. Any extrinsic action spoils the water; stopping to rest on a bench, doing any deed other than required for the rite itself—these disrupt the circle of sanctification within the world of uncleanness that the burning of the cow has required. So the facts lead us to the critical question at the heart of matters: why does the state of human intentionality govern in the confrontation with corpse-uncleanness?

Man's supreme act of will, embodying intentionality in highly-purposive activity, can overcome even the effects of death. If the Halakhah wished to say, man can overcome death through the correct and deliberate attitude, it could not have embodied that message in more powerful language than the activities required for the formulation of purification-water. Man's act of will overcomes the uncleanness of death, just as man's act of deliberate rebellion brought about death to begin with. Man restores what man has disrupted. As to the rest, man refrains from deliberate action, and nature, providing purifying water from heaven, accomplishes the restoration. That is because the other forms of uncleanness come about by nature's own failure to realize itself, so nature provides the medium of the removal of the consequence: water that Heaven supplies naturally matches nature's condition.

f. *Sanhedrin-Makkot*

The Halakhah set forth in the tractate of Sanhedrin—Mishnah, Tosefta, Yerushalmi, Bavli—deals with the organization of the Israelite government and courts and punishments administered thereby. The court system is set forth in the Mishnah's statement of matters at M. 1:1-5:5, the death-penalty at 6:1-11:6, and extra-judicial penalties at 9:5-6, 10:1-6. The penalties other than capital are set forth in tractate Makkot, covering perjury (with variable penalties), banishment, and flogging. While Scripture supplies many facts, the Oral Torah organizes and lays matters out in its own way. Where the Written Torah does not provide information that sages deem logical

and necessary, they make things up for themselves. Where verses of
Scripture play a role in the Halakhic statement of matters, they are
cited in context. The details of the organization of the court system
do not derive from the Written Torah, nor are the specificities of the
death penalty supplied there. The contribution of the Written Torah
is therefore episodic. Dt. 16:18-20 specifies appointing judges, Dt.
17:8-13 provides for an appellate system, "If any case arises requiring
a decision between one kind of homicide and another, one kind of
legal right and another, or one kind of assault and another, any case
within your towns that is too difficult for you, then you shall arise and
go up to the place that the Lord your God will choose...." The death
penalty for murder is specified at Num. 35:30, on the testimony of
two or three witnesses, Dt. 17:6-7. The comparison of the high priest
and the king at M. San. 2:1ff., rests on Lev. 21:10-12 for the high
priest and Dt. 17:14-20 for the king. The death penalty involving
hanging the body on a tree until night but burial the same day is at
Dt. 21:22-23; the stubborn and rebellious son at Dt. 21:18-21. The
city that is wiped out because of idolatry is treated at Dt. 13:12-18.
The upshot is that at specific topics, Scripture, cited here and there,
contributes facts, but the shape and program of the tractate as a
whole is not to be predicted on the basis of the Written Torah. On
that basis I classify the dual-tractate as I do.

An outline of the Halakhah as set forth in the Mishnah-Tosefta-
Yerushalmi-Bavli provides an overview of the treatment of the topic:

i. The Court System
    A. Various Kinds of Courts and their Jurisdiction
    B. The Heads of the Israelite Nation and the Court System
    C. The Procedures of the Court System: Property Cases
    D. The Procedures of the Court-System: Capital Cases
ii. The Death Penalty
    A. Stoning
    B. The Four Modes of Execution that Lie in the Power of the Court
       and how they are Administered
    C. Stoning
    D. Burning or Decapitation
    E. Strangling
    F. Extra-Judicial Punishment
    G. Death At the Hands of Heaven: Denial of Eternal life

This final item is as follows:

> M. 11:1 [Mishnah = 10:1, and so throughout] All Israelites have a
> share in the world to come, as it is said, "your people also

shall be all righteous, they shall inherit the land forever; the branch of my planting, the work of my hands, that I may be glorified" (Is. 60:21). And these are the ones who have no portion in the world to come: He who says, the resurrection of the dead is a teaching which does not derive from the Torah, and the Torah does not come from Heaven; and an Epicurean.

Once we see whole and complete the Halakhah in its classical statement, we find no difficulty in defining the problematics of the topic. The topic is sanctions for the protection of the social order, that is treated in the category-formation defined at tractate Sanhedrin. The problematic is revealed in the exposition of the topic. What captures sages' interest in the topic is a hierarchization of sins or crimes as indicated by the severity of the penalties that are imposed, matched, also, by the formality and procedural punctiliousness of the courts' process. Stated simply, we may say that sages find important in the category-formation, criminal justice, the issue, which sin is more severe than the other, and how does the penalty fit the crime in a set of hierarchized sins with matching sanctions? That is the center of the matter. Once that question is asked of this topic—the problematics of hierarchization as that pertains to criminal justice—the order of presentation is set, the sequence dictated, start to finish, with only a few flaws.

Makkot concerns itself with the judicial sanctions of flogging and banishment. The order of the topical exposition is somewhat puzzling, since Chapters One and Three belong together. The following outline shows the picture clearly:

i. Penalties for Perjury
ii. The Penalty of Exile (banishment)
   A. Those Who are Sent into exile
   B. The Cities of Exile
iii. The Penalty of Flogging
   A. Those Who Are Flogged
   B. The Conduct of the Flogging

Within Israel's social order the Halakhah addresses from a theological perspective the profound question of social justice: what shall we make of the Israelite sinner or criminal? Specifically, does the sin or crime, which has estranged him from God, close the door to life eternal? If it does, then justice is implacable and perfect. If it does not, then God shows his mercy—but what of justice? Seeing the Halakhic statement whole, we see how the topics set forth by Scripture are reworked in an original and fresh way to frame an independent proposition, integral to the Torah viewed whole. We can understand the answer only if we keep in mind that the Halakhah takes for granted the resurrection of the dead, the final judgment, and the life of the world to come beyond the grave. From that perspective, death becomes an event in life but not the end of life. And, it must follow, the death penalty too does not mark the utter annihilation of the person of the sinner or criminal. On the contrary, because he pays for his crime or sin in this life, he situates himself with all of the rest of supernatural Israel, ready for the final judgment. Having been judged, he will "stand in judgment," meaning, he will find his way to the life of the world to come along with everyone else.

g. *Zebahim*

Of the issues that predominate in the category-formation of Zebahim —especially the role of intentionality in linking God and Israel— Scripture knows little or nothing. But wherever they can, the Oral Torah's sages find in Scripture the starting point for their own systematic reflection. For its part, Scripture's governing provisions for animal offerings are set forth at, Lev. 1:1-9, Lev. 1:14-17, Lev. 3:1-5, Lev. 4:27-31, Lev. 6:27-28, Lev. 7:1-7, and Lev. 17:3ff. The Priestly Code organizes information within its governing categories, just as does the Oral Torah; these categories go over the same topics, but each focuses facts in its own way. The category-formation is new, because the Oral Torah aims at treating as a single classification a set of distinct rules, there with respect to the diverse meal offerings, here, the diverse animal offerings. Where Scripture differentiates and then compares and contrasts, the Oral Torah homogenizes, subjects to a single body of governing principles. The starting point should not be missed. While Scripture presents the transaction that takes place at the altar by classifying types of offerings, e.g., the burnt-offering, sin-offering, guilt-offering, peace offerings, firstling, tithe of cattle, and the Passover, the Oral Torah forms its own classifications, setting forth rules that apply to all (or most) classes of offerings throughout. So the Oral Torah systematizes by identifying the four cultic acts that, properly performed by the priest, render the animal-sacrifice suitable for yielding parts for the altar fires and parts for the priests' consumption. These four acts pertain to all classifications of offerings of beasts.

The focus and dynamic of the work of systematization remain to be identified. These emerge from the problematic of the Oral Torah and come to full exposure in the account of the generative religious principles that the Oral Torah embodies and actualizes. The Oral Torah sets forth, in connection with animal offerings, four bodies of rules, most of them addressing issues not taken up in Scripture but precipitated by Scripture's account of matters. Out of and in line with the elaborate account of the Written Torah, the Oral Torah identifies its own concerns. It wants to know, specifically, about the role of intentionality in the sacrificial cult, an issue not explicitly addressed in the Written Torah's treatment of the same subject but deemed implicit therein. Further interest encompasses issues systematically addressed in the Oral Torah's examination of a broad variety of topics, e.g., issues of mixtures and confusion of categories, rules of precedence, and the like. Here too, the Written Torah supplies the hard facts that the Oral Torah systematizes, in which the Oral Torah finds indicative traits susceptible to ordering. Finally, while Scripture does not differentiate among the locations at which the altar is located, the Oral Torah systematizes information on the same matter and deals with the diverse rules governing sacrifices at the several locations at which Israel made offerings prior to the building of the Temple. The entire enterprise of the Oral Torah proves to be one of generalization and systematization, but at the same time, the Oral Torah contains within itself remarkably fresh initiatives of inquiry. Were we engaged by the question of how the Oral Torah responds to that of the Written one, we should find here the exemplary cases for defining principles of that response.

The facts derive from Scripture, the generative problematics from the resources of the Oral Torah. Take the case of the blood-rite itself: the effect depends entirely on proper attitude, even when not matched by correct action. The blood-rite forms the center of the transaction between Israel and God at the altar. That is shown in the answer to the question, At what point is the offering validated, so that the disposition of the animal bears consequences? It is when the blood has been properly sprinkled or tossed. The basic conception is, when the rite is performed properly with the correct intentionality, it accomplishes its goals (it is "valid"). When the rite is performed properly but classified incorrectly, it is invalid. The Oral Torah bears no messages concerning the meaning of the blood-rite, only the conditions that are required for its effective accomplishment. The Oral

Torah takes as its problem an issue on which the Written Torah makes no statement within the framework of normative prescriptions, but makes an elaborate statement indeed within the setting of narrative of exemplary events and transactions from the beginning to the end. So in the present setting the Oral Torah takes as its task the embodiment in ritual of the Written Torah's myth.

Why the stress on intentionality, and what outcome for Israel's relationship with God do we discern? The simple fact is, the Israelite has the power to change the status of a beast from secular to sacred, and this he does by an act of will. He designates a beast as sacred, specifying the purpose of the act of sanctification. So the entire process of presenting personal offerings (as distinct from the public ones) depends upon the act of will effected by the individual Israelite. And since the rites are carried out at the critical turnings by the priest, the attitude that governs his activities likewise must register. Neither the Israelite nor the priest is portrayed as an automaton, nor do the actions of the two parties emerge as coerced or automatic. What the Israelite does realizes his will, which is why the deed makes a difference, and, the Oral Torah takes for granted, the priest too engages through an act of will. Both are deemed to have, and to make, choices, and these choices respond to the intentionality that motivates the entire transaction, start to finish. So the Oral Torah portrays the cult as the stage on which Israel—priest and Israelite alike —work out in concrete actions the results of their interior reflections.

We should not miss the negative, for it yields a positive result. It is not enough that the Israelite designate the animal; God must know that the priest has prepared it in accord with the definition of the sanctification that has taken hold of that animal by reason of the Israelite's act of sanctification: the priest must carry out the action within the same framework of purpose established by the Israelite for the beast. So it does not suffice for the priest to impose his judgment upon the disposition of the beast; the initial act of sanctification has imposed limits upon his purpose. The Israelite requires priestly conformity to his, the Israelite's, act of will in designating the beast. The priest effects the correct offering only when he subordinates his will to that of the Israelite. The Israelite attains atonement and reconciliation with God only when, after an unintended violation of the Torah, he demonstrates that, in giving something back (whether a costly beast, whether a bird of no account), he subordinates his will to that of God. We find matched acts of willful and deliberate subordination—the priest's to the Israelite's, the Israelite's to God's.

God closely attends to the match of deliberation and deed, and only when the Israelite's intent and the priest's intent coincide does God confirm his gracious acceptance of the result, propitiation resulting. So while the presentation of offerings superficially places the human side of the transaction at the center—it is the Israelite's, then the priest's parts that effect the relationship—in fact, it is God's engagement with the same transaction, his close and careful surveillance of the match of intent and action, word and deed, that makes all the difference. In the cult Israel relates to God intimately and concretely. Once the Israelite undertakes by an act of will to engage in a deed of sanctification, God's participation in the process, step by step, his close attention to the interior of the activities consequence upon the undertaking—these responses embody God's intense interest in the Israelite's attitude, to which God responds. That is why "intentionality" takes on very concrete and specific meanings in the setting of the offering to God of the gifts of the Land, meat, wine, oil, grain and the like. When an Israelite expresses his intentionality to sanctify a particular animal for a specified offering, that consecrates the beast for God's service at the altar. But the intentionality of the Israelite then requires a corresponding attitude on the part of, with a confirming action by, the officiating priest. If he does the deeds of the sacrifice for some purpose other than the announced one of the Israelite, he denies the Israelite the benefit of confirmation of his intentionality by a cultic action. What is the result of the priest's misconceiving of matters? Where the beast can serve for some appropriate cultic purpose, it does so. That is to say, the original action of the Israelite in sanctifying the beast is not nullified by the contradictory intentionality of the priest. But where the beast is designated for a very particular purpose and can then serve no other, the sacrificial act is lost.

What about the Oral Torah's rules for the regulation of the altar? These go over five distinct issues: disposing of sacrificial portions or blood that derive from diverse classes of sacrifices and have been confused; what the altar sanctifies, which is what is appropriate to it, but not what is not appropriate to it; precedence in use of the altar; blood of a sin-offering that spurts onto a garment; and the division among the eligible priests of the meat and hides of sacrificial animals. Of these five matters three yield encompassing generalizations, the other two producing ad hoc rules that articulate the Written Torah's details. The program of the Oral Torah aims at sorting out confusion in a practical, rational way. If animals are confused, so that some may be suitable for the altar, some not, we wait until a blemish disqualifies the beasts and sell them, using the proceeds for the altar. A correct but practical solution resolves the matter, the sanctity imparted to the beast by the act of consecration not indelibly affecting the animal; it is relative to the animal's own suitability for its purpose. The value is consecrated, the body of the animal not.

So too, the altar sanctifies what is appropriate to it but has no affect upon what is not appropriate to it. Sanctification does not inhere in the altar, such that mere contact with the altar transforms what touches the altar into something permanently sacred. And along these same lines, perfectly rational considerations govern questions of precedence. In all three instances of the disposition of "the sacred," we find sanctity not an inherent trait but one that depends upon circumstance and suitability. The full meaning of these important components of the Oral Torah emerges only when we consider the Written Torah's judgment of the same matter, which is stated at Ex. 29:37: "the altar shall be most holy; whatever touches the altar shall become holy." That of the Oral Torah significantly qualifies that statement, adding the language "that is appropriate" to the phrase, "whatever touches...." The issue is whether sanctification is indelible or stipulative.

Schismatic opinion holds that what is sanctified in the sanctuary is indelibly sanctified so is not removed from the altar. If, then, the cause of invalidation for the altar took place in the sanctuary, the sanctuary accepts the thing in any event and it is not removed from the altar. If its invalidity did not take place in the sanctuary, the sanctuary does not accept it and it should be removed from the altar. But that position concerning sanctification by being assigned to a named sage as against "sages" is labeled as not normative, and consequently the Oral Torah underscores the logic of its generative position, which is, sanctification affects status, not substance.

XVII. *Kaleidoscopic Discourse*

To gain perspective on the category-formations before us, I invoke as a metaphor, the kaleidoscope. Invented in 1817, it is "an optical instrument consisting of from two to four reflecting surfaces placed in a tube, at one end of which is a small compartment containing pieces of colored glass. On looking through the tube, numerous reflections of these are seen, producing brightly colored symmetrical figures, which may be constantly altered by rotation of the instrument" (*Oxford English Dictionary* [Oxford, 1971], s.v.). The Halakhic topics are the colored glass. Their juxtapositions in the category-formations just now surveyed result from the Oral Torah's counterpart to "the rotation of the instrument." The symmetrical figures that we perceive in our survey of the Oral Torah's independent definition of category-formations then come about by reason of the character of the reflecting surfaces, the planes and angles, concave or convex formation, and the like. The Oral Torah affords not only a glimpse at the fixed light but, properly perceived, the surfaces that shape the light into the fixture we now perceive. To apply the metaphor: when we have identified the distinctive rationality of the Oral Torah viewed whole, we shall know the counterpart to those planes and angles, concave or convex formations, that govern the light of the colored glass and produce the galaxy of combinations of the kaleidoscope.

The greatest categorical achievement of the entire Oral Torah, the unitary Halakhah of Baba Qamma, Baba Mesia, and Baba Batra, utilizes colored glass of its own as well as of Scripture, but (as is the fact, by definition) on its own has polished the surfaces that shape the light into the patterned reflection we perceive. It is a fixed pattern, one that cannot change in the rotation of the tube; indeed, to cross the bounds of the metaphor, the Oral Torah forms the tube and fixes its parts into a working whole: one that will not move. The point of insistence—the stasis of the well-ordered society, its interplay with the disruptions of intentionality—then forms a statement that the individual participant, with his own attitudes and wishes, may register, but the normal, and normative, society will transcend what variegates and disrupts. It will establish what is not only fair but also enduring, what man by an act of will has upset, man by an act of will must restore, the whole assessed by appeal to the proportionality of classes of causation. So intentionality intersects with responsibility, yielding an original category-formation and, by the way, a set of topical inquiries precipitated by the new combination.

When, at Hagigah, the Oral Torah's category-formation joins the topic of the pilgrimage with the topic of cultic cleanness, it produces the remarkable exercise in the comparison and contrast of categories of cultic cleanness—the layman, the priest's, the cult's—that in the very details of the law form a single construction of the two subjects. If one keeps cultic cleanness at home, that requires one class of observances, one level of alertness; when he does so to enter the Temple, that requires a higher level of alertness. Then the laws of cultic cleanness vary, and that is in accord with the intentionality of the Israelite participant. If he intends to become cultically clean for one purpose, he takes one set of steps, and for another, a different set of steps. His wishes then classify his obligations in the matter of cultic cleanness, even though the status on the surface remains uniform, that is, unclean or clean. Once we add, unclean and then clean for this purpose, in this context, the variable of intentionality takes over.

Kelim constructs a complex grid, one that holds together within a single framework these variables: the materials of which objects are made; the forms that objects require to be serviceable, e.g., forming a receptacle or flat; the state, as to manufacture, of the utensils, incomplete or complete; the condition of the utensils, whole, broken, or only partially usable; and the attitude of the person who is to use the utensils, how and for what purpose he intends to utilize them. All of these distinct planes of analysis are held together in a coherent and encompassing composition, one in which three dimensions comprehend the whole: form, function, and the user's purpose or attitude. The entire composite, the category-formation and its components, attests to the contribution of the Oral Torah. Nothing in the Written Torah precipitates speculation, whether in concrete or abstract form and language, upon the matter of how the human will interacts with the material world of things.

Megillah and Moed Qatan bear in common the quality of joining incongruous topics. Megillah's incongruity derives from the disproportion of juxtaposing rules on the reading of a particular book of Scripture with rules on the conduct and governance of synagogue affairs all together, with a focus upon reading Scripture in general. Moed Qatan jars because celebration of the intermediate days of the festival and burial of the dead represent opposed activities, the one joyful, the other mournful. Each makes its statement, and the two statements bear the traits of coherence and cogency. Here the analogy to the kaleidoscope works well: fixed colors when differently refracted combine into new shades.

When the Oral Torah organizes Scripture's facts into its own category-formation, it does so because it wishes to make a statement that only that reconstitution of givens brings about. At Miqvaot we find a key to the mode of thought that yields the particular message. It is one of comparison and contrast of categories. If we wish to think in the manner in which the Oral Torah carries out its analytical inquiry, then, we have to identify the foundations of comparison and the purpose of contrast. Here we establish a shared genus, which is, water that purifies. Then we speciate. The grounds of speciation— whether or not man may intervene in the collection of the water; whether or not the water may be collected in utensils, that is, by human action; how water not collected by man must be treated to form a pool; how the diverse classes of water are utilized to effect purification and the like—these once more form an exercise in the interplay of human will and the material facts of nature.

Only by forming the category, penalties for sin and crime viewed altogether (Sanhedrin-Makkot) can the Oral Torah deliver its message on the way God balances justice and mercy. Specifically, the social order brings about justice in this world, which is an act of mercy because it opens the way for the sinner or criminal to enter into the world to come.

We have already noted how Menahot systematizes and organizes a vast corpus of data of the Written Torah. Zebahim accomplishes the same work, but in laying out generalizations to hold together Scripture's facts concerning animal offerings, the Oral Torah's counterpart, generalizing category-formation also makes an original statement. That statement plays itself out on two planes, formed into a grid. The one has to do with intentionality, the other, sanctification. The one brings about the other. But is sanctification substantive or relative, an intrinsic characteristic of that which has been sanctified, or a contingent characteristic responsive to context, circumstance, and will? The grid of these two basic principles holds together most, though not all, of the systematic, analytical expositions of law in this category-formation.

In all of these cases, therefore, the Oral Torah has invented category-formations in response to its own requirements: to deliver the message at hand, only the fabricated category can serve as the effective medium. And for the most part, though not entirely so, the particular message that the Oral Torah wishes to set down concerns the power, and the limits, of the human will: where man makes consequential choices, where his will bears no weight whatsoever, and the in-between cases that fill up the agenda of the Halakhah. A clear picture of the program and plan of the Oral Torah takes shape. Where the Oral Torah redefines what matters in the category-formations of the Written Torah, that shape becomes still more vividly exposed.

XVIII. *Same Letter, New Spirit: When the Oral Torah Asks its Own Questions about the Written Torah's Topical Program*

This account of the Oral Torah's own contribution reaches its climax when we ask, what happens when the Oral Torah takes over and makes its own the category-formations and expositions of the Written Torah? Now, by contrast to the category-formations considered in Chapter Four, the Oral Torah reveals its autonomous program, and, properly described, analyzed, and interpreted, we contemplate a truly original and subtle one at that. Here the Oral Torah places on display its particular and distinguishing traits of mind, doing so by how it defines a received category-formation and expounds it. The Oral Torah in the identified category-formations thereby recasts matters so as to make a fresh and distinctive statement of its own. And when we examine all of the statements and ask the interpretive question, how do they fit together and what do they say seen whole, the answer proves quite remarkable. Pursuing a program of problems, indicative of its own sustained problematic, one that in Halakhic discourse the Written Torah in no way adumbrates, the Oral Torah defines its own character. And, as we shall see at the end, that self-definition frames the Oral Torah as the necessary complement, the fulfillment, in the social order, of the Written Torah's narrative of Israel: one whole Torah indeed.

That is what I mean when I identify category-formations defined by the Written Torah but entirely reframed, not just recapitulated and amplified, by the Oral Torah. The Oral Torah presents itself as original and recapitulative in a fresh, necessary language. The full originality of the Oral Torah, its imparting a new spirit to a received letter—these remarkable traits emerge with clarity and force. But when we grasp the statement that the Oral Torah sets forth, we shall see why the Written Torah required, made absolutely necessary, the achievement of, the Oral Torah. No more compelling evidence of the character of the Oral Torah comes to hand than what follows. It vastly transcends the formulation of a wholly new set of questions to address to a received topical program. What we contemplate in the Oral Torah emerges as the reworking of the Written Torah, in the Written Torah's own spirit, into a wholly new statement of a single, enduring truth. Stated simply: we shall see exactly how the letter of the law gives life to the spirit of the story the Torah tells about man.

a. *Besah*

Besah (a.k.a., Yom Tob, festival) deals with the preparation of food on the festival day itself. Scripture permits doing so: "On the first day you shall hold a holy assembly, and on the seventh day a holy assembly; no work shall be done on those days; but what everyone must eat, that only may be prepared by you" (Ex. 12:16). What is permitted on the first and seventh days of Passover also is permitted on Pentecost and on the first and seventh days of Tabernacles. The statement of the topic in Scripture in no way prepares us for the remarkable category-formation set forth in the name of Besah. The exposition of the topic shows the complete independence of the Halakhic presentation:

I. Preparing Food on the Festival Day
   A. Cases and their Implications
   B. Designating Food before the Festival for Use on the Festival
   C. Doing Actions Connected with Preparing Food on a Festival Day in a Different Manner from on Ordinary Days. Other Restrictions
   D. The Status of a Person's Possessions in Respect to the Sabbath Limit

Clearly, at issue are considerations not contained within Scripture's laconic statement. The issues encapsulated in the governing principles, none of them dictated by Scripture's treatment of the subject, are these: [1] must food for use on the festival be available and designated for that purpose, actually or potentially, prior to the festival? Further, [2] may or may not one carry on the preparation of food on the festival in exactly the same way in which one does so on an ordinary day? Next, [3] may or may not one prepare what is required for the preparation of food, that is, secondary or tertiary acts of labor, in the way in which one may do so on an ordinary day? Finally, [4] may or may not one do such acts of labor at all? The Sabbath supplies the governing analogy. The tractate asks about distinguishing the actual preparation of food, which the Written Torah

permits, from acts of labor required for food but not directly pertaining thereto; acts of labor indirectly involved in food preparation. The
analogy of the Sabbath is ever present. We deal with one of the
triumphs of the Halakhic imagination. The generative premises of
the Halakhah form a natural connection to the topic at hand, but
every one of them works well, also, in other contexts altogether, and
none is particular to the topic, let alone insinuated by Scripture's
meager statement on the topic, of festival cooking. What we have
before us is a quite independent development of a subject rather
casually stated by Scripture. All of the complexities, and the premises
that generate them, derive from other minds altogether, even though,
one may fairly claim, all of the participating intellects concur on
everything important within the governing logic that comprehends
the law of Scripture and the Halakhah of the Oral Torah—both.

One may prepare food on the festival days of Passover, Pentecost,
and Tabernacles. Scripture is explicit on that point. But the
Halakhah of Besah wishes to raise searching questions. If I had to
select the single most pervasive principle of Halakhah, it is the insistence on designating food before the festival for use on the festival, on
the one side, and linking the status of the household to the status (e.
g. , as to location) of his possessions, on the other. In advance of the
householder must designate for use on the festival what he is going to
prepare on the festival. That represents an act of particularization,
this batch of food for this festival in particular, and it is entirely
familiar to us in another context altogether. Once more we observe
the Halakhah's recurrent stress on the particularity of intentionality.
Here the principle is, one must in advance of the festival designate
for use on the festival whatever one is going to utilize on that day.
When it comes to things other than edibles, advance planning is
absolutely required. These reflections on intentionality intersect with
deep thought on the potential and the actual to create a complex grid
of analysis of cases by appeal to the one principle or to the other. But
they lead to a theological principle that the sacred, e. g., sacred time,
must be designated and differentiated as an act of intentionality. One
must prepare in advance for the advent of the festival by designating
what is going to serve the legitimate tasks of that day. Once more the
Tosefta states a case that bears the principle: ashes from a fire which
one lit on the festival day do they not use to cover blood of a beast
slaughtered on that festival day, for they are not that which was
made ready before the festival day.

b. *Erubin*

The Halakhah set forth by Erubin focuses on the verses, Ex. 16:29-30, that link the act of eating with the locus of residence:

> "See! The Lord has given you the Sabbath, therefore on the sixth day he gives you bread for two days; remain every man of you in his place; let no man go out of his place on the seventh day. So the people rested on the seventh day."

The prohibition of "going out of one's place" on the Sabbath is linked to eating meals in one's place on the holy day. The juxtaposition of a double-supply of bread for Friday and Saturday and remaining in place leaves no doubt that [1] one stays home, on the one side, and that [2] home is where one eats, on the other. By extension, one must remain within the limits of one's residence on the Sabbath. The Written Torah defines the Sabbath in part by sending Israel to its tents on that occasion. Repose involves entry into a stationary condition. The given of the Halakhah of 'Erubin is that people are to stay in their place on the Sabbath day. That means each person has a place, defined as four cubits (enough for a burial plot), and, further, that he may move from that place for the distance of two thousand cubits in any direction. Scripture yields the proposition at hand, though if that is the case, then Scripture is remarkably reticent to define any details of the law.

In play throughout the exposition of the Halakhah of Erubin are these propositions: [1] one may not transport objects from private to public domain, but [2] there are types of domain that are neither the one nor the other, specifically, the courtyard linking a number of private properties, and the alleyway onto which a number of courtyards debauch. To these givens the Halakhah of Erubin takes for granted a number of propositions, upon which all else is founded. These are as follows:

[1] Remaining in one's place does not mean one may not leave his house; one may move about his own property; he may move to the limit of 2,000 cubits from one's own residence.

[2] Through a fictive meal or an *'erub*—a meal of commingling—one may commingle ownership of a courtyard shared with others. Similarly, through a fictive meal, or a *shittuf*, a meal of partnership, an alleyway into which a number of courtyards debauch may be formed into a common courtyard; this is signaled by marking the alleyway as a single domain by establishing a gateway, and then the

shared meal establishes that all of the private domains are commingled as to ownership.

[3] One must remain in his own village, that is, the settled area and its natural environs.

[4] One may establish residence at some place other than his own household, by making provision for eating a meal at that other place. The meal must be located in its place by sundown on the Sabbath, but a verbal declaration accomplishes the same purpose. That fictive residence permits him to measure his allotted area for travel from that other place. The Written Torah has therefore defined the category-formation, but the Oral Torah, its meaning and significance.

Why do sages devote their reading of the Halakhah of Erubin above all to differentiating public from private domain? The Halakhah has independently developed a topic that, to begin with, Scripture introduces without elaboration. Yet all of Erubin and a fair component of Shabbat focus upon that matter. The answer derives from the governing theology of the Sabbath. The Written Torah at Gen. 1:1-2:3 represents the Sabbath as the climax of creation. The theology of the Sabbath put forth in the Oral Torah's Halakhah derives from a systematization of definitions implicit in the myth of Eden that envelopes the Sabbath. Sages' thinking about the Sabbath invokes in the formation of the normative law defining the matter the model of the first Sabbath, the one of Eden. The two paramount points of concern—[1] the systematic definition of private domain, where ordinary activity is permitted, and [2] the rather particular definition of what constitutes a prohibited act of labor on the Sabbath—precipitate deep thought and animate the handful of principles brought to concrete realization in the two tractates. We can make sense of the Halakhah of Shabbat-Erubin only by appeal to the story of Creation, the governing metaphor derived therefrom, the sages' philosophical reflections that transform into principles of a general and universal character the case at hand.

Both an 'erub-fence and an 'erub-meal render private domain public through the sharing of ownership. The 'erub-fence for its part renders public domain private, but only in the same sense that private domain owned by diverse owners is shared, ownership being commingled. The 'erub-fence signals the formation for purposes of the sanctification of time of private domain—but with the ownership commingled. So what is "private" about "private domain" is different on the Sabbath from in secular time. By definition, for property to be private in the setting of the Sabbath, it must be shared among house-holders. On the Sabbath, domain that is totally private, its ownership not commingled for the occasion, becomes a prison, the householder being unable to conduct himself in the normal manner in the court-yard beyond his door, let alone in other courtyards in the same alleyway, or in other alleyways that debauch onto the same street. And the Halakhah, as who do not offer their proprietorship of their households for commingling for the Sabbath. What happens, there-fore, through the 'erub-fence or 'erub-meal is the re-definition of proprietorship: what is private is no longer personal, and no one totally owns what is his, but then everyone (who wishes to participate, himself and his household together) owns a share everywhere. So much for the "in his place" part of "each man in his place." His place constitutes an area where ordinary life goes on, but it is no longer "his" in the way in which the land is subject to his will and activity in ordinary time. If constructing a fence serves to signify joint ownership of the village, now turned into private domain, or constructing the gateway, of the alleyway and its courtyards, what about the meal? The 'erub-meal signifies the shared character of what is eaten. It is food that belongs to all who wish to share it. But it is the provision of a personal meal, also, that allows an individual to designate for him-self a place of Sabbath residence other than the household to which he belongs.

So the Sabbath loosens bonds, those of the householder to his property, those of the individual to the household. The advent of the Sabbath forms communities, the householders of a courtyard into a community of shared ownership of the entire courtyard, the indi-vidual into a community other than that formed by the household to which he belongs—now the community of disciples of a given sage, the community of a family other than that in residence in the house-hold, to use two of the examples common in the Halakhah. Just as the Sabbath redefines ownership of the Land and its produce, turn-ing all Israelites into a single social entity, "all Israel," which, all together, possesses the Land in common ownership, so the Sabbath redefines the social relationships of the household, allowing persons to separate themselves from the residence of the household and des-ignate some other, some personal, point of residence instead. The Sabbath recapitulates the condition of Eden, when Adam and Eve could go where they wished and eat what they wanted, masters of all they contemplated, along with God. Israel on the Sabbath in the

Land, like Adam on the Sabbath of Eden that celebrates Creation, shares private domain and its produce. The Oral Torah has shown how this is accomplished.

c. *Gittin*

The topic, writs of divorce, derives from Scripture, which is explicit that at the cessation of the marital bond (for which in Scripture the language of sanctification does not enter) a writ of divorce be handed to the woman. The pertinent verse of Scripture, Dt. 24:1-4, is as follows:

> "When a man takes a wife and marries her, and it happens that she finds no favor in his eyes because he has found some uncleanness in her and he writes her a certificate of divorce, puts it in her hand and sends her out of his house, when she has departed from his house and goes and becomes another man's wife, if the latter husband detests her and writes her a certificate of divorce, puts it in her hand and sends her out of his house, or if the latter husband dies who took her as his wife, then her former husband who divorced her must not take her back to be his wife after she has been defiled; for that is an abomination before the Lord, and you shall not bring sin on the land that the Lord your God is giving you as an inheritance."

Scripture lays emphasis upon the prohibition of a divorced woman, once remarried, to return to the husband who has divorced her. The Halakhah of the Oral Torah, by contrast, finds its focus of interest in the subordinated details of the transaction set forth in Scripture. The topical program does not signal the foci of interest that the Halakhah will identify for itself. Here is the outline of the Halakhah as set forth by the Mishnah-Tosefta-Yerushalmi-Bavli:

I.   The Writ of Divorce
    A.   Transmitting the Writ of Divorce
    B.   The Writ of Divorce and the Writ of Emancipation of Slaves
    C.   Preparing a Writ of Divorce
II.   Rules of Agency and Writs of Divorce
III. Rulings Pertinent to the Writ of Divorce Made for Good Order of the World, and Other Rulings in the Same Classification
IV.   The Slave
V.   The Wife's Receipt of the Writ of Divorce
VI.   The Husband's Instructions on the Preparation & Delivery of the Writ
    A.   Instructing Agents to Prepare the Writ
    B.   The Conditional Writ of Divorce

VII. The Impaired Writ of Divorce
  A. The Writ of Divorce that is Subject to Doubt
  B. The Writ of Divorce that is Subject to Flaws or Imperfections
  C. An Invalidating Restriction in a Writ of Divorce
  D. Confusing Writs of Divorce

The Halakhah takes as its principal problem the delivery of the writ of divorce to the wife. Not only must the document be particular to that women, but it must also accommodate her preferences as to its delivery. That underscores her active role in the procedure; she must be fully cognizant of the matter. Since the document must conform to the law or yields no effect and leaves her sanctified to that particular man, she has to make sure it is validly prepared at its critical points. That is why she dictates the conditions of the writ's delivery. While she cannot initiate the procedure—Scripture has accorded her no role in the transaction but the passive one of receiving the document—her will governs where and how the writ will be handed over to her. What is at stake in these requirements? They serve to make certain the writ is valid and takes effect, so that all parties to the transaction know that the woman's status has changed irrevocably. But that means, even an imperfection without any bearing on the substance of the transaction, such as misdating or misidentifying the writ (using the wrong date, or misidentifying the locale of the husband, suffices to invalidate the writ. So too, if the scribe erred and gave the writ of divorce to the woman and the quittance to the man, rather than giving the writ to the man to give to his wife and vice versa, it is a complete disaster. Both cases and comparable ones bring to bear the most severe penalties. Then, if the actually-not-divorced wife should remarry on the strength of the impaired writ of divorce, her entire situation is ruined. She has to get a new writ of divorce from the first husband and from the second; she loses her alimony; she loses many of the benefits and guarantees of the marriage-settlement. And the offspring from the marriage fall into the category of those whose parents are legally unable to wed, e.g., the offspring of a married woman by a man other than her husband. Everything is lost by reason of the innocent actions of the wife in remarrying on the strength of an impaired writ, and that means, the wife has an acute interest in, and bears full responsibility for, the validity of the writ. The husband's only unique power is to direct the writing and delivery of the writ; otherwise, the wife bears equal responsibility for the accurate preparation of the document, the valid delivery (hence insistence that she be alert to the transaction), and the fully-correct details inscribed therein.

The passage of Scripture pertinent to writs of divorce in no way prepares us for the issues of the Halakhah. Critical to the Oral Torah is the conception that Heaven, not only the husband and wife, concerns itself with the change in the woman's status as holy. Where, in the repertoire of the Halakhah, does that concern express itself? It is in the valid preparation of the document itself. That document—properly written, properly witnessed, properly handed over—serves to deconsecrated the woman, as surely as the rites of disposition of the consecrated animal not used for its correct purpose deal with the change in status of that beast. So it is the document that is the medium of effecting, or of annulling, the status of consecration. And what gives the document effect? The answer is in two parts. First, we know, the witnesses are the key-element in the process; the document is validated by valid witnesses, and lacking valid witnesses, even though it is correctly written and delivered, it has no effect at all. In the end the particular witnesses attest not only to the facts of what is incised in the writing but also to the specificity of the writing: this man, this woman, this document.

Then what is to be said about the witnesses to the preparation of the document, for whom do they stand? The witnesses validate the document and give it effect because they stand as Heaven's surrogates. Israelite males not related to the parties, the witnesses accord cognizance on earth in behalf of Heaven to that change in intentionality and status that the document attests. When the witnesses to the validity of the writ prepared overseas say, "Before us it was written and before us it was signed" (that is, by the witnesses to the document itself), they confirm what is at stake in the entire transaction: Heaven has been informed of the change of intention on the part of the husband, releasing the wife from her status of sanctification to him. So the change in intentionality must be attested on earth in behalf of Heaven. And that which is certified by the witnesses is not only the validity of the writing of the document but the explicit transaction that has brought about the writing: the husband has instructed the scribe to write the writ of divorce, that particular writ of divorce, for his wife, for the named wife and no other woman (even of the same name). When he has done that, pronouncing his intent to nullify the relationship of sanctification that he proffered and the woman accepted, then all else follows. But, second, Heaven wants something else as well. Not only must the intention be articulated, and explicitly in the transaction at hand and no other. The document itself must give evidence of counterpart specificity. What makes all the difference? The Halakhah specifies irregularities of two classes, first, those that do not fundamentally invalidate the transaction, second, those that so completely invalidate the transaction that the original status of sanctification retains effect, despite what the husband has said, despite what the wife has correctly received by way of documentary confirmation of the change of intentionality and therefore status, his and hers, respectively. That represents a most weighty result, with long-term consequences.

In two circumstances the husband's intentionality does not register with Heaven, so M. 8:5 (and M. 8:8):

> M. 8:5 If he wrote the writ of divorce dating it according to an era which is not applicable, for example, according to the era of the Medes, according to the era of the Greeks, according to the building of the Temple, according to the destruction of the Temple, [if] he was in the east and wrote, "In the west," in the west and wrote, "In the east," she goes forth from this one [whom she married on the strength of the divorce from the former husband] and from that one [the first husband]. And she requires a writ of divorce from this one and from that one.

Who then has the power to nullify even the effect of the intentionality of the husband? It is the scribe. If he errs in dating the document, or if he errs and writes down the wrong location of the participant, then, whatever the husband's intentionality and whatever the wife's (wrong) impression of what has taken place, the writ is null, and the result is as specified, chaotic. So too if the scribe made a mistake in transmitting the documents that are to be exchanged, the transaction is null. Why has the scribe so critical a role in the transaction that he can utterly upset the intentionality of the one and the consequent conclusion drawn by the other party, husband and wife, respectively? The Halakhah attributes to the scribe a role in the transaction as critical, in its way, as the role of the husband in commissioning the document and the wife in receiving it. And what is it that the scribe can do to ruin the transaction? First, he can commit the unpardonable sin of not delivering the document to the correct party at the husband's instructions. That is, the husband has told him to deliver the writ of divorce to the wife, but he has given her the quittance instead. The woman has never validly received the writ. The scribe must realize and not thwart the husband's intentionality. But what about the other matter, misdating the document, misidentifying the parties? Here what has happened is that the writ no longer pertains to those mentioned in it. The scribe has placed the parties in a different period from that in which they live, dating them, by reason of the document, in some other time; or he has placed them in a different locale from the one where they are situated. He has set forth a document for some others than the ones before him, and he has given to those before him a spurious time and place.

So the Halakhah raises yet again its requirement on the acute localization of the piece of writing: this woman, here and now, her and her alone, this man, here and now, him and him alone. That is to say, the Halakhah has underscored the conception, the conviction really, that the moment and act of sanctification are unique, specific, not to be duplicated or replicated in any way or manner. When God oversees this holy relationship, he does not wish it to be confused with any other. That is why, when God is informed of the change of intentionality that has brought about the consecration of the woman to the man, he must be given exact information. The Halakhah before us rests on profound reflection about the character of intentionality and its effects. What the law ascertains encompasses not only the intentionality and will of the husband, not only the conscious, explicit cognizance of the wife, but the facts of the case. Specifically, the Halakhah insists that the husband's act of will carries effect only when confirmed by valid action. Intention on its own is null. The full realization of the intention, involving valid provision for all required actions, alone carries effect. Not only so, but a third party, the scribe, intervenes in the realization of the husband's will. That means, facts beyond the husband's control and the wife's power to secure a right to supervise and review matters take over—with truly dreadful and permanent results. But the scribe possesses no intentionality in the transaction (other than the will we assume motivates his practice of his profession, that is, professionalism). The very role accorded to the scribe, not to the contracting parties, underscores the position of the Halakhah. It is that intentionality not confirmed by the correct deeds in the end does not suffice.

d. *Hallah*

The Hallah- or dough-offering is given to the priest, so Num. 15:17-

21. Sages understand the verses to require the separation of a portion from the bread; it is to be coarse meal, taken to mean unbaked bread-dough. Mishnah-tractate Hallah also explores two matters on which Scripture is silent: first, the precise point in the processing of the dough at which the dough becomes liable to the offering; and, second, the amount that one must separate." Three principal considerations intersect: what constitutes bread that is liable to dough-offering, when liability takes effect, and where the offering is required? When we know the answers to these three questions, we realize how fresh and original is the thought of the Halakhah on Scripture's topic. Bread is a baked food product that is made of flour that, upon being moistened and kneaded and fermented, rises. What derives from flour that does not leaven is not liable to dough-offering and not classified as bread for purposes of Passover either. Two criteria of liability coexist, one marking the beginning, the other the end, of the spell. First, people snack on dough without giving dough offering until the dough is made into a ball or is rolled out in a solid mass. But formal liability takes effect when a crust forms, which is to say, when the enzyme that brings about leavening dies. These points of demarcation—when the liability commences, when the liability must be met—correspond to the points at which the crop in the field *may* be tithed, at the outset, and *must* be tithed, at the end of the harvesting-process. So the spell of liability commences with the mixture of flour and water and the working of the two into a mass, and it is fixed with the conclusion of the same process. The upshot is, the span of susceptibility coincides with the process of fermentation: the activation of the enzyme, at the outset, then the cultivation of the fermentation process, and finally the realization of the goal of that process in the forming of a crust, the conclusion of fermentation. We may say that the critical criterion is [1] dough that has incurred liability within the Land of Israel and [2] that is consumed by Israelites in the Land, So there is a very specific point of intersection that dictates which dough is liable to dough-offering: [1] dough prepared from wheat and comparable flour, which, when mixed with yeast and water, has the power to ferment; [2] dough at the point at which the fermentation-process has realized its goal. Leavening then is the key to the definition of bread. Taken as a natural process, leavening is perceived as animate.

At the moment of adding water to the yeast and dough when making bread, life renews itself through the life-precipitating touch of

water to the flour and the yeast. Here considerations of uncleanness
and those of sanctification intersect. That is the point that precipitates concern with the forces of death, prime source of cultic uncleanness. Then, to preserve purity, Israel goes on the alert for the danger
of pollution: at the moment when yeast, flour, and water ignite the
processes of animation. So too for all of their counterparts: "if water
be put on the seed," (Lev. 11:34, 37) take care. Now we see the other
half of the story. Unclean or otherwise, the dough congeals, the yeast
ferments and yields gas, and so, life-processes having commenced,
though death and its surrogates threaten. Then the householder goes
on the alert—if he cares, if by an act of deliberation he has made life
happen. And there too, by sharing the outcome of the fermentation
with God, the householder acknowledges the opposite of death,
which is life, embodied in the living processes by which the bread
comes into being, and resulting in the presence, within the dough, of
a portion subject to sanctification: donation to the priest in the
present instance. It is the processing of flour into bread to sustain life
where fermentation represents life marks the occasion for the affirmation of God's presence in all life-forms and processes: God lays his
claim to his share, because God's claim upon the Israelite householder extends to the outer limits of vitality. While Scripture surely
concurs on all these points, the Halakhah, not Scripture, has identified the generative premises and the critical tensions and points of
special concern that it brings to the subject Scripture has defined.

e. *Hullin*

As at the Babas, so here too, Scripture provides a considerable corpus
of facts, but the Halakhah recasts and reshapes these facts and makes
of them a statement that is quite independent of Scripture's presentation of the same topic. What the Halakhah does, essentially, is to
form diverse facts into a single coherent construction and through
them to make a striking point. The verses of Scripture that pertain
are Dt. 12:20-24, Ex. 22:30, Dt. 14:21, Lev. 22:28, Lev. 17:13-14,
Gen. 32:33, Dt. 18:3, Dt. 22:6-7. What is it that the Halakhah makes
of these several rules about meat-preparation in the household? The
category, Hullin, covers the preparation of meat for the table at
home, its counterpart being Zebahim, on the preparation of meat for
the altar in the Temple. When it comes to the preparation of meat,
the Halakhah deals with three settings: [1] the Temple, [2] the Land

of Israel, and [3] foreign land. And for all three, it insists, the same rules pertain, even despite the considerable differences that apply. Since all territory outside of the Land of Israel is by definition unclean, the premise of the Halakhah is that, despite that fact, Israel is to consume its secular meat in accord with those rules of sanctification that pertain to food and its preparation. The laws of cultic cleanness may apply to the household in the Land of Israel but cannot pertain abroad; nonetheless, the other principal admonitions apply overseas. The existence of the Temple or its destruction makes no difference.

The topical program of the Halakhah, as set forth in the Mishnah-Tosefta-Bavli, is as follows:

    i.   Rules of Slaughtering Unconsecrated Animals for Use at Home or in the Temple
        A. General Rules of Slaughter
        B. Specific Regulations. *Terefah*-Rules
        C. Slaughter and Illicit Sacrifice
        D. *Terefah*- and Valid Carcasses
        E. The Affect of Valid Slaughter on the Parts of a Beast's Body, e.g., on the Foots
    ii. Other Rules Governing the Preparation of Food, Principally for Use at Home
        A. Not Slaughtering "It and Its Young" (Lev. 22:28)
        B. The Requirement to Cover Up the Blood (Lev. 17:13-14)
        C. The Prohibition of the Sciatic Nerve (Gen. 32:32)
        D. The Separation of Milk and Meat (Ex. 23:19, 34:26, Dt. 12:21)
        Connection for the Purposes of Contracting Uncleanness
        F. The Gifts to the Priest Taken from a Beast Slaughtered for Secular Purposes: The Shoulder, Two Cheeks, and Maw (Dt. 18;3)
        G. The Gift to the Priest of the First Fleece of a Sheep (Dt. 18:4)
        H. Letting the Dam Go from the Nest When Taking the Young (Dt. 22:6-7)

Scripture clearly has contributed a substantial repertoire of subjects. Here the governing problematics defines a remarkably cogent exposition of diverse, related topics, the same point being made concerning various subjects within the larger agendum at hand: killing animals for meat. The governing problematics derives from the premise that the altar and the table compare, belonging to a single continuum of sanctification and conforming to a single set of cogent rules. So the generative issue throughout is, how is the table like the altar? And that draws in its wake the complementary issue, how is it different?

Then how the circumstance of the one imposes a different rule from that of the other will demand detailed attention. Since the table compares with the altar, how and where and why is it subject to a different rule from that pertaining to the altar?

That the Oral Torah independently develops Scripture's topic is clear. The Halakhah states in so many words what it wants to know, which is whether [1] the destruction of the Temple and cessation of the offerings, 2] the degradation of the Land of Israel, and [3] the exile of the holy people, Israel, from the Holy Land, affect the rules of sustenance in the model of the nourishment of God in the Temple, in the Land, among the holy people. The answer is, whatever the condition of the Temple and its altar, whatever the source—the Holy Land or unclean gentile lands—of animals, and whatever the location of Israel, whether enlandised or not, one thing persists. The sanctification of Israel, the people, endures [1] in the absence of the cult and [2] in alien, unclean territory and [3] whatever the source of the food that Israel eats. Israel's sanctity is eternal, not contingent, absolute. The sanctification that inheres in Israel, the people, transcends the Land and outlives the Temple and its cult. These propositions form a remarkably fresh statement concerning the received topic.

The Halakhah to make its statement about the eternal sanctification of the people, Israel, explicitly responds to three facts: [1] Israelites live not only in the holy land but abroad, in unclean land; [2] the Temple has been destroyed; [3] and, consequently, animals are slaughtered not only in the Temple in the Land but in unconsecrated space and abroad, and the meat is eaten not only in a cultic but in a profane circumstance. Anyone who wonders whether the Halakhah that applied to the Temple and the home when the Temple was standing and Israel was in the Land of Israel continues to apply with the Temple in ruins and Israel in exile here finds his answer. Although the sanctity of the Temple stands in abeyance, the sanctity of the Israelite table persists; although Israel is in exile from the Holy Land, Israel remains holy; although in the Temple rules of uncleanness are not now kept, they continue in force where they can be. Birds and animals that flourish outside of the Land when prepared for the Israelite table are regulated by the same rules that apply in the Land and even (where relevant) at the altar. So Israel, the people, not only retains sanctity but preserves it outside of the Land, and the sanctity of Israel transcends that of the Temple and its altar.

The Written Torah supplies a law that contains the entire message, when it imposes the same requirements that pertain to slaughter of an animal sacrifice for the altar in Jerusalem to killing an animal for the use of Israel at home. That means meat Israel eats is subject to the same regulations that apply to meat God receives on the altar-fires. The same law is explicit that meat for those who are not holy, that is, gentile-idolaters, is not subject to the same rules (Ex. 22:30, Dt. 14:21). So the point cannot be missed: food for God and for Israel must be prepared in comparable manner, which does not apply to food for gentiles. How does that principle affect animals raised abroad? The laws of Hullin apply to them, because the laws apply to unconsecrated animals as much as consecrated ones. The destiny—nourishing Israel—is what counts, that alone. The beast intended for Israelite consumption at the table even in a foreign country must be prepared as though for God on the altar in Jerusalem, and that can only mean, because the beast is intended (by the act of correct slaughter) for Israel, the use of the beast by Israel sanctifies the beast and necessitates conformity with the rules of slaughter for God in the Temple. Israel, even abroad, renders the food that it eats comparable to food for the altar. The Halakhah rests on generative premises of its own, responding to a set of questions in no way proposed by Scripture.

f. *Moed Qatan*

The Halakhah of Moed Qatan deals with two distinct matters and joins them into a single category-formation: first, actions that are permitted or prohibited on the intermediate days of Passover and of the Festival of Tabernacles, with special reference to farming and commerce, and, second, special problems involving burial of the dead on those days. The governing principles for the former corpus of Halakhah are [1] one may carry out an act of labor that prevents substantial loss, but only if the act is not onerous; and [2] that work that ought to have been done prior to the festival may not be left over to be done on the intermediate days. These may not be treated as ordinary work days, even though they also are not observed as festival days are, with the complete cessation of all labor except for cooking. Scripture knows prohibitions of labor for the opening and closing days of the specified festivals (Ex. 12:16, Lev. 23:7-8, Num. 28:18, 25, 29:12-35). Num. 28:18-25 provide for offerings for Passover and the intervening days. For the Festival of Tabernacles, Num. 29:12-35 provides a huge toll of animal sacrifices. It follows that the intermediate days are observed in the Temple. The intermediate days require sacrifices designated for that occasion, so are differentiated from days that require merely everyday offerings in the Temple. But no explicit restrictions govern conduct on the intermediate days. The premise of the Halakhah, that the intermediate days of the Festivals of Passover and Tabernacles are subjected to restrictions comparable to, though of lesser severity than, those for the opening and concluding Festival days themselves, requires explanation. The topical program of the Halakhah is indicated by the following outline of the tractate in the Mishnah-Tosefta-Yerushalmi-Bavli:

    i.   Labor on the Intermediate Days of the Festival
       A. In the Fields
       B. Miscellanies
       C. Cases of Emergency and Loss
    ii. Commerce
    iii. Burial of the Dead, Mourning on the Intermediate Days of a Festival

The generative premise of the Halakhah stands behind two distinct issues: [1] restricting labor on the intermediate days of the festival, and [2] linking the intermediate days of the festival in a single category-formation with the laws on mourning. Neither one is invited by Scripture's presentation of the topic; both represent the results of independent development of the subject.

    First, what made sages suppose to begin with that any restrictions at all should pertain on the intermediate days of the Festival as comparable to those for the Festival, though subject to diminished restrictions? The answer emerges when we consider the activities in the Temple on those same days. Num. 28:17ff. for Passover, Num. 29:12-35 for Tabernacles, as we have seen, provide for Temple rites in observance of the intermediate days, over and above the daily offerings. The upshot is, the Temple offerings respond to the sanctity of the intermediate festival days. The household then does no less. The household on the intermediate days is brought into a continuum with the Temple; the advent of the festival, like the Sabbath, transforms the household in exactly the way the Written Torah emphasizes: as to the acts of labor performed therein. Second, what links the two subjects of the category-formation at hand? The Mishnah, and therefore within the discipline of the Halakhah's presentation, also the Tosefta, Yerushalmi, and Bavli, in dealing with the topic, the intermediate days of the Festivals, all focus a sizable proportion of the Halakhah upon the rules of burial. What has death to do with the intermediate days of the festival? To answer that question we remind ourselves how the Halakhic founders, the framers of the Mishnah, conducted their speculative thought. The principal mode of thought of the Mishnah is that of comparison and contrast. Something is like something else, therefore follows its rule; or it is unlike the other, therefore follows the opposite of the rule governing that something else. How do death and mourning compare to the intermediate days of the festival? The point of opposition—the contrastive part of the equation—then proves blatant. Death is the extreme opposite of the celebration of the festival. The one brings mourning, the other, joy. And the Mishnah's inclusion of the mourner on its list of those whose special situation must be taken into account then precipitates thought about the item on the list—the mourner—that most clearly embodies the special circumstance of all items on the list.

g. *Maaserot*

Ma'aserot through a mass of small rules sets forth a message of broad consequence in amplifying Dt. 14:22. The Halakhah answers three questions: at what point does produce become liable to the designation and separation of tithes, what produce falls into the category of tithing, and when is the act of tithing required? The answers to these Halakhic questions appeal to a single theological conception. The questions logically amplify the simple fact that Scripture sets down. The answers carry us far beyond the framework of the fact that Scripture supplies. The basic principle is that when the produce is suitable for use by its owner, then it becomes subject to tithing and may not be used until it is tithed. But crops *must* be tithed when the farmer claims the produce as his own. Nothing in Scripture leads to such a distinction between "may" and "must" be tithed, nor does the conception that produce must be tithed when the owner claims it as his own derive from Scripture's law. So what makes the difference? It is not the condition of the produce at all, but, rather, the attitude toward the produce that is taken by the farmer who has grown it. That attitude takes effect through the farmer's act of ownership, beyond possession. Asserting ownership takes place when he brings untithed produce from the field to the courtyard or prepares it for sale in the market. At that moment, the farmer having indicated his claim to the produce and intent to use it for his own purposes, God's interest is aroused, his share then is due. God responds to man, specifically, God's attitudes correspond to those of man: when (Israelite) man wants to own the crop and dispose of it as he wishes, then, God demands his share.

The principal religious issue of the Halakhah of Maaserot is simple: the distinction between possession, which is conditional, and ownership, which is absolute. Israel possesses the Land, God owns it, and the Halakhah aims at establishing the relationship of Israel to God, through the use of the Land, as a relationship that is stipulative, a gift and not a given. In this regard, one must invoke the category of covenant, as the Written Torah does when speaking of the Land, and state very simply, the governing religious principle of Ma'aserot is, Israel's possession of the Land is subject to the conditions of the covenant, and Israel's rendering to God what God requires as his share of the produce forms a principal expression of Israel's relationship with God. It follows that the Halakhah rests upon the principle that, while Israel possesses it, God owns the Land, and the agricultural offerings that Israel sets aside for those designated by God as his scheduled castes—the priest, the poor, the support of Jerusalem, for example—represent God's share of the crops. God and man lay claim to the produce of the Land. Only when the produce is shown by the actions of the farmer to be valuable to the farmer does God's claim emerge. The farmer may use the produce as his own only when he has acknowledged God's claim, not eating the produce as if it were his own, but only after setting aside God's share. If the farmer prepares to make a meal of the produce in the field or claims to be sole owner, he loses his right to eat the food until he tithes. Meeting God's claim, the farmer may then use the produce.

When the farmer who possesses the Land proposes to exercise the rights of ownership of the Land, specifically by making his own the produce of the Land, then God enters his rights of ownership and expects his share of the crop. Israel possesses the Land but does not own it, God owns it, and the relationship between Israel and God is worked out in that distinction between what amounts to usufruct and what represents absolute domain. In attitude and emotion, Israel is like God, in the concrete case, the Israelite farmer and God see matters in exactly the same way when it comes to assessing the value and use of the Land and its crops. Both parties—Israel and God—

value the Land. Both lay claim to it, and both affect and are affected by what takes place on it. But while in Scripture, possession of the Land forms a critical component of the history of Israel, in the Oral Torah possession of the Land defines how God and Israel relate through the natural world, through creation. How is it that Israel and God relate in so concrete and specific a situation as is defined by the course of nature, the ripening of the crops? It is because, the Hala-khah takes for granted, God and Israel bear the same attitudes, feel the same emotions, form corresponding intentions. On the foundations of that conviction the Halakhah builds its structure.

h. *Makhshirin*

In connection with imparting susceptibility to uncleanness to produce, Scripture contributes the facts, sages the problematics. That is to say, sages understand Lev. 11:34, 37, to hold that produce that is dry is unaffected by uncleanness from any source and falls outside of the system. Only when produce is wet down is it susceptible. They further take as a fact that produce that is wet down by the intent of the owner is affected, but that wet down inadvertently, under duress, or by third parties is not. We look in vain for the Written Torah's recognition of that fact. The treatment of the topic shows how the Halakhah has defined matters within the framework of its own interests, not in response to the data Scripture has provided:

I.   Intention: Divisible or Indivisible
II.   Water Capable of Imparting Susceptibility Mixed with Water Incapable of Imparting Susceptibility
III.   Absorption of Water
IV.   Water Used for One Purpose: Its Status as to a Secondary Purpose
V.   The Stream as a Connector
VI.   The Insusceptibility of Liquids that are Not Used Intentionally
VII.   The Liquids that Have the Power to Impart Susceptibility to Uncleanness

The Halakhah before us forms a sustained essay on the problematics inherent in the theme, human intentionality. The opening question is, what happens if I change my mind? If I want something but then decide I do not want it, does that change of attitude affect the outcome? No, the Halakhah maintains, it does not. Concomitantly, do I have the power by an act of will to overcome a physical actuality? If liquid is unclean, can the fact that I do not want the liquid to wet

down my produce prevent contamination of my produce? Predictably, since uncleanness works *ex opere operato,* uncleanness takes effect
at the very moment of contact with the produce, and my will that the
produce stay dry is null: Unclean liquids impart uncleanness
[whether they are] acceptable or not acceptable. Intention is tempo-
rally indivisible. Liquid gains but never loses the capacity to impart
susceptibility to uncleanness and to render that on which it falls
susceptible. The really critical and generative question asks about the
relationship of action to intentionality. Do we decide on the basis of
what one has done the character of his prior intention, that is, of
what he intended to do? We have a variety of positions. The first is,
[1] intention without action is null; [2] action is retrospectively deter-
minative of the character of intention—we judge the intention by the
result. A further view is that prior intention plays a balancing role in
the interpretation of the status of the water. We do not decide solely
by what one has done, by the ultimate disposition of the water.

What Scripture treats as a matter of fixed and final classification—
something is either wet or dry—is transformed by the Halakhah of
the Oral Torah into a matter that is relative and contingent. What
results is that the consideration of whether or not something is wet
down in the end is subordinated to attitude and circumstance. As in
Kelim and Tohorot, for utensils and food alike, the householder has
the power to inaugurate the working of the system. The susceptibility
to uncleanness of utensils and food is relative to the attitude and will
of the householder. What is wet is not necessarily susceptible to uncleanness. The matter is relative, not absolute, extrinsic and contingent, not material and inexorable; it is dependent on circumstance
and intention, not uncontingent. It would be difficult to state more
explicitly, or radically, the position that all things are relative to intentionality than in the Halakhah that differentiates in connection
with the same bundle of leeks water that imparts susceptibility to
uncleanness from water that does not. The entire corpus of Halakhah
at hand celebrates the primacy of human wishes: water that has in its
history conformed to a man's wishes—at some point man has lifted it
up and shown that he wants it for some purpose—has the capacity to
impart susceptibility to uncleanness, and water that has not remains
neutral in the system. The upshot of the Halakhah may be stated
very simply:

[1] Liquids impart susceptibility to uncleanness only if they are
useful to man, drawn with approval, subject to human deliberation
and intention.

[2] Liquids that can impart susceptibility to uncleanness do so only if they serve a person's purpose, are deliberately applied to produce, irrigate something through human deliberation and intention.

Preserving the cultic purity of food, including clothing and utensils, so that the household may take its place upon that continuum that the indelible sanctification of holy Israel establishes by its very presence, defines what is at stake. Remembering what one has done and what has happened, remaining ever alert to the dangers of pollution and the opportunities of sanctification represented by one's own restraint—these too derive from the Torah as the sages read it. Here is an instance in which sages do much with very little.

i. *Ohalot*

Corpse-uncleanness embodies in a viscous liquid the effect of the soul when upon death it leaves the body and flows out. It is "the uncleanness effected by the soul" (tuma't hannepesh). Scripture defines but does not characterize, the uncleanness and its effects as the Halakhah portrays them. The Halakhah of the Oral Torah takes up the task of defining, in concrete terms, the character and workings of corpse-uncleanness as portrayed at Num. 19:11-22. Uncleanness is transmitted through contact ("touching"), and, in addition, corpse-uncleanness is conveyed through the effects of the Tent, that is to say, the overshadowing of the corpse by a roof, which transmits the corpse-uncleanness to whatever is overshadowed, except for the contents of tightly sealed clay utensils, through which, it is held, the corpse-uncleanness cannot penetrate. The exposition of the Halakhah follows the outline below, set forth in the Mishnah and paramount in the Tosefta as well:

I.   Corpse-Uncleanness, its Affects on Man and Utensils
    A.   The Matter of Removes
    B.   The Comparison of Susceptibility of Man and Utensils to Corpse- and Other Uncleanness
    C.   Defining the Corpse or corpse-matter that conveys corpse-Uncleanness
    D   Defining Corpse-matter that Does not Convey Corpse-Uncleanness through Overshadowing, but only through Contact and Carrying
    E   Defining Corpse-matter that Does not Convey Uncleanness at All

     F. Corpse-matter that Is Divided; Corpse-Matter that is Joined Together, to form the Requisite Volume to Convey Uncleanness
II. The Opening of a Handbreadth Squared Affords Passage to Uncleanness or Interposes against the Transmission of Uncleanness
     A. Effecting Contamination and Affording Protection
     B. The Utensil and the Tent: Effecting Contamination and Affording Protection
     C. Man, Utensils and the Tent
     D Corpse-Matter in a Wall
III. Defining the Tent: Its Sides, its Apertures, the Materials of which it is Constructed
     A. The Sloping Sides of the Tent
     B. The Apertures
     C. The Materials of Which the Tent Is Constructed
     D. The Utensil and the Tent, Illustrated by The Hive and the Tent
     E. The Hatchway of the Tent
IV. Dividing the Tent or House; Dividing Utensils. Interposition
     A. Dividing the Household and its Appurtenances
     B. Walling off the Flow of Corpse-Uncleanness in Various Circumstances
     C. Holes in the Walls of Tents and Utensils and the Passage of Corpse-Uncleanness, and Diminishing the Dimensions of the Hole to Impede the Flow of Corpse-Uncleanness
     D. Wall-Projections and the Flow of Corpse-Uncleanness
     E. Other Media of Interposition
     F. Dividing the House/Room by Filling It with Dirt and Stone
     G. The Moving Tent
V. Graveyards and Contaminated Dirt

The uncleanness of the corpse bears no traits particular to itself that require exposition, but the way in which corpse-uncleanness is disseminated does. And nearly the entire exposition of the Halakhah focuses upon problems of dissemination. First comes dissemination of corpse-uncleanness through direct contact with the corpse, and that involves the differentiation of the effects of contact with a corpse upon man and upon utensils (e.g., clothing, vessels). Second, we deal with carrying corpse-matter even though not touching it. But the paramount mode of the dissemination of corpse-uncleanness comes about through the effects of overshadowing.

The shank of the Mishnah's and Tosefta's presentation of the Halakhah occupies itself with an abstract reading of "the tent." Numbers 19 does not prepare us for this discussion. A "tent" is defined as a contained space of a cubic handbreadth: thus a cubic handbreadth introduces the uncleanness and interposes before the uncleanness.

Here "the tent" matters because it affords passage to, or prevents entry by, corpse-uncleanness. Accordingly, we concern ourselves, in particular, with the space that serves to permit the passage of corpse-matter or to prevent the entry of corpse-matter. Corpse-uncleanness is defined in the dimensions of a handbreadth, and it is further understood to function as does a liquid, that is, if it is compressed, it shoots upward and downward, and if not, it spreads laterally. The generative problematics of the Halakhah then takes shape in response to three large issues, each with its subdivisions and its formulation in terms of concrete problems of conflict among established principles:

1   the workings of the opening of a handbreadth squared in affording passage to uncleanness or interposing against it, involving the comparison of the tent and the utensil,

2   the definition of the tent with special attention to its apertures, on the one side, and the materials of which it is constructed, on the other, now with a further comparison of the utensil and the tent, and finally,

3   subdivisions of the tent or the house (or room), once more requiring attention to the comparison of the tent and the utensil.

These rules form simple exercises in problems of the dynamics of fluids and leave no doubt of the Halakhic conception of this form of uncleanness as essentially palpable and material. Scripture cannot be said to have dictated the main lines of the development of this topic. The Halakhah contains within itself a profound conception, which we may uncover by identifying the following governing principle: corpse-uncleanness passes through a handbreadth of open space; its passage is impeded by a handbreadth of closed space. It is a trait of corpse-uncleanness that Scripture does not indicate. The handbreadth in breadth, depth, and height, sufficient to contain the corpse-uncleanness that exudes from a corpse or corpse-matter, has no relationship with a tent except in abstract form and (equally abstract) function. What exactly does the contained space of a cubic handbreadth contain? It contains a kind of thick liquid, which flows and dissipates in the airspace that is contained by the tent as defined in the pure abstraction, A cubic handbreadth introduces uncleanness and interposes before uncleanness. To that statement we need only add, what is contained in the cubic handbreadth of contained space is the uncleanness of the corpse, which is to say, that invisible matter that flows like liquid from the body of the deceased. Then we refer to what leaves the body at death, having been contained therein through life. What exudes from the corpse at death, that viscous matter that is unseen but attaches itself to whatever in the contained space of the tent is not tightly sealed, is a fourth of the volume that a person occupies in the space of the world. That is, a human being deemed to occupy three cubits for purposes of Sabbath rest. That is the physical dimension of the ordinary person. The body retains its physical dimensions in death, so the cubic handbreadth of viscous fluid that the body emits, that which animates the body in life, defines the uncleanness of the corpse. To state matters as bluntly as sages do, corpse-uncleanness stands for "the uncleanness of the soul."

The Written Torah speaks of a tent or house in which whole and healthy people live. Revising the terms of discussion in a highly abstract manner, the Oral Torah speaks of a tent as a space that is capable of containing that which exudes from the body at the moment of death, a tent that replaces the body and holds what the body held or transmits that portion of the person that exudes at death. The handbreadth that is at the foundation of dissemination or interposition is the space through which the effects of the corpse makes its way. A tent is not the same thing as a house or building in which people can live; it is the contained space that holds the gaseous effusion of the corpse. When we say that a tent must measure a handbreadth squared, either to prevent uncleanness from entering an enclosed space or to keep uncleanness within an enclosed space, we speak of not what holds the body but what holds the part of the person that exudes at death, the soul. If corpse-uncleanness is something that can be contained by a tent, and a tent is something that can contain or interpose against corpse-uncleanness, then we deal, in a tent, with the function equivalent of the body. The tent takes the place of the body, makes a place for that which, in the body, leaves at the point of death. It is to be understood then as a surrogate for the body, restoring the imbalance that has taken place with the leaving of the body by that which exudes from it. Death has released this excretion or effusion, the tent can contain it. What exudes from the corpse at such a viscosity as to pass through an open space of at least a handbreadth is the uncleanness of the corpse; it is the soul, the spirit surviving after death and requiring a new locus. That notion is expressed in so many words by Philo, when he says (Special Laws 3:206-7, trans. F. H. Colson, p. 605):

"Those who enter a house in which anyone has died are ordered not to touch anything until they have bathed themselves and also washed the clothes that they were wearing. And all the vessels and articles of furniture and anything else that happens to be inside, practically everything is held by him to be unclean. For a man's soul is a precious thing, and when it departs to seek another home, all that will be left behind is defiled, deprived as it is of the divine image. For it is the mind of man that has the form of God, being shaped in conformity with the ideal archetype, the Word that is above all."

Whether sages will have found Philo's explanation for the uncleanness of what the soul leaves behind I doubt, since in their view, it is that effusion—that which leaves the corpse—that constitutes what is unclean. The tent serves as a broken utensil. The utensil when whole cannot hold back uncleanness, when broken it can. Then the object is not susceptible to uncleanness and cannot be acted upon by uncleanness. The soul, having left its broken utensil, the corpse, finds a domicile only in another broken utensil. What I find critical in the Halakhah is the intense engagement with the issue of how the uncleanness that exudes from the corpse, which we corresponds to the soul leaving the body, is domiciled in the long interval between death and resurrection.

j. *Parah*

Scripture defines a distinctive process of purification from corpse-uncleanness in particular. This it does by providing for the preparation of purification-water, a mixture of the ashes of a red cow and water, and for the application of that water upon a person or object that has suffered corpse-uncleanness. The mixture is applied on the third and seventh days after contamination, and on the seventh day the unclean person immerses and regains cleanness with the sunset, so Numbers 19:1-22. Scripture says little, and the Halakhah much, about the collection and mixing of water and ash, the protection of both from uncleanness, the role of intentionality in the procedure, and the like. Moreover, Scripture's rules leave open the generative question that the Halakhah takes as the center of its program: how does a rite conducted outside of the Temple courtyard ("the camp") relate to the rules governing rites conducted inside? And how can the mixture of ash and water that purifies derive from a rite that contaminates all of its participants, and how can that same purification-water both purify the person that is made unclean by a corpse and also contaminate the person that applies the water? The rite as set forth in Scripture and amplified in the Halakhah of the Oral Torah encompasses two paradoxes, involving the creation of cleanness out of uncleanness, and uncleanness out of cleanness. The first paradox is that it is possible to create a realm of cultic cleanness in the unclean world that lies outside the boundaries of the Temple—the world of death. This is expressed in the proposition that the cow is burned outside of the camp, that is to say, outside of the Temple, in an unclean place. Its blood is tossed not on the altar but in the direction of the altar, toward the front of the tent of meeting. Then the cow is burned outside of the Temple, the ashes are gathered and mixed with water, and the purification-water is then prepared. So the Halakhah underscores that, in the condition of uncleanness, media for achieving cleanness from the most virulent source of uncleanness, the corpse, are to be brought into being.

The second paradox is that, even encompassing those who have gained the highest level of purification, uncleanness envelops the world, for all death is ever-present. Thus those who have attained and maintained the extraordinary level of consciousness required to participate in the rite of burning the cow, collecting the ashes, gathering and transporting water, and mixing the ash and the water, as well as those who propose to utilize the purification-water so brought into being—all by virtue of their very activity in creating media of purification are deemed unclean. They have defied death in the realm of death and overcome—but have contracted uncleanness nonetheless, indeed a paradox: out of a contaminating rite comes water for purification, and, still, the one who sprinkles the purification-water also becomes unclean. Now sages explore the requirements of an offering conducted in a condition of uncleanness, in a place that is unclean by definition, by priests who contract uncleanness (but not corpse-uncleanness) by participating in the rite. Does that mean we impose more stringent purification-rules, to create a circle of cleanness in the unclean world? Or do we impose diminished rules, taking account of the givens of the circumstance? Along these same lines, do we perform the rite exactly as we should in the Temple at the altar, or do we perform the rite in exactly the opposite way, that is, as a mirror-image of how it would be done in the Temple? These parallel questions provoked by the twin-paradoxes of Scripture's and the Halakhah's rules for the rite, respectively, define the problem addressed by the Halakhah, which contains the Oral

Torah's deepest thinking upon the meaning of sanctifying the secular, ordinary world.

The Halakhah decisively answers the generative question: the highest level of alertness, the keenest exercise of caution against uncleanness—these alone will create that circle of cleanness in the world beyond the Temple courtyard that, by definition, is unclean. That accounts for the bizarre arrangements for transporting the youngsters with the stone cups from the Temple, where they have been born and brought up, to the Siloam pool and thence to the Mount of Olives—all to avoid corpse-matter buried at great depths. And still more to the point, the Halakhah suspends the strict purity-rules protecting from contamination not only common food or priestly rations but even Holy Things and imposes much more stringent ones. This it does three ways. First, while hand-washing suffices for eating in a state of cleanness food in the familiar classifications, to purify oneself for participating in preparing the purification-water, total immersion is required; the familiar distinction between hands and body falls away. Second and more decisive, purification-water contracts uncleanness (and so is rendered useless) at any number of removes from the original source of uncleanness, even one hundred; that is to say, we do not count removes. Everything is unclean by reason of its history—a history of which we may well be ignorant. Third, persons involved in preparing the mixture—collecting the ashes, gathering the water, mixing the two—must remain not only constantly alert but perpetually active. From the beginning to the end of their work, they may do only what concerns the task. If they sit down on a chair or lie down on a bed, they automatically contract uncleanness, for what can contract uncleanness is deemed unclean for them. And intentionality enters in at critical points in the classification of actions, e.g., whether or not they are extrinsic to the rite. Perfect concentration on the task, uninterrupted by any extrinsic action or even consideration, alone suffices.

These rules form the paradigm of what it means, of what is required, to attain cultic cleanness: the most intense, best focussed, concentration on the matter at hand. Cultic cleanness beyond the cult is possible, only through the exercise of enormous resources of will and concentration. But however devotedly Israel undertakes the work, the perpetual prevalence of uncleanness persists: the person who has attained an astonishing level of cleanness to participate in the rite and who has concentrated all his energies and attention upon the rite and succeeded—that person, Scripture itself decrees, emerges unclean from his labor in perfect cleanness to prepare purification-water. The one proposition—to participate, the highest, most extraordinary level of cleanness is required—requires the other—one emerges unclean from the labor. Thus cultic cleanness beyond the cult is possible, but the world beyond the Temple remains what it is—no matter what. Having created the instruments for removing corpse-uncleanness, the parties to the rite immerse just as they ordinarily would, wait for sunset, and only then eat their evening meal in the condition of cultic purity that the Halakhah makes possible: the ordinary immersion-pool, the quotidian sunset suffice, but only provisionally. Tomorrow is another day, and it already has begun, if in the state of cleanness that is, or ought to be, the norm for Israel. To the formulation of that message, Scripture has contributed facts. The Halakhah has provided the insight and the dynamics to translated the insight into detailed norms.

k. *Shabbat*

The Written Torah sets the stage. The Sabbath marks the celebration of creation's perfection (Gen. 2:1-3). Food for the day is to be prepared in advance (Ex. 16:22-26, 29-30). Fire is not to be kindled on that day, thus no cooking (Ex. 34:2-3). Servile labor is not to be carried on that day by the householder and his dependents, encompassing his chattel (Ex. 20:5-11, Ex. 23:13, 31:12-17, 34:21). The "where" matters as much as the "when" and the "how:" people are supposed to stay in their place: "Let each person remain in place, let no one leave his place on the seventh day" (Ex. 16:29-30), understanding by place the private domain of the household (subject to further clarification in due course). No Halakhic category comes to more explicit formulation in Scripture than Shabbat at Mishnah-Tosefta-Yerushalmi-Bavli. Yet none reshapes the topic more distinctively than the one at hand. In the setting of its topic, the Sabbath, the Halakhah of Shabbat articulates only a few generative conceptions. But these, expressed in acute detail, encompass the whole. The result of the applied reason and practical logic, most, though not all, of the concrete rulings embody those few conceptions. Six governing principles cover nearly the entire Mishnah-tractate, and, it follows, nearly the whole of the Halakhah (since the Tosefta mainly amplifies and refines the principles initially stated by the Mishnah, and the Talmuds contribute little Halakhah to begin with).

The conceptions are of two types, the one distinctive to the Sabbath, the other pertinent to a broad spectrum of Halakhic categories but here illustrated by cases involving the Sabbath. We begin with the more general. The latter type supplies the larger number of generative conceptions, concerning, first, intentionality, second, causality (cause and effect), and, third, how many things are one and one many. These constitute philosophical, not theological problems. Let us consider the recurrent concerns that transcend the Sabbath altogether, starting with intentionality:

1. Intentionality: The classification of an action is governed by the intention by which it is carried out, so too the consequence:
   A. One is not supposed to extinguish a flame, but if he does so for valid reasons, it is not a culpable action; if it is for selfish reasons, it is. If one deliberately violated the Sabbath, after the Sabbath one may not benefit from the action; if it was inadvertent, he may. We consider also the intentionality of gentiles. One may not benefit indirectly from a source of heat. But what happens *en passant*, and not by deliberation, is not subject to prohibition. Thus if a gentile lit a candle for his own purposes, the Israelite may benefit, but if he did so for an Israelite, the Israelite may not benefit.
   B. If one did a variety of actions of a single classification in a single spell of inadvertence, he is liable on only one count.
   C. In the case of anything that is not regarded as suitable for storage, the like of which in general people do not store away, but which a given individual has deemed fit for storage and has stored away, and which another party has come along and removed from storage and taken from one domain to another on the Sabbath—the party who moved the object across the line that separated the two domains has become liable by reason of the intentionality of the party who stored away this thing that is not ordinarily stored.
   D. The act must be carried out in accord with the intent for culpability to be incurred. The wrong intention invalidates an act, the right one validates the same act. Thus a person breaks a jar to eat dried figs from it, on condition that he not intend [in opening the jar] to make it into a utensil.
   M. 2:5, T. 2:16, T. 2:14, T. 2:17-18, 21, M. 7:1-2, 10:4, 22:3-4
2. Not only direct, but indirect consequences are taken into account.
   A. Since one may not perform an act of healing on the Sabbath, one may not consume substances that serve solely as medicine. But one may consume those that are eaten as food but also heal. One may lift a child, even though the child is holding

something that one is not permitted to handle or move about; one may handle food that one may not eat (e.g., unclean) along with food that one may eat. One may not ask gentiles to do what he may not do, but one may wait at the Sabbath limit at twilight to do what one may ask another person to do. Thus: they do not go to the Sabbath limit to wait nightfall to bring in a beast. But if the beast was standing outside the Sabbath limit, one calls it and it comes on its own.

M. 3:3, 4, 5, M. 4:2, M. 14:3-4, 16:7-8, 21:1-3, 23:3-4, 24:1-4

3. In assessing culpability for violating the Halakhah of the Sabbath, we reckon that an action not only may be subdivided but it also may be joined with another action, so that multiple actions yield a single count of culpability.

A.   Thus whoever forgets the basic principle of the Sabbath and performs many acts of labor on many different Sabbath days is liable only for a single sin-offering. He who knows the principle of the Sabbath and performs many acts of labor on many different Sabbaths is liable for the violation of each and every Sabbath.

B.   He who knows that it is the Sabbath and performs many acts of labor on many different Sabbaths is liable for the violation of each and every generative category of labor. He who performs many acts of labor of a single type is liable only for a single sin-offering.

M. 7:1-2, 22:5

A program of questions of general applicability to a variety of topics of the Halakhah clearly shaped the problematics of Shabbat. Intentionality, causality, and classification of the many as one and the one as many—these standard themes of philosophical inquiry turn out to shape the presentation of the Halakhah at hand. If we were composing a handbook of Halakhic exegesis for a commentator intent on covering the entire surface of the Halakhah, the issue of the many and the one would take its place, alongside the issues of causality, direct and indirect, and the taxonomic power of intentionality. But the specificities of the Halakhah of Shabbat in no way then provide more than the occasion for a routine reprise of these familiar foci of exegesis. So if we had to stop at this point and generalize upon our results, we should conclude that the Halakhah on the Sabbath serves as a mere vehicle for the transmission of philosophical principles of general applicability. Such a result even merely on the face of things would prove dubious. For we should be left with a body of law disconnected from the religious life that accords to that law origins in revelation and authority in God's will. The Halakhah would emerge as the concretization of philosophical reflections bear no consequence for the knowledge of God and what God has in mind for holy Israel.

Let me specify what I conceive to be the encompassing principles, the generative conceptions that the laws embody and that animate the law in its most sustained and ambitious statements. They concern three matters, [1] space, [2] time, and [3] activity, as the advent of the Sabbath affects all three. The advent of the Sabbath transforms creation, specifically reorganizing space and time and reordering the range of permissible activity. First comes the transformation of space that takes effect at sundown at the end of the sixth day and that ends at sundown of the Sabbath day. At that time, for holy Israel, the entire world is divided into public domain and private domain, and what is located in the one may not be transported into the other. What is located in public domain may be transported only four cubits, that is, within the space occupied by a person's body. What is in private domain may be transported within the entire demarcated space of that domain. All public domain is deemed a single spatial entity, so too all private domain, so one may transport objects from one private domain to another. The net effect of the transformation of space is to move nearly all permitted activity to private domain and to close off public domain for all but the most severely limited activities; people may not transport objects from one domain to the other, but they may transport objects within private domain, so the closure of public domain from most activity, and nearly all material or physical activity, comes in consequence of the division of space effected by sunset at the end of the sixth day of the week.

1. Space: On the Sabbath the household and village divide into private and public domain, and it is forbidden to transport objects from the one domain to the other:
   A. Private domain is defined as at the very least an area ten handbreadths deep or high by four wide, public domain, an unimpeded space open to the public. There one may carry an object for no more than four cubits, which sages maintain is the dimension of man.
   B. The sea, plain, *karmelit* [neutral domain], colonnade, and a threshold are neither private domain nor public domain. They do not carry or put [things] in such places. But if one carried or put [something into such a place], he is exempt [from punishment].
   C. If in public domain one is liable for carrying an object four cubits, in private domain, there is no limit other than the outer boundaries of the demarcated area of the private domain, e.g., within the walls of the household.

> D. What is worn for clothing or ornament does not violate the prohibition against carrying things from private to public domain. If one transports an object from private domain to private domain without bringing the object into public domain, e.g., by tossing it from private to private domain, he is not culpable.
>
> M. 1:1, M. 6:1-9, 11:1-6

2. TIME: What Is to be Used on the Sabbath Must Be So Designated in Advance.

> A. For example, on the Sabbath people do not put a utensil under a lamp to catch the oil. But if one put it there while it is still day, it is permitted. But they do not use any of that oil on the Sabbath, since it is not something which was prepared [before the Sabbath for use on the Sabbath.
>
> B. What one uses on the Sabbath must be designated in advance for that purpose, either in a routine way (what is ordinarily used on the Sabbath, e.g., for food preparation, does not have to be designated especially for that purpose) or in an exceptional manner. But within that proviso, all utensils may be handled on the Sabbath, for a permitted purpose. If something is not ordinarily used as food but one designated it for that purpose, e.g., for cattle, it may be handled on the Sabbath.
>
> M. 3:6, 17:1-8, 18:2, 20:5, 22:2

3. ACTIVITY: On the Sabbath one is liable for the intentional commission of a completed act of constructive labor, e.g., transporting an object from one domain to the other, if one has performed, in the normal manner, the entire action beginning to end.

> A. If one has performed only part of an action, the matter being completed by another party, he is exempt. If one has performed an entire action but done so in an-other-than-ordinary manner, he is exempt. If one transports an object only to the threshold and puts it down there, he is exempt, even though, later on, he picks it up and completes the transportation outward to public domain.
>
> B. He one performed a forbidden action but did not intend to do so, he is exempt. If one performed a forbidden action but in doing so did not accomplish his goal, he is exempt: If one transported an object or brought an object in—if he did so inadvertently, he is liable for a sin offering. If he did so deliberately, he is subject to the punishment of extirpation.
>
> C. All the same are the one who takes out and the one who brings in, the one who stretches something out and the one who throws [something] in—in all such cases he is liable. By observing Sabbath prohibitions prior to sunset, one takes precautions to avoid inadvertent error.
>
> D. One is liable for constructive, but not destructive acts of labor, and for acts of labor that produce a lasting consequence but not ephemeral ones.

E. One is liable for performing on the Sabbath classifications of labor the like of which was done in the tabernacle. They sowed, so you are not to sow. They harvested, so you are not to harvest. They lifted up the boards from the ground to the wagon, so you are not to lift them in from public to private domain. They lowered boards from the wagon to the ground, so you must not carry anything from private to public domain. They transported boards from wagon to wagon, so you must not carry from one private domain to another.

F. But moving the object must be in the normal manner, not in an exceptional way, if culpability is to be incurred.

G. An entire act of labor must involve a minimum volume, and it must yield an enduring result. An act of destruction is not culpable. Thus, as we recall, he who tears [his clothing] because of his anger or on account of his bereavement, and all those who effect destruction, are exempt.

H. Healing is classified as an act of constructive labor, so it is forbidden; but saving life is invariably permitted, as is any other action of a sacred character that cannot be postponed, e.g., circumcision, saving sacred scrolls from fire, saving from fire food for immediate use, and tending to the deceased, along with certain other urgent matters requiring a sage's ruling.

> M. 1:1, 2, 3, 10-11, 2:7, 8, 7:2, M. 7:3-4,
> M. :1-6, 9:5-7, 10:1, 10:2-4, 10:5-6, 12:1-5,
> M. 13:2-7, 14:1-2, 15:1-3, 16:1-8, 18:3, 19:1-6,
> T. 15:11ff., M. 22:1, 22:6, 23:5, 24:5

This systematic, extensive, and richly detailed account of the activity, labor, that is forbidden on the Sabbath but required on weekdays introduces these considerations, properly classified:

A. *Preconditions*
   1. intentionality: the act must carry out the intention of the actor, and the intention must be to carry out an illicit act of labor
   2. a single actor: culpability is incurred for an act started, carried through, and completed by a single actor, not by an act that is started by one party and completed by another
   3. analogy: an act that on the Sabbath may be carried out in the building and maintenance of the tabernacle (Temple) may not be performed in the household, and on that analogy the classification of forbidden acts of labor is worked out
B. Considerations
   1. routine character: the act must be done in the manner in which it is ordinarily done
   2. constructive result: the act must build and not destroy, put together and not dismantle; an act of destruction if not culpable

C. Consequences
  1. completeness: the act must be completely done, in all its elements and components
  2. permanent result: the act must produce a lasting result, not an ephemeral one
  3. consequence: to impart culpability, a forbidden act of labor must involve a matter of consequence, e.g., transport of a volume of materials that people deem worth storing and transporting, but not a negligible volume

What is the upshot of this remarkable repertoire of fundamental considerations having to do with activity, in the household, on the holy day? The Halakhah of Shabbat in the aggregate concerns itself with formulating a statement of how the advent of the Sabbath defines the kind of activity that may be done by specifying what may not be done. That is the meaning of repose, the cessation of activity, not the commencement of activity of a different order. To carry out the Sabbath, one does nothing, not something. And what is that "nothing" that one realizes through inactivity? One may not carry out an act analogous to one that sustains creation. An act or activity for which one bears responsibility, and one that sustains creation, is [1] an act analogous to one required in the building and maintenance of the tabernacle, [2] that is intentionally carried out [3] in its entirety, [4] by a single actor, [5] in the ordinary manner, [6] with a constructive and [7] consequential result—one worthy of consideration by accepted norms. These are the seven conditions that pertain, and that, in one way or another, together with counterpart considerations in connection with the transformation of space and time, generate most of the Halakhah of Shabbat.

Scripture contributes the topic of the Sabbath, but the Halakhah goes its own way in defining that topic through normative laws. Scripture declares that Israel on the Sabbath in the Land like God on the Sabbath of Eden rests from the labor of creation. That means, no acts of work—and the Halakhah commences where Scripture concludes, an archetypal case of independent development of a received subject. That brings us to the question, What about that other principle of the Sabbath, the one set forth by the Halakhah of Shabbat? The richly detailed Halakhah of Shabbat defines the matter in a prolix, yet simple way. It is that on the Sabbath it is prohibited deliberately to carry out in a normal way a completed act of constructive labor, one that produces enduring results, one that carries out one's entire intention: the whole of what one planned, one has accomplished, in exactly the proper manner. That definition takes into account the shank of the Halakhah of Shabbat as set forth in the Mishnah-tractate, and the amplification and extension of matters in the Tosefta and the two Talmuds in no way revises the basic principles. Here there is a curious, if obvious, fact: it is not an act of labor that itself is prohibited (as the Ten Commandments in Exodus and Deuteronomy would have it), but an act of labor of a very particular definition.

The details of the Halakhah then emerge out of a process in which two distinct sources contribute. One is the model of the tabernacle. What man may do for God's house he may not do for his own—God is always God, the Israelite aspires only to be "like God," to imitate God, and that is a different thing. The other is the model of the creation of the world and of Eden. Hence to act like God on the Sabbath, the Israelite rests; he does not do what God did in creation. The former source supplies generative metaphors, the like of which may not be done; thus acts like sowing, like harvesting, like lifting boards from public to private domain, and the like, are forbidden. The latter source supplies the generative principles, the abstract definitions involving the qualities of perfection and causation: intentionality, completion, the normality of the conduct of the action, and the like. The mode of analogical thinking governs, but, as we see, a double metaphor pertains, the metaphor of God's activity in creation, the metaphor of the priests' and Levites' activity in the tabernacle. Creation yields those large principles that we have identified: the traits of an act of labor for God in creation define the prohibited conditions of an act of labor on the Sabbath. By appeal to those two metaphors, we can account for every detail of the Halakhah.

XIX. *Old Dog, New Tricks*

Having taken up the asymmetry of the Oral Torah's presentation of categories defined in detail by the Written Torah, with the descriptive task complete, we focus upon the results seen whole: the analytical and interpretive stages. How does the Oral Torah renew received category-formations? To answer that question, we endeavor to see matters whole and complete, and so ask: Do the tractates before us fall into coherent categories? I see three taxonomic possibilities.

First comes grouping the topical category-formations by large, general themes, with the following result: [1] the particularization of time: Besah, Erubin, Shabbat, Moed Qatan; [2] the interplay of uncleanness and sanctification: Makhshirin, Ohalot, Parah; [3] nourishing Israel's life as God is maintained in the time: Hallah, Hullin, Maaserot; [4] the family: Gittin. I discern no pattern here. When we identify as our indicative trait topical concerns, the result is un-illuminating.

But, second, what if we ask the same question of all categories? Then we find a somewhat more useful point of differentiation. In light of the foregoing description, the analytical criterion of classification obviously derives from intentionality. Here are the category-formations in which where intentionality makes a difference: Maase-rot, Makhshirin, Parah, Besah, Shabbat-Erubin, Gittin (the wife's responsibility within the transaction), Moed Qatan, Hallah. Within the same framework, correlatively, comes the one in which intention-ality makes no difference, Ohalot. That contrary entry is readily predicted, for intentionality is null in the face of a source of unclean-ness, even as intentionality forms the operative criterion of differen-tiation when the working of uncleanness is at issue. The only cat-egory-formation I can discern where intentionality plays no role then is Hullin, which asks a range of questions on sanctification of Israel to which, curiously, intentionality makes no contribution. It follows that where the Oral Torah identifies for sustained inquiry a category-formation defined by the Written Torah, that category-formation will provide an opportunity for deep reflection upon the role of man's will, with special attention to the interplay between man's will and the material world. That result serves, but only in general terms. It is too abstract to illuminate the details or to lead us from analysis to an interpretive theory of the whole. That is because I cannot identify a bridge from the Halakhah in its particularity to the system in its fullness: Aggadah and Halakhah all together. And that goal—to show how the principal native categories, Halakhah and Aggadah, join together into a single, whole statement, permeating the culture of the system—defines the criterion of analytical success: making sense of the whole, but in detail and with entire regard for particular-ity. So intentionality is necessary but not sufficient as an organizing hermeneutics for the Oral Torah's distinctive contribution, seen in detail.

Then, third, a further analytical initiative, one neither too concrete nor too abstract, comes under consideration. Specifically, I identify three fundamental issues that encompass the Oral Torah's reworking of the Written Torah's category-formations: [1] creation and the Sabbath, [2] intentionality, and [3] uncleanness and sanctification. Within those rubrics the Oral Torah frames its statement on the received topics of Scripture—and, as we shall see, we can identify a narrative that, in Aggadic terms, infuses the Halakhah and makes of it a single, coherent construction. Now I shall make those twin-claims stick.

Creation, the Sabbath, Domains and Acts of Labor

Shabbat-Erubin systematically defines private domain as against public domain, and the act of labor prohibited on the Sabbath. Both topics respond to the narrative of Gen. 1:1-2:3, that is, the presentation of creation. Erubin recasts proprietorship, forming of private domains a commingled domain. Shabbat defines the kind of action that one may not carry out, and it is not generic acts of labor, but those acts of labor that produce enduring results, that are carried out by a single person, bearing responsibility for the whole; they are completed acts of constructive labor, producing lasting effects. The interplay of space, time, and activity is sorted out as well. Other restrictions on ordinary labor demand attention. People may work on the intermediate days of the festivals, but within severe restrictions. The work may not be onerous; not doing the work must bring about heavy loss; the work cannot have been set aside for performance on the festival season.

Issues of intentionality

Certainly the Oral Torah's most original statement comes in Maaserot, where the Halakhah unfolds within the principle that God responds to the attitude of the Israelite householder. When the household values the crop and wishes to take possession of it, then God values the crop and wants his share. Not the condition of the produce but the attitude of the farmer governs, as we noted above. So God's and man's feelings, attitudes, and emotions correspond; they are consubstantial. Makhshirin forms a second exercise in the matter, now introducing the consideration of the interplay of actuality and intentionality. If water is intentionally put on produce, then the produce becomes susceptible to uncleanness. But if the produce is wet down on its own, not with the owner's intentionality, the water is null. Then the question arises, do we assess intentionality in terms of outcome: how things worked out is how the farmer wanted them to work out? As we saw, some opinion deems intention without action null; some deem action retrospectively to dictate the character of intention. In the hands of the Oral Torah, Scripture's rule that one may cook on the festival day, yields Besah, which asks questions of the actual as against the potential embodied in the designation of food in advance of the festival for use on the festival, thus the interplay of intentionality and the actualities of the material world; then the comparison and contrast of the festival day and the ordinary day; the extent to which it is permitted to conduct labor at all. Designation in advance of the Sabbath of what is to be used on the Sabbath also plays a role. One must prepare in advance for the Sabbath, and then the activity, embodying one's proper intentionality, is permitted. Shabbat pursues the issue of intentionality in a different way, in the principle that the classification of an action is governed by the intention by which it is carried out, along with the consequence of the same. An act is neutral, it may or may not violate the law, depending upon the intent of the actor. The issue of an individual's idiosyncratic intentionality generates its own issues; what people generally do not value a particular person may deem useful, and the rest follows. At Gittin the issue of intentionality is framed in terms of active engagement. The woman cannot initiate the divorce-process, but she bears full responsibility for the correct conduct of her part of the transaction and bears heavy consequences of that part is improperly carried out.

Uncleanness unto Death and Purification for Sanctification for life (eternal, beyond Death!)
In the Oral Torah, the opposite of the holy is the unclean. Corpse uncleanness, the most virulent source of uncleanness, embodies the soul as it leaves the body; that fluid and the body from which it has exuded impart severe uncleanness. And that has no relationship to attitude or intentionality; uncleanness is effective eo ipse and unconditionally; a source of uncleanness embodies uncleanness, no matter the attitude of the person that embodies that source, e.g., the Zab and Zabah of Lev. 15, the menstruating woman of the same chapter, as much as the corpse. What removes corpse-uncleanness—the mixture of the water and the ashes of the red cow—is prepared with the highest possible level of attentiveness. Parah stipulates that the persons engaged in collecting the water and transporting it to the ashes

and mixing the water and the ashes contract uncleanness if they merely sit down; they disqualify the water if they otherwise engage in an act of labor not involved in the process itself. So if, as we shall see, death comes about willy-nilly, the removal of the effects of death demands the opposite: an extreme of intentionality. And the upshot for the system as a whole is not to be missed. If uncleanness stands for death, then cleanness leading to sanctification stands for life. And, within the narrative of Eden, life was meant to be forever. Death came about by reason of the working out of improper intentionality.

Sanctification and uncleanness intersect at Hallah, which forms a small exercise in a large principle. It is, uncleanness embodies death, sanctification, life. Death threatens life. When the dough comes alive, with the mixing of flour, yeast, and water, the water rendering the mass susceptible to uncleanness, then the householder goes on the alert. At that point, God is owed his due for the life that creation has brought about. Sanctification forms the issue in another context altogether, one in which intentionality does not figure, and to which uncleanness does not, by definition, form a consideration. Hullin introduces into the formation of the law adventitious circumstances: the fact that the Temple is destroyed and Israelites are located in unclean territory. The message is, taking life for man's sustenance accords with the rules of the Temple, even when the Temple life in ruins and Israelites reside abroad. The rules of the Torah govern life-sustaining activities; "the blood is the life" and similar principles transcend the locative and temporal limits of the Temple and its cult. That is because Israel remains holy wherever it is located, even outside of the holy Land, even in the absence of the cult. The conditions that sustain its life continue to apply. Life persists within the people, without regard to circumstance or context.

If these cogent category-formations provide an encompassing and proportionate structure for the Oral Torah's own contribution, the question arises, what turns the structure into a system? When at the end of Chapter Seven we follow as a single, continuous story the three category-formations I have imputed in the inductive analysis of the Oral Torah's laws as I describe them, how do they set forth a coherent, compelling narrative and to what narrative in the Written Torah do the Oral Torah's laws correspond? In the Preface I alleged that the Oral Torah's Halakhah translates the Written Torah's narratives into exemplary cases, the cases into rules, and the rules into governing, abstract principles. So I claim the Written Torah's story about the creation of the world and the formation of Israel, and its laws for the construction of Israel's "kingdom of priests and holy people" come to realization in the rules and principles embodied in the Oral Torah's Halakhah. The formulation as abstractions of principles out of rules, and rules out of cases turns the entire Halakhic corpus of the Pentateuch from a set of composites of inert information into a proportionate and coherent structure and a working system. It is nearly time for me to keep the promise I made in the Preface. But first comes one final corpus of category-formations, wherein I test the taxonomy proposed just now.

XX. *When the Oral Torah Finds Fresh Issues in Received Information*

We come to the most subtle problem, the identification, within received categories and their laws, of fresh hermeneutical principles. When the Oral Torah takes over a category-formation of the Written Torah and amplifies the received Halakhic program therein, it sometimes produces something distinctive to itself, not a mere extension but a quite original variation on a theme. That is because in amplifying the received category-formation and its rules, the Oral Torah's formulation of the same category-formation and derivative rules identifies and reproportions propositions that the Written Torah's category-formation and its rules encompass, if without emphasis or amplification. In going over familiar topics in established ways, through details deftly devised, the Oral Torah redirects matters. So working with the Written Torah's Halakhic premises and facts, the Oral Torah creates variations on a theme, indeed, managing to make quite new music altogether. In these independent reconfigurations of the Written Torah's facts following the Written Torah's category-formations, we discern the Oral Torah's remarkable capacity to deliver its message through a received language about a ready-made topic. Here the Oral Torah accomplishes its task in a deft and subtle manner, with results as striking as those we found in Chapter Six.

a. *Kilayim*

The Halakhah of Kilayim elaborates upon Lev. 19:19 and Deuteronomy 22:9-11. The Halakhah in its own terms derivatively amplifies the simple rules just now cited, spelling out what seems to me implicit in them. At the same time, as we examine the Halakhic propositions, we find, time and again, propositions that vastly transcend the limits of the data of Scripture. The Halakhah thus raises issues of clarification that Scripture clearly invites, but it also frames the topic in terms that Scripture scarcely requires. On that basis, I have classified the category-formation as I have: independent development of a topic Scripture has defined.

The following outline shows the topical program of the Halakhah as laid out in the Mishnah-Tosefta-Yerushalmi:

I.   Raising Together Diverse Species of Plants
     A.   Plants That Are or Are Not Classified as Diverse Kinds
     B.   Grafting
     C.   Sowing Together or in Adjacent Spaces Diverse Species of Crops
     D.   Sowing Crops in a Vineyard
II. Mating Animals of Different Species
     A.   Prohibition of Hybridization
     B.   Prohibition of Yoking Diverse Species of Beasts
III. Mingling Wool and Linen Fibers
     A.   The Prohibition
     B.   Application of the Prohibition

At no point does the Halakhah introduce a topic not invited by Scripture's own formulation of matters. But the way in which the topic is developed is quite independent of Scripture's provision of inert information.

The main point that the Halakhah investigates has to do with the priority of appearance over actuality—a case of reproportioning the category-formation and its received law, not inventing a fresh problematic for an existing category-formation. What looks like a confusion of diverse kinds constitutes a violation of Scripture's law. What does not give such an appearance in no way violates that law. So the issue of the tractate is, what appears to constitute mixed species, and how is that appearance to be removed? Mixing classes or species—plants, animals, fibers, thus, whether plants, crops in a vineyard, kinds of animals, or diverse sources of fabrics, linen from the earth and wool from animals—violates the principles of order established in creation, when each species was set forth in its own category ("according to its name"). But what defines a class? The Halakhah takes the view that man does. Man has the power to do in the Land of Israel what God did in creating the world at Eden, that is, establish order, overcome chaos, perfect the world for the occasion of sanctification. The Halakhah that elaborates the commandments on the present topic set forth in Scripture makes man God's partner in overcoming chaos and establishing order. It is man's perspective that governs, man's discernment that identifies chaos or affirms order. When the Halakhah leaves matters relative to appearance to man, the actualities of mixed seeds no longer matter, or matter so much as appearances. And that requires a second reason as well. For if God cares that "you shall not sow your field with two kinds of seed and that you shall not sow your vineyard with a second kind of seed," surely the actuality, not the appearance, ought to prevail—unless another consideration registers. That consideration comes into play when we ask, how, through the shared engagement with the Land, do God and Israel collaborate, and to what end?

The answer to that question exposes the second, and I think, principal, explanation for the emphasis of the Halakhah upon how man sees things, Israelite man being the subject throughout. Israel is in charge of the Land. Israel not only bears responsibility for what happens in the land, but also bears the blame and the penalty when matters are not right. Israel relates to God through Israel's trusteeship of the Land. The tractates that deal with the enlandisement of the relationship of Israel to God, Kilayim and the others, present Israel as the trustee of the Land and, as we see in the present tractate, assign to Israel the task of cultivating the Land in a manner appropriate to the perfection of creation at the outset. No wonder, then, that Israel's view of matters must prevail, for Israel bears full responsibility on the spot for how things will appear to Heaven. To treat the Land as holy means to farm it in such a way that order prevails, that confusion, embodying chaos, is overcome. So the Land must look like the embodiment of the perfection of Creation, all things in place and in order, everything in its correct category or species, no two species confused.

b. *Orlah*

Tractate Orlah elaborates the Torah's commandment, at Lev. 19:23-25. The produce of the fourth year after planting is treated as equivalent to second tithe, that is, it is brought to Jerusalem ("for jubilation before the Lord") and eaten there. The tractate deals only with the prohibition of the fruit for the first three years. The topical program of the Halakhah gives the misleading appearance of a systematic, low-level exposition, as the following outline indicates:

In fact, as with Kilayim and for much the same reason, we cannot characterize the Halakhic category at hand as a merely derivative amplification. When we examine the details of the law as portrayed in the Oral Torah (here encompassing Sifra's points of stress), we discern a systematic reconstruction thereof, for details of the law point to profound reconsideration of the topic. That comes about because the category-formation spins out its logic by asking a question Scripture does not raise but nonetheless provokes. It concerns the role of man in precipitating the effect of the prohibition takes priority. Scripture's laconic statement assigns to human intention no position in the application of the law. Man has a role in bringing about the prohibition of the law, but man cannot by his intentionality change the facts of the case. It is man's assessment of the use of the tree that classifies the tree as a fruit-tree or as a tree of some other category, e.g., one meant for lumber. But man cannot declare as a fruit-tree, so subjecting the produce to the prohibition for three years from planting, one that does not bear fruit at all. Man's actions reveal his original intentionality for the tree, e.g., how the tree is planted. Intentionality dictates whether or not a tree that can bear fruit actually is covered by the prohibition. Trees not used for fruit are not affected by the prohibition, so the farmer may use the lumber even in the first three years from planting; and parts of trees not intended for fruit are not subject to it either, so may be pruned off and used for fuel. But intention cannot classify what nature has already designated for one or another category.

Further points explored by the Oral Torah's reading of the category include the principle that the law takes effect only from the point at which Israel enters the land. That trees produce fruit matters only from Israel's entry onward. Second, Israelite intentionality is required to subject a tree to the 'orlah-rule. If an Israelite does not plant the tree with the plan of producing fruit, then the tree is not subject to the rule. If the tree grows up on its own, not by the act and precipitating intentionality of the Israelite, the orlah-rule does not apply. It is Israel's own intentionality—not God's—that imposes upon every fruit-bearing tree—and not only the one of Eden—the prohibition of three years. So once Israel wants the fruit, it must show that it can restrain its desire and wait for three years.　To find the context in which these rules make their statement, we consider details, then the main point. First, why three years in particular? Fruit trees were created on the third day of creation. Then, when Israel by intention and action designates a tree—any tree—as fruit-bearing, Israel must wait for three years, as creation waited for three years. Then the planting of every tree imposes upon Israel the occasion to meet once more the temptation that the first Adam could not overcome. Israel now recapitulates the temptation of Adam then, but Israel, the New Adam, possesses, and is possessed by, the Torah. By its own action and intention in planting fruit trees, Israel finds itself in a veritable orchard of trees like the tree of knowledge of good and evil. The difference between Adam and Israel—permitted to eat all fruit but one, Adam ate the forbidden fruit, while Israel refrains for a specified span of time from fruit from all trees—marks what has taken place, which is the regeneration of humanity.

So when Israel enters the Land, in exactly the right detail Israel recapitulates the drama of Adam in Eden, but with this formidable difference. The outcome is not the same. By its own act of will Israel addresses the temptation of Adam and overcomes the same temptation, not once but every day through time beyond measure. Adam could not wait out the week, but Israel waits for three years—as long as God waited in creating fruit trees. Adam picked and ate. But here too there is a detail not to be missed. even after three years, Israel may not eat the fruit wherever it chooses. Rather, in the fourth year from planting, Israel will still show restraint, bringing the fruit only "for jubilation before the Lord" in Jerusalem. That signals that the once-forbidden fruit is now eaten in public, not in secret, before the Lord, as a moment of celebration. In the fifth year Israel may eat on its own, the time of any restraint from enjoying the gifts of the Land having ended. That sequence provides fruit for the second Sabbath of creation, and so through time. How so? Placing Adam's sin on the first day after the first Sabbath, thus Sunday, then calculating the three forbidden years as Monday, Tuesday, and Wednesday of the second week of creation, reckoning on the jubilation of Thursday, we come to the Friday, eve of the second Sabbath of creation. So now, a year representing a day of the Sabbatical week, just as Leviticus says so many times in connection with the Sabbatical year, the three prohibited years allow Israel to show its true character, fully regenerate, wholly and humbly accepting God's commandment, the one Adam broke. By its own act of restraint, the New Adam, Israel, in detailed action displays its repentance in respect to the very sin that the Old Adam committed, the sin of disobedience and rebellion. Facing the same opportunity to sin, Israel again and again over time refrains from the very sin that cost Adam Eden. So by its manner of cultivation of the Land and its orchards, Israel manifests what in the very condition of humanity has changed by the giving of the Torah: the advent of humanity's second chance, through Israel. Only in the Land that succeeds Eden can Israel, succeeding Adam, carry out the acts of regeneration that the Torah makes possible. This message is produced wholly by the Halakhah, on its own and when expounded in Sifra, and while I think it is implicit in the Written Torah, it emerges only in the Oral Torah's reconfiguration of the Written Torah's laws.

c. Tebul Yom

Here is yet another case in which, while Scripture introduces the topic, the Halakhah frames its own program of inquiry. The Tebul Yom is a person or object that has been immersed but awaits sunset for the realization of the restoration of the natural condition of cleanness. Living or flowing water by itself purifies the one who has had a discharge. When the Written Torah refers to washing, bathing, and laundering in the context of attaining cleanness from uncleanness in particular, by contrast, it specifies that the object remains unclean until sunset. So ordinary water is distinguished from spring or living (flowing) water and is not understood as a substance that purifies something from uncleanness. What accomplishes the purification is sunset. Pertinent verses of Scripture include Lev. 11:31-2, Lev. 15:13, Lev. 11:32, Lev. 11:40, Lev. 14:8, Lev. 15:5, Lev. 15:16, Lev. 15:21, Lev. 15:27, Lev. 16:28, Lev.17:15, Lev. 22:6-7, Num. 10:7, Num.

17:17, and Dt. 23:11:1. Along these same lines, the status of Tebul
Yom—one who has immersed on the selfsame day and awaits sunset
for the completion of the rite of purification—is assigned by the
Halakhah of the Oral Torah to a person or object immersed in forty
seahs of still water of an immersion pool for the remainder of the day
on which the immersion takes place. That status ends at sunset, at
which point the person or object is clean. The status of that person or
object in Scripture is unambiguous; Scripture is explicit: that person
or object is unclean until sunset, then he or she or it is clean. But
sages take the view that the immersion has affected the uncleanness,
removed some of its virulence, even while not wholly effecting cleanness. The Halakhah of Tebul Yom asks, in what way is the Tebul
Yom clean and in what way is he unclean? Is he essentially clean, but
unclean in some minor aspect, or is he essentially unclean, but in a
lesser status of uncleanness than before immersion? The deeper question, the power of sunset, is not addressed in the Halakhah, only
taken for granted. But it is there that the Halakhah finds its animating convictions, and only there that we grasp the source from which
emanates the intangibles of relationship and circumstance, which is,
the turning of the light.

Scripture leaves no doubt that what has been washed in water is
unclean until the evening, then when the sun has set, it is clean. The
Halakhah of the Oral Torah further registers that the Tebul Yom is
in the second remove of uncleanness, imparting unfitness to heave
offering. The logical next question is, does that mean what has been
immersed is really unclean until evening, therefore falling into the
same status as all other sources of uncleanness? Or is what has been
immersed really clean, therefore imparting unfitness to heave offering
in accord with the distinction between what is primary and what is
secondary? The issue of classification is addressed at the point of
acute interstitiality, which is connection. There we want to know
whether the object affects the status of what is attached to it, whether
the attachment (the stem to the fruit) is deemed detached therefrom.
So we shift the analysis of the intermediate status of the Tebul Yom
to the status of what is intermediate in the object of uncleanness. And
there we further ask yet another relativizing question: what is primary and what is subordinate in a mixture, what is essential and
what is peripheral in a composite. And, we note at the very outset,
for the first and only time in considering the sources of cultic uncleanness that contaminate the Israelite household, we even intro-

duce the variable of intentionality. For an original, free-standing essay on interstitiality and mixture, the Halakhah of Tebul Yom provides an ideal setting.

Concerning the character of cultic uncleanness in the household, the Halakhah of the Oral Torah could not have made a more vivid statement than it does here. What it stresses is the negative, that uncleanness is not intrinsic but imputed, and the positive, that the attitudes and arrangements of the householder vis à vis sources of uncleanness directly affects the effects of those sources, which is to say, the power of a source of uncleanness to contaminate is mediated by, even vitiated within, the circumstances that govern. The person has immersed but the sun has not set, so now, but not before, the person's intentionality plays a role, on the one side, and issues of connection resolved in terms of primary and subsidiary utilization of parts of a composite require resolution, on the other. Then what difference does sunset make? The Halakhah of the status, not condition, of the Tebul Yom alerts the householder that if he wishes to know the condition of his property and possessions, he must pay attention to sunset. That is in two aspects. Until sunset he not only is not to use for purposes of preparation of food in conditions of cleanness what has just been immersed, he has also to notice the relationships between what has just been immersed and what not. The matter of connection brings about the same heightened consciousness as the matter of removal from uncleanness on the inner side of immersion, before the rinsing. Just as removes from the source of uncleanness require us to know not only the condition of an unclean object but also the subsequent history, from the moment of contamination, of that same object, so connection in the differentiation by reason of immersion imposes alertness not only as to the primary but also the secondary and peripheral contacts of the object that has been immersed.

Sunset marks the creation of the new day, hence the commencement of a new span of time that tells the story of the struggle of Israel, naturally clean, to remain clean from the sources of uncleanness round about. Uncleanness does not accumulate, but, when the householder determines by the act of immersion to bring uncleanness to closure, terminates at sunset, the end of the old day. Whatever the condition of persons or objects as to uncleanness, once the process of cleanness has properly commenced with the act of immersion, the result is inexorable: Israel becomes clean as surely, as reliably, as the sun sets. No wonder, archaeology now shows, people wanted immersion-pools in their houses, signaling as they do the authentic condition of Israel.

d. *Temurah*

Building upon Scripture, the Halakhah of Temurah underscores the limitations that God sets upon Israel's command of taxonomic, transformative language. Specifically, once the Israelite has made a statement, he cannot nullify it. Nor can he change his mind, declaring profane a beast designated as holy and replacing that beast with some other. Scripture (at Lev. 27:10) is explicit that the beast designated as a substitute becomes holy and the beast that was already consecrated remains holy. That fact in hand, the sages of the Oral Torah register a number of important convictions, wholly coherent with the established program of the Halakhah governing the altar and the encounter that takes place there. The Halakhah of Temurah makes the point that the status of sanctification is not only indelible but immutable. The language that effects the act of sanctification produces that change in classification that turns the common into the holy, and once spoken, words work. But precisely how the candidate for substitution becomes holy, what it means for the candidate to enter into the status of, become like, the already-holy beast—these define problems that require much thought.

The law of substitution encompasses an anomaly: an act contrary to the Torah produces effects of which the Torah takes account. One is not permitted to substitute one beast for another. If one does so, however, consequences follow. The issue is, what is the law governing the consequence of performing an action that, on its own, is illegal and null? Does a person bear the sanctions for an action that produces no legal effects? The basic issue of the Halakhah of Temurah is whether or not the status, as to sanctification, of that which is sanctified is subject to revision. And the position of the law is that once something has been sanctified, not only is the sanctification indelible (except through the Halakhah's own media of secularization) but it is permanent in its character. The Oral Torah contributes to the Written Torah's category a secondary layer of logical development. I find two considerable points that the Oral Torah sets forth in its amplification of the logic of the Halakhah of the Written Torah, both of them consistent with the Oral Torah's

Halakhah elsewhere—but not here. The first proposition is, language is not magical. The formula that transforms a secular beast into a sacred one accomplishes its act of transformation only when the prior condition is met that the one who uses the language has the right to use it. The language, on its own, bears no coercive quality, is not a formula that works without regard to circumstance. The Oral Torah, second, insists that the actualities of the originally-consecrated offering play no role whatsoever. The beast declared a substitute need not belong to the same category as the beast that has already been sanctified; the analogy—"this in place of that"—focuses upon the "this," not the "that." The trait of the initially-sanctified beast that registers is only its classification as holy, not the particularity of that for which it has been sanctified. And that violates the rule that one may not change the status, as to sanctification, of a designated beast. If it has been declared Most Holy Things, it cannot be reclassified as Lesser Holy Things, and so throughout. When it comes to the transformation of the substitute, by contrast, we ignore considerations of classification—specificities and particularities—and invoke only a single criterion: the classification of sanctification *per se*. God responds to the language and circumstance but need not take account of irrelevant details in the transaction at hand. So one may substitute an animal for others different from it—an amazing point that fits entirely within the present rationality. The upshot is, the entire system of matching intentionality to actuality, the will of the sacrifier to the deed of the priest and the intentionality as to the offering expressed by the priest, here is suspended.

e. *Terumot*

Among the various agricultural tithes and offerings, the single most important is called "heave-offering," that which, as a matter of chance and not deliberate selection, is raised, or heaved-up, out of the crop. The pertinent verses of Scripture are at Num. 18:8-13. The questions that the Halakhah of the Oral Torah takes for its own are, first, how a quantity of produce becomes sanctified, and, second, what happens when such produce is mixed with common food, more broadly, what to do when produce designated as heave offering is used as if it were secular food and so is eaten by a non-priest? The outline of the Halakhah as set forth in the Mishnah-Tosefta-Yerushalmi is as follows:

Scripture's presentation of the topic does not suggest what the Halakhah will deem of critical importance in that topic, even though the Oral Torah's exposition of matters coheres in detail with that of the Written Torah; I claim that that exposition is implicit here and explicit in other classifications of the Pentateuchal law, so what the Oral Torah contributes once more is a reproportioning and a harmonization of details into a single, whole construction. A statement of the generative premise of the Halakhah suffices to show that fact: the Halakhah of Terumot constitutes a vast exegesis of a single religious principle: the Israelite has the power by an act of will confirmed (where required) by a concrete deed to sanctify what is common. The Israelite then is accorded by God the remarkable power to designate as holy, by reason of the Israelite's own uncoerced will, what is otherwise ordinary and not sacred.

Not the only category of the Halakhah to embody in concrete actions that considerable proposition, the Halakhah of Terumot nonetheless forms a remarkably apt medium for delivering that message. That is because of the stress in the Halakhah at hand on considerations of particularity: the householder's act of sanctification pertains to a very specific batch of produce, the consequence of sanctification invokes a very particular teleology inherent in the type of produce that has been sanctified. The Israelite householder has the power to initiate the entire process of sanctification, to transform the classification of produce and to subject that produce to the logic that inheres in its very character: its own teleology. The householder then restores to God his share in the crop and imposes upon God's share the discipline required by the logical character of that particular crop. A productive corollary insists that the intentionality of the Israelite pertain to a very specific, differentiated corpus of produce. While holiness does not inhere in a given batch, so that the heave-offering of one batch may serve for several, nonetheless batches must be formed of like produce. That means that one's intentionality pertains to the species, not to the genus: olive oil, not olives in general, and so throughout. The particularity of the focus of intentionality cannot be overstated; the Halakhah stresses the matter in a wide range of cases, e.g., they may not separate oil as heave-offering for olives which have been crushed, nor wine as heave-offering for grapes which have been trampled but the processing of which has not yet been completed.

Man's intent for a given object accordingly bears the power to classify as sacred that particular object. God's intent in making that same object controls the legitimate use of the object that is sanctified. So the plan or attitude or program of each party to the transaction—the householder's, God's—governs. But that takes place for each party in his own way. Man's intentionality dictates the classification of the object as God's (that is, as sanctified) and then, God's, the disposition, of the object now subjected to his ownership. That is where the teleology of things enters in. We may then say, once man has assigned ownership to God (through God's surrogates), God's plan in making an object, the teleology that inheres in that object, takes over. No wonder, then, that the Halakhah so emphasizes the specificity of the transaction: this particular object (batch of produce), serving the natural purpose that inheres in this particular object, forming the transaction at which man and God intersect. In assigning to the status of sanctification a portion of the crop, the householder gives up his possession of, thus his right to subject to his own will, a batch of produce and assigns that which he gives up to God's domain, therefore makes the produce subject to God's will. God's will then extends to Israel in its way, to nature in its context. Stated in this way, the transaction in heave-offering represents an act of submission by man's to God's will that is very specific and concrete. The importance of the specificity of intentionality, on the one side, and the particularity of the teleology that governs the use of heave-offering, on the other hand, now merges. Israel and nature relate to God in accord with the same rules, in the same way, but in quite different dimensions.

f. *Yadayim*

The topic derives from Scripture, which is explicit that priests in the tabernacle "sanctify" (=wash) their hands and feet before performing priestly functions at the altar (Ex. 30:19-21, 40:12, 31-32): "Command the priests that they shall wash their hands and feet lest they die" (Ex. 30:21). Hand-washings punctuate the high priest's conduct of the rite on the Day of Atonement (Lev. 16). Perceiving what is implicit in the Pentateuchal provisions, the Halakhah deems the hands ("hands and feet"—but not the rest of the body) to form a distinct entity for purposes of cleanness and uncleanness. So the isolation of the hands as a distinct realm of uncleanness, with their own rite of purification, can appeal to Scripture. Then the Oral Torah further discerns in Scripture's fact what is implicit: if the hands form a distinct realm for purification, then they ought also to have their own distinct medium of purification, and, given the inner dynamics of the system, to the hands also will be imputed a status, as to uncleanness, that also is particular to them in context. That is what I think the Oral Torah has intuited, and I should claim, it is only what is contained within the Written Torah's formulation of matters.

Then, once we realize the difference between immersion for persons and objects that have contracted uncleanness from a Father of uncleanness and hand-washing for hands that are simply assumed to have contracted uncleanness even from an Offspring of uncleanness, we find ourselves in the realm of the Halakhah of the Oral Torah alone.

To begin with, by the Halakhah, the hands are deemed perpetually unclean, a realm of uncleanness—fingertips to wrist—distinct from the rest of the body, which then may be uncontaminated by the condition of the hands and vice versa. But the Halakhah also regards the hands as a distinct source of uncleanness among the animate sources. And the hands also are subject to their own rite of purification, the area from the wrists to the fingertips forming a separate area not only for contracting uncleanness but also for removing it. All of this is not suggested by Scripture's treatment of the subject. The hands are deemed constantly active, whether or not the person pays attention, and so are assigned a position in the second remove of uncleanness. That is to say, even though the person may know what he or she may or may not have touched, the person cannot know with what the things the hands have touched themselves have had contact—thus leaving the hands perpetually in the second remove of uncleanness. Accordingly, as I explained, flowing from the fact dictated by the Pentateuchal formulation, it follows that the hands form a distinct realm of uncleanness and require their own rite of purification.

The entire context scarcely requires attention, being the given of both the Pentateuch and the Oral Torah's Halakhah. Purifying the hands has no bearing on whether or not they are actually free of dirt. What is required is a cultically-prescribed action to respond to a cultically-designated source of uncleanness. Accordingly, the required hand-washing in the Halakhah has no bearing on hygienic cleanliness. It is performed in accord with cultic rules, an act of cultic purification of a demarcated part of the body. The hands, up to the wrist, are restored to cleanness not through immersion in an immersion-pool but through rinsing. The water that hits the hands affects but is affected by them, and that water too requires a rinsing—hence, as we shall see, a cultic purification through a repeated act of rinsing. Further, how the water is collected and administered defines a rite of purification for a component of the person that bears its own traits of cultic uncleanness. The human being's hands then constitute an animate source of uncleanness. The Halakhah as set forth in the Mishnah-Tosefta takes up the following matters:

I. Washing Hands. A Repertoire of Rules
II. Washing Hands. The Status and Condition of the Water. First and Second Pourings of Water
III. The Status of Uncleanness Imputed to Hands
IV. The Uncleanness of Sacred Scriptures

Now an important point registers. What serves to purify the body does not serve to purify the hands and vice versa. How is the purification of the hands different from other modes of purification? To wash hands one must make use of a utensil, just as for the purification-rite one draws water with a utensil. For immersion pools one does not make use of water drawn in a utensil. So for hand-washing human intervention, with a high degree of alertness, is required in the collection and disposition of the water. To wash hands, one must make use of water that has never been used before. Further, an act of labor extraneous to the rite itself spoils the water used for washing hands. The same rule applies to the water for use in preparing purification water. An act of labor extraneous to the rite spoils that water that is to be mixed with the ashes of the red cow in the making of purification water. But the water of an immersion pool may be used again and again, and that is not so for the water used for washing hands.

Thus the rules of washing hands clearly depend on the analogy drawn to rules of water used for purification water. The rite of the red cow depends upon cleanness established and attained outside of the Temple, and the rite of washing hands leads to cleanness for eating food outside of the cult, so in both cases, human agency, guided by an alert human being, is required, by contrast to rainwater, which is collected naturally upon the ground and would be spoiled for an immersion pool if human action intrudes. The difference between the uncleanness of the hands and of the rest of the body and removing that uncleanness through a process guided by its own distinctive rules derives from the Written Torah, which identifies the hands (and feet) as a realm of uncleanness unto themselves and specifies a process of removing that uncleanness distinct from the process that pertains to the rest of the body. And it uses its own language for the one and for the other. The key-language derives from Scripture, using the word "sanctify" to refer to the cultic rinsing of hands and feet. Take, for instance, the very vocabulary at hand.

The word for wash for purposes of cultic cleanness used in the Halakhah of Yadayim is "sanctify," as at T. 1:7: Priests sanctify [=wash hands and feet] in the sanctuary only with a utensil. The analogous actions then involve the purification rite, sprinkling purification-water, pouring water for hand-washing. The uncleanness of hands and the purification thereof carry us deep into the Halakhic theory of the interpenetration of household and sanctuary. Here the model of the cult, for both uncleanness and cleanness in the home, is most explicit. The language of Scripture for rinsing persons and objects from uncleanness for purpose of restoring cleanness is "rinse" or "wash" (rhs), and Scripture is always explicit that after such dunking in an immersion-pool, the object remains unclean until sunset. So matters could not have been made more explicit.

And that difference between "sanctifying" hands and "rinsing/ washing" persons or garments leads to the question, What about the contrast between uncleanness and sanctification? That too is drawn explicitly. The Halakhah expresses the contrast between death and sanctification, but it makes its statement of the match of opposites in its own way. That is in a variety of details, but the most important concern the character of the utensil used in connection with water for sanctifying hands as against water for rinsing, and the preparation of the water used for sanctification as against that used for removing uncleanness. As to the utensil, here is how: a utensil that cannot be used for drawing water for hand-washing does not require a tightly-sealed cover to serve to interpose against uncleanness, and one that does also requires a tightly sealed cover in the Tent of a corpse. So the areas of Halakhah are deemed corresponding and opposite. The contrastive force of death and sanctification renews itself in the present matter.

But there is a still more blatant expression of the same contrast. The gathering of the water used for sanctifying the hands conforms in the definition of the required attitudes and actions to the requirements for collecting the water used for mixing with the ashes of the red cow (Num. 19:1ff.) in preparing purification-water for the removal of corpse-uncleanness. The collection of the water for combining with the ashes, not only the appropriate utensil for use in that connection, involve strict and rigid rules. These same rules govern here as well, so far as sages can apply them. The act must be purposive, the water gathered deliberately, by human action, in a valid utensil. Water for the immersion pool must collect naturally, unaffected by human action, and may not be collected in a utensil. The same rules govern water for mixing with ashes to make purification-water for the removal of corpse-uncleanness and water for use in sanctifying the hands. It follows that uncleanness of hands is removed by water, and preparation of the water accords with the rules pertinent to purification-water utilized for mixing with the ashes of the red cow, Num. 19:14ff. That governing analogy is made explicit, e.g., they draw, and they mix water with the ash of the red cow, and they sprinkle purification water, and they pour water for hands only with a utensil. The analogy of the immersion pool and its water is rejected. Deliberate human action effected through a whole, useful utensil is required.

What statement emerges from the facts now adduced, [1] that the hands are deemed always just one remove away from corpse-contamination, and [2] it is through water analogous to that used for preparing purification-water for the removal of corpse-uncleanness that the hands are sanctified (not merely cleansed of uncleanness, with sunset required to complete the process of purification) even for eating food in the status of priestly rations? What I hear from the Halakhah is the statement, death is ever-present, if not in what is touched, then in what has touched what is touched or in what has touched that. So the hands are always in the second remove of uncleanness, meaning, death is always just a few steps away from contact with what is meant to be kept holy, clear of death. And that is—in the context of the hands and when they are sanctified—food for the nourishment of Israel. But death and all that death overspreads can be kept beyond the boundary of the household table by deliberate action defined by perpetual concern: the right intention, especially for the meal. So with that first bite of bread at the meal, the stakes are very high indeed. I need hardly note, to Scripture, these conceptions are simply beyond all imagining. Yet it is Scripture that has defined the category and provided the facts that the Oral Torah has reconfigured into one of its most profound statements that the dynamics of sanctification embody the struggle of life and death, purpose and creation, aimlessness and chaos. A simple conclusion follows from the law of Yadayim. Nature is created for a purpose, which is life, and when nature does not carry out its purpose, death results; the condition of sanctification denotes life, uncleanness, death. Then, we may say, uncleanness, an ontological condition, comes about in consequence of unrealized teleology. And that brings us to the climactic achievement of reconfiguration on the part of the Oral Torah in its dialogue with the Written Torah, Zabim and Niddah, to which we now turn.

g. *Zabim and Niddah*

Like the corpse, the Zab and Zabah and the menstruating woman disseminate contamination in both the familiar way—through touching or being touched—and otherwise, e.g., intangible dissemination through positioning or overshadowing. The Zab or Zabah transmits uncleanness to that on which they sit or lie, even though they do not touch the chair or bed. The Halakhic givens derive mainly from first, Lev. 12:1-8, for the woman after childbirth, then Lev. 15:1-33, encompassing in a single statement both the flux (*zob*) of the Zab and the Zabah, and semen and menstrual blood, that is, excretions of the sexual organs that do not, and that do, pertain to the cycle of procreation, the former breaking, the latter establishing, that cycle. Scripture's point of emphasis throughout is on three matters, [1] the character of the discharge that signifies flux-uncleanness, [2] the effects of the status of uncleanness: objects that are subject to uncleanness, and [3] how the uncleanness is transmitted; and the mode of purification and attendant cultic rite signifying the regaining of the normal status of cleanness.

The contribution of the Oral Torah in the articulation of these facts proves not only formidable but intellectually fructifying, as sages explore the considerations of teleology embedded in Scripture's own statement of the matter. Whether sages have penetrated into the logic inherent in the Written Torah's Halakhah, or whether they have brought to bear a set of considerations all their own in reframing the inherited Torah into the dense and subtle formation that they set forth, remains to be seen. In the Halakhah of the Oral Torah we deal with semen or vaginal blood that cannot carry out the purpose that by nature the one or the other realizes, which is participation in the process of procreating life. Such non-productive semen, such vaginal flow outside of the normal cycle of procreation—these violate their own innate teleology. They do so on their own, not by man's or woman's intervention. Of such violations of the natural law and the purposive definition of the media of procreation, the Israelite householder has to take heed. If he wishes to preserve the cleanness of the household, its food, and (in the present case) its beds and chairs, he will not introduce into his household either gentiles as a rule or Israelites as an exception. So we shall wonder what is special about the bed and comparable objects that subjects those objects to a particular kind of uncleanness, transmitting in a quite distinctive way: using those objects for the purpose for which they are manufactured.

That classification of uncleanness, called midras- or pressure-uncleanness, pertains only to objects that ordinary are used to bear weight or pressure, that is, beds and chairs and things analogous to them. The Halakhah of Kelim rules that objects not used for sitting or lying, e.g., pots and pans, are not susceptible to the midras- or pressure-uncleanness transmitted by a Zab or a Zabah, so the question is a real one. And midras is a severe uncleanness, comparable to the corpse-uncleanness that affects receptacles and persons, requiring a period of seven days in which the source of uncleanness does not renew itself, on the one side, and a rite of purification in the Temple, on the other. Accordingly, in Zabim we deal with the animate form of uncleanness that falls into the classification of the counterpart inanimate form, that is, *zob* (flux) compares with corpse-matter, the Zab or the Zabah with the corpse. And, the logic of the Halakhah requires, the media of dissemination will prove comparable as well.

At issue in the distinction between menstrual or niddah-blood and zibah-blood is the character of a woman's vaginal secretions or blood: when does it appear, how is it classified? The distinction between menstrual or Niddah-blood and Zibah-blood, the former part of the procreative cycle, the latter not, yields very little difference in actuality, except at the point of purification. The one is vaginal blood that flows during the woman's established menstrual cycle. The other is vaginal blood that flows during the eleven clean days between one cycle and another; these are called Zibah-days, in that blood that flows during the eleven days between menstrual cycles is deemed *Zob*, as we have already established in the Halakhah of Zabim. In some ways—those that have to do with actualities—the two types of vaginal flow are comparable, in others, they contrast. The menstruating woman and the Zabah convey uncleanness through touch, and both serve as Fathers of uncleanness, setting into the first remove of uncleanness whatever they touch. One who touches what they have lain upon or sat upon immerses, awaits sunset, and is then clean. As to sexual relations, the menstruating woman imparts her own status to the one with whom she has sexual relations, and he imparts pressure-uncleanness by sitting and lying as well. As to the Zabah, touching produces the same result; no provision is made for sexual relations. A cultic purification-rite is provided for her, but not for the menstruating woman, who, at the end of her period, simply immerses and waits for sunset. She is then in the first remove, her period having concluded.

So while the concrete effects of the respective sources of vaginal uncleanness coincide, the purification-rite contrasts sharply. The Zabah purifies herself in a blood-rite at the tabernacle. The purification-rite, not required for the menstruating woman, marks the woman as suitable to reenter the procreative cycle; the flux has removed her from that cycle, the cessation signifies her suitability once more. We have, therefore, to distinguish Niddah- from Zibah-blood (*Zob*). The facts at hand suffice to show that Zibah-blood signifies an aberration in the procreative cycle, Niddah-blood proves integral to that cycle. The one is irregular and disrupts normal sexual relations, marking the woman as one who, at that point, may not reproduce life (any more than, from sages' view, the semen emitted by a flaccid penis can reproduce life). The other is regular, integral to the normal sexual cycle, and marks the woman as one wholly integrated to the cycle of reproduction. Then the entire sequence—eleven Zibah-days, seven Niddah-days—forms an account of the woman's relationship to the procreative cycle, which involves three possibilities: she wholly participates, having sexual relations, receiving semen and not emitting blood; she is wholly excluded, not having sexual relations at all, and she is temporarily excluded but remains sexually accessible, which is why the Torah makes provision for the status of one who, in her period, does have sexual relations with her.

The character of *Zob* and of its flow guides us to the center of the religious world-view at hand. It is genital discharge that by its nature cannot accomplish that for which it is created, its purpose or teleology. In a word, the physical world portrayed here finds its definitive traits in the teleology of things, which yields the meetings and the matchings that produce the Halakhah of Zabim. The uncleanness generated by sexual fluids that do not realize their teleology passes via pressure, analogous to that of the sexual relation, to objects that serve for sexuality. When the teleological physics of sexual fluids accomplish their goal, they bring about life. Then, consequently, a minor uncleanness is brought about by semen properly ejaculated, and so too with vaginal blood of an episodic character outside the regular period. When the teleology—the procreation of life—of the

sexual parts, encompassing further the objects used for sexual intercourse, and extending even to the activities and exertions characteristic thereof, including the exertion of weight or pressure in coitus—
when that teleology is not realized, then severe uncleanness results,
comparable to the uncleanness of seven days that the corpse exudes.
That uncleanness then overspreads each of the components of procreation that has not realized its purpose:

[1] the fluid itself, now source of uncleanness analogous to corpse-
uncleanness;

[2] the activity, exerting pressure, now medium for disseminating
not life but uncleanness, and

[3] the bed and analogous objects, now the focus of not procreative activity but contamination.

Now, not realizing their tasks within the teleological physics at
hand:

[1] the fluid is unclean,

[2] the bed and analogous objects become the unique foci of the
uncleanness of said fluid, and

[3] the activity—pressure—serves as the medium not of life but of
anti-life, such as, we now realize, cultic uncleanness disseminated
through midras-uncleanness in particular represents.

How are we to compare and contrast the uncleanness of the soul,
the seven-day uncleanness of the corpse and corpse-matter, with the
uncleanness of *Zob?* When we examine, the uncleanness exuding
from the Zab or Zabah, encompassing not only the flux itself,
whether semen or blood, but the body-fluids, e.g., the spit, the urine,
of a person so afflicted, we find an interesting fact. Zob does not
constitute a Father of Fathers of Uncleanness as the corpse does. The
Zabah or Zab is a Father of uncleanness, contaminating the garments and utensils of someone who touches her or him, also those
things that bear her or his weight. These are made unclean in the
first remove. So the virulence of the escaping soul vastly exceeds that
of the genital excretions that do not realize their purpose. Now how
are we to differentiate the gaseous corpse-uncleanness, which does
not respond to pressure, from comparable *Zob*-uncleanness, which
does? A difference in (imagined) viscosity ought to explain matters.
Corpse-uncleanness flows within a guiding framework (under pressure, spurts upward and downward, we recall). But it does not perme-
ate and pass through intervening fabric ("tent") or other materials.
Zob-uncleanness under pressure is not guided along the lines of that

which conveys the pressure—the tent for example—but flows right into, and through, the fabric or other material that contains it. Hence seen in physical terms, the former is dense, glutinous and semifluid, the latter attenuated, spare and light.

But those physical traits on their own do not suffice to explain the difference as to the modes of movement between the uncleanness exuding from the corpse and that emitted by the sexual organs, male or female. Specifically, why should the latter classification of uncleanness flow so as to pass through the stone on which the Zab exerts pressure through direct contact, as well as weight, to the bed beneath, on which the Zab exerts pressure not through contact but only through weight? Why should a receptacle contain corpse-uncleanness but not the uncleanness of *Zob*, that is, why should a receptacle be unaffected by midras- or pressure uncleanness of a Zab or Zabah? Asked in that way, the question bears its own answer. We deal in *Zob* with a kind of uncleanness that matches, that responds to, its own origin, assignment, and character: origin in sexual organs, assignment, procreation, and character defined by a dysfunction in those organs. Sexually-generated fluid that, by (sages') definition cannot accomplish the purpose that, by nature, sexually-generated fluid is supposed to achieve—procreation of life—affects, as we noted in another context, those sorts of objects that serve sexually, ones used for lying and the like, but not those sorts of objects that under normal circumstances do not serve sexually, receptacles, for example.

That brings us to the paradoxical fact of the Halakhah that overshadowing serves corpse-uncleanness and *Zob*-uncleanness, but with powerful distinctions, and each in its own way. What overshadows a corpse contracts corpse-uncleanness, and what a corpse overshadows is contaminated by corpse-uncleanness. That is without regard to the character of the objects. We do not, furthermore, differentiate between the two locations of the corpse relative to the object in relationship thereto. So locative relationship and substantive character play no role in the transmission of corpse-uncleanness through overshadowing. The corpse that overshadows or is overshadowed produces its effects without regard to what is affected. But that is not how matters are with *Zob*-uncleanness. Here we do differentiate, in the situation of overshadowing, between the character of classes of objects. And, concomitantly, we also differentiate locatively, between the two locations that said classes of objects take up: above, below the Zab. So we have two variables as to the character of objects, and two variables as to their location, and, further, these variables produce opposite results, the locative for the substantive, as the case requires.

Here again, a teleological logic comes into play through analogical-contrastive dialectics, then, with the things that enjoy their natural relationship to the Zab subject to his effect, those not, not; and then the opposite comes into force: what the Zab cannot use for lying that is located where the Zab cannot lie down is affected by the Zab! So considerations of fulfilling the physical purpose for which the thing is shaped take over, even here. To state matters simply: teleological physics dictates the course of contamination by *Zob* and the results, for things affected by that contamination, as well. And it is a simple teleology, which we identified at the very outset: what serves for procreation is distinguished, in respect to *Zob*-uncleanness, from what does not. And the rest follows.

What we confront, therefore, is a physics permeated by teleology: the flow of fluids in response to the condition or purpose of that to which, or from which, they flow, and not in response only to their own character, e.g., to the density of the atoms that comprise the fluid and define its viscosity. That which matches the character of an object or its purpose flows to that object or its purpose, and the invisible flow itself conforms to the character of the activity conducted with said object. The bed, used for lying or sitting, then is affected by pressure, carried on in acts of lying or sitting; the particular uncleanness at hand, sexual excretions in a non-procreative framework, affects those objects that by their nature serve, through those actions that by their nature produce, procreation.

When sexual activity bearing the potential of procreation takes place, a transient uncleanness results—that of healthy semen, which passes upon immersion and sunset, as Scripture says. When sexual excretions lacking that potential take place, a virulent uncleanness takes over, life replaced by anti-life, by a form of death nearly as virulent as the death that takes over the life of a man and causes the excretion of the soul. The soul of the fully-realized man or woman is thick, the unrealized, proto-soul of *Zob*, thin. But the former can be contained in physical limits, as it was in the body, while the latter flows teleologically, its character and therefore its purpose overriding the substantive, physical traits, or physical traits responding to teleological matches (whichever formulation better serves).

Intentionality plays no role in the capacity to transmit uncleanness imputed to the animate beings; the corpse transmits uncleanness *ex opere operato,* from the moment of death, about which the deceased was not consulted, and so too the menstruating woman, man afflicted with flux or the Zab, and the woman or the Zabah afflicted with flux outside of her regular period, effect uncleanness willy-nilly. The woman's period does not depend upon her intentionality. And equally probatively, the Oral Torah lays great stress that the flux of the Zab and the Zabah that bears the power to contaminate—semen from the one, blood from the other—make its appearance on its own. The blood or semen must come about without the connivance of the afflicted party. The teleological principle that permeates the whole underscores the exclusion of man's or woman's will. As to what contracts uncleanness, man disposes, but as to what imparts uncleanness, nature imposes. In the Halakhah of the Oral Torah we deal with semen or vaginal blood that cannot carry out the purpose that by nature the one or the other realizes, which is participation in the process of procreating life. Such non-productive semen, such vaginal flow outside of the normal cycle of procreation—these violate their own innate teleology. They do so on their own, not by man's or woman's intervention. Of such violations of the natural law and the purposive definition of the media of procreation, the Israelite householder has to take heed. If he wishes to preserve the cleanness of the household, its food, and (in the present case) its beds and chairs, he will not introduce into his household either gentiles as a rule or Israelites as an exception.

What is special about the bed and comparable objects that subjects those objects to a particular kind of uncleanness, transmitting in a quite distinctive way? It is using those objects for the purpose for which they are manufactured. That classification of uncleanness, called midras- or pressure-uncleanness, pertains only to objects that ordinary are used to bear weight or pressure, that is, beds and chairs and things analogous to them. The Halakhah of Kelim rules that objects not used for sitting or lying, e.g., pots and pans, are not susceptible to the midras- or pressure-uncleanness transmitted by a Zab or a Zabah, so the question is a real one. And midras is a severe uncleanness, comparable to the corpse-uncleanness that affects receptacles and persons, requiring a period of seven days in which the source of uncleanness does not renew itself, on the one side, and a rite of purification in the Temple, on the other. Accordingly, in Zabim we deal with the animate form of uncleanness that falls into the classification of the counterpart inanimate form, that is, *zob* (flux) compares with corpse-matter, the Zab or the Zabah with the corpse. And, the logic of the Halakhah requires, the media of dissemination will prove comparable as well. All of this represents a remarkably independent development of Scripture's topic.

XXI. *Original Variations on Borrowed Themes*

Now comes a metaphor from music. Great composers find pleasure in taking over themes of predecessors and through daring and imagination entirely renewing them, Benjamin Britten's variations on a theme by Purcell being a commonly-familiar case. Variations on themes supply an apt analogy for the Oral Torah's reconfigurations in the rather subtle exercises in the cases before us. In them we identify what is particular to the Oral Torah even in its re-presentation of the available categories and laws.

Without further ado, I adopt the classification-system already set forth, which encompasses all of the cases before us in one of three category-formations.

Restoring Eden
Israel demonstrates it has learned the lessons of Eden, restoring on its own in the Land the world lost through rebellion. Israel orders the Land, all things in their correct classification, as God ordered Eden. At Orlah, man works out the sequence of creation, reenacting the drama over the fruit tree, now with a different outcome. At Tebul Yom the pattern of the end of one day and beginning of the next, at sunset, takes over, with the message that the new day restores the natural condition, the condition of cleanness, to what has been made unclean.

Man's Attitude
The Israelite has the power by an act of will to sanctify what is susceptible of sanctification, as much as he has the power by an act of will to render susceptible to uncleanness what falls within the realm of cleanness or uncleanness. Terumot works out the theme that an act of will confirmed by a concrete deed sanctifies what is secular. God's intentionality governs the disposition of what is sanctified. Here once more we follow man's subordination of his will to God's will. When, at Kilayim, the Oral Torah amplifies and clarifies the

facts of Scripture within the framework defined by Scripture, it lays down the judgment that appearance takes priority over actuality, meaning, man's perspective on matters determines how things are judged. The issue is correct classification, the proper ordering of the Land, and the problematic, how to resolve cases that depend upon man's attitude. Man's intentionality supplies the key to the classification of fruit-trees in Orlah. When it comes to uncleanness, a matter that is imputed and not intrinsic, man's intentionality plays a role, so we see at Tebul Yom. Specifically, he stays alert and pays close attention to the time of day, before or after sunset in particular. Can an act expressing an intent contrary to the Torah bear consequence? Not at all, Temurah underscores, for once one has declared the intent to sanctify something, the Torah does not permit reneging, and man's intent to the contrary is null. Not only so, but the Torah allows man to classify something as sacred but not to determine the category, among the taxa of sanctification, that pertains.

Sanctification and Uncleanness

Human intentionality plays no role in matters of uncleanness, indeed, it is rigidly excluded. But God's intentionality then governs, and when God's purpose is not carried out, uncleanness comes in consequence. At Zabim and Niddah the Oral Torah frames the category-formation and its law into a massive statement that uncleanness marks that which does not realize its teleology—blood, semen, the life-force of man's vitality in that which exudes from the body upon death above all. Uncleanness then weighs in the balance against sanctification, which characterizes that which fully realizes its teleology—Israel is meant to be holy, and its cleanness marks its natural condition. In accord with God's will, the world of creation and Israel within it are meant to be sanctified—and the rest follows. How does Israel's will then produce sanctification and can Israel's will reverse itself? No, once Israel by an act of will sanctifies, that status is irreversible. God's will takes over. Once Israel declares something sanctified, it remains so; at Temurah, it is made clear, the power of man to classify, and so transform the status of, things of value comes to its outer limit. Israel cannot use language to reverse the result of already-used, transformative language. The hands are always busy, so before one touches what is meant to be kept cultically clean, one has to "sanctify" the hands, so Yadayim, and that means an act of deliberation, carried out with full intentionality, comparable to the act of collecting water and mixing water with the ash of the red heifer to produce purification-water. What is required to overcome uncleanness is a high degree of concentration, the use of a utensil, the collection of water for this purpose by an act of will, and that is what produces cleanness, in this case, "sanctification of hands."

CHAPTER TWO

THE MISHNAH AND ITS TIMES:
THE THREE STAGES
IN HALAKHIC CATEGORY-FORMATION

I. *The Starting Point: Second Temple Times*

The Halakhic category-formations commence their development in Second Temple Times. By "Second Temple times," within the framework of the history of religious ideas, I mean, the period between the closure of the Pentateuch and the initial phases of the Halakhic structure and system culminating in the Mishnah-Tosefta-Yerushalmi-Bavli. The year 450 B.C.E. stands for the former, some time before and soon after 70 C.E., the latter. By "the Halakhah," I mean the normative laws of Rabbinic Judaism. By "Rabbinic Judaism" I mean that Judaism, among the several Israels and their Torahs and distinctive traditions that flourished in late antiquity, the Judaism that sets forth the myth of the dual Torah, written and oral, revealed in writing and in memory through formulation and transmission from master to disciple, by God to Moses "our rabbi." That is the Judaism that identifies, among the vast corpus of writings produced by various Judaisms of the age, as its canon only Scripture, the Mishnah, Talmuds, Midrash-compilations, and related documents, all of them marked by sayings attributed to specific rabbis and, within the system, deemed part of the one whole Torah of our rabbi Moses. Among all Judaic, and even Jewish-ethnic, writings of antiquity, only Rabbinic ones cite rabbis, and they are, therefore, the only ones that tell us what is particular to that Judaism.[1]

What premises and principles that animate the Mishnah, and the Halakhah more generally, originated in the period between 450 B.C.E. and 70 C.E., and what are we able to say about the formative history of the Halakhah thereafter? These premises and principles shaped into cogent category-formations I identify out of the particu-

---

[1] One may wish even to claim, it is in particular that Judaism that privileged the Pentateuch among the writings of Scripture, but for the present purpose such a claim need not be entered, though I think it can be defended.

lar cases and examples of the Halakhah that can be shown through
the correlation of attributions and logical progression to belong to the
period before 70, or, in some cases, to form the foundations of cases
and examples in the earliest phases of the Halakhah beyond 70.
When we work systematically forward from the Pentateuch and
backward from the earliest phases of the Mishnah's Halakhah, we
designate temporal limits of the history of ideas, fore and aft. Thus
the closure of the Pentateuch serves as the starting point or terminus
a quo, and the beginning of the articulation of the Halakhah at its
logically-primitive base of the Mishnah and the Tosefta (here treated
for the present purpose as correlative) as the end-point or *terminus ante
quem,* that is to say, the final decades of Second Temple times. Why
ca. 70? For most, though not all, the categorical structures of the
Halakhah, points of disputed law rest on undisputed premises that
originate among authorities at the beginning of the Halakhic process
in late Second Temple times. These undisputed premises form the
foundations for the structure of law culminating in the Mishnah,
Tosefta, baraita-corpus, Yerushalmi, and Bavli.

History of ideas in any familiar sense, establishing a sequence in
which ideas took shape in succession and identifying a given idea
with a determinate time, place, and circumstance, does not emerge
for Second Temple times, which I treat as an undifferentiated span of
time. While the ideas I identify certainly had to have taken shape, in
the category-formation in which we now know them, between ca.
450 B.C.E. and ca. 70 C.E., I have no notion of when, in that half-
millennium, a given conception germinated and sprouted nor, in
particular context, why. I do not even know where. Nor do I claim
that these ideas are particular to the circles the successors of which
produced the writings of Rabbinic Judaism, only that, in those writings, these ideas form critical components of the Rabbinic system.
For that long period we have no plausible evidence of named authorities, together with issues they confronted or ideas they held. But
what I do promise is to describe the main points and identify where
in the Halakhah they surface.

It follows that I am working with two boundaries, then, the point
from (or after) which an idea can have emerged, and a point *before which*
it must have reached articulation (if not in words we now have).
Sages cannot have begun their work prior to the Pentateuch, and
sages had to have completed the processes of thinking outlined here
by 70: that is what I allege.

The former hardly requires amplification. The Pentateuch viewed as a coherent system marks for the Halakhah of Rabbinic Judaism (also seen as a system) the sole possible starting point, the *a quo*. To be sure, no one would claim that the generally-prevailing date for the Pentateuch of the late sixth through the mid-fifth centuries B.C.E. also tells us when everything within the Pentateuch originated as well. But it does tell us when the system seen whole initially made its appearance. Nor would anyone allege that facts, conceptions, or other data encompassed within the Halakhah of Rabbinic Judaism originate solely in Scripture; the opposite has been shown many times over. Cultural artifacts from diverse times and places formed a common heritage of culture in the Near and Middle East. But in the context of Rabbinic Judaism, these commonplaces of civilized transactions take on consequence for the study of that system only within the framework of that system—a truism, an established point hardly demanding amplification. What is at issue therefore is not where and when episodic facts originate, but how and why facts are taken over and put together into that remarkably cogent structure and system of thought that is embodied by the Halakhah of Rabbinic Judaism— thus the *a quo* of the Pentateuch, which, privileged by Rabbinic Judaism, at the starting point dictated the structure and system of that Judaism in their principal lines of structure and order.

What about the point before which, or by which, a given principle had to have attained authoritative status within the circles of sages, that is, the *ad quem?* It is indicated not by the appearance of the Mishnah, in ca. 200 C.E., but by the very initial marks of the beginnings of thought that ultimately yielded the Halakhah (whether expressed in the Mishnah or set forth only in subsequent compilations).[2] Given the verifiable aspects of the attributions of sayings to authorities—I shall explain presently how we can show a correlation between the order, by generations, of sages and the sequence, in logic, of what is attributed—the beginnings of the Mishnaic law also marks the end-point of the generally-undocumented age. Then—in general by 70—important categorical issues were settled and the generative problematic of a variety of subjects identified. On that basis, on the

---

[2] My *The Halakhah. An Encyclopaedia of the Law of Judaism* (Leiden, 1999: Brill) treats *the Halakhah*, not only the Halakhah of the Mishnah, hence the formulation given here. But nearly the whole of the Halakhah of formative Rabbinic Judaism occurs in the Mishnah and the Tosefta, only a small portion of the entire complex first surfacing in categorical terms in the two Talmuds, and that fact has long been known among historians of the Halakhah.

foundations of ideas set forth here, the work that produced the Halakhah as we should know it got underway in the age before and after 70. With what do I deal in particular? It is with the processes of thought, the period of fermentation, of ideas founded on the Penta-teuch but not articulated therein, or not founded on the Pentateuch at all, and those taken as givens. So for Second Temple time I por-tray the premises of the Halakhah and the bases for its articulation and development as documented in the Mishnah and the Tosefta and baraita-corpus. The results of those processes can be recon-structed.

How, exactly, do I conceive that interim-period in the formation of Rabbinic Judaism, between the Pentateuch and the foundations of the Mishnah (and the Tosefta)? My conception of matters is best expressed in the very terms of the Halakhah on which I have been working for thirty years. Hence, not surprisingly, a Halakhic concept supplies a metaphor in helping me to explain the conception at work here, the conception of the critical interval between the periods that the successive documents demarcate. My illustrative metaphor de-rives from the Halakhah of the dough-offering, Hallah, and may be stated very simply as embodying the difference between *may* and *must* and explaining it. Specifically, there is a point in the making of a loaf of bread at which dough offering may be separated (thus: *a quo*), and there is a point at which it must be separated (thus *ad quem*), and when we identify the characteristics of that interval, a time of fer-ment, between the beginning and the end of a process, we can under-stand full well precisely the conception of this work.

So let me introduce some Halakhic facts. At what point is it per-mitted to designate a portion of dough as dough-offering, and at what point is it required to do so?[3] Dough-offering *may not* be sepa-rated, e.g., from dry flour, before the flour has been wet down and so made into dough. If one does so, it is not dough-offering. Dough offering *may* be separated once the flour has been wet down with the yeast and the fermentation process commences. When the dough forms a crust in the oven, however, then the dough *must* yield its dough-offering. I cannot think of a more vivid way of linking the obligation to separate dough-offering to the fermentation-process. Such a process must be possible—hence the five species but no oth-

---

[3] The same principle takes effect for all manner of tithes, and its counterpart pertains to the inauguration of susceptibility to uncleanness, but that is another story.

ers—*and it must be underway.* Then the consideration of God's share in the dough registers.

There are then two boundaries, one fore, the other aft: the point at which liability descends, the moment at which the liability must be met. And what do the boundaries signify? The answer is, the commencement and the conclusion of a process of fermentation. The former comes when the flour is brought to life by water and yeast; then the life of the loaf commences, so God's claim on the bread registers. The dough, when alive and expanding, encompasses a share belonging to God. By sharing the outcome of the fermentation with God, the householder acknowledges life embodied in the living processes by which the bread comes into being, and resulting in the presence, within the dough, of a portion subject to sanctification: donation to the priest in the present instance. So that is when the dough offering may be separated for the priest. What about the end-point? The formation of the crust marks the death of the yeast. So when the process of fermentation has come to an end, with the formation of the crust and the death of the yeast, then the obligation to give dough-offering must be met. God's claim cannot be postponed, if man wishes to derive benefit from the fermentation process, now concluded, by eating the bread.

Now briefly to apply the metaphor to our problem: [1] the closure of the Pentateuch marks the starting point of a process of fermentation; [2] the commencement of the documented, Halakhic process culminating in the Mishnah and the Tosefta marks the end. Like that period of fermentation from the mixture of flour, yeast, and water to the formation of the crust, the period between the Pentateuch and the initial formation of the Halakhah marks a time of remarkable activity, the life of the mind corresponding to the life of the growing nourishment: bread from the earth matching Torah from heaven.

II. *Methodological Foundations:*
Correlating Sequences of Sages with Sequences of Rulings

What logic sustains the theoretical account of ideas framed posterior to the Pentateuch but prior to the earliest identifiable conceptions of the Halakhah that comes to formulation in the Mishnah-Tosefta-Yerushalmi-Bavli? From the beginning, in 1972, of my work on the history of the Halakhah, starting with the Mishnah and the Tosefta, I have carried forward the approach of the greatest practitioner of Talmudic history ever to work in the field, Y. I. Halevy, in his magnum opus, *Dorot Rishonim* (Vienna and Berlin, 1923, in five parts). Addressing the problem of the history of the Halakhah of the Mishnah-Tosefta-Yerushalmi-Bavli in his history of "the Oral Torah," Halevy asked, What is taken for granted but not subjected to dispute? And what is taken for granted in such everywhere-taken-for-granted principles? Therein he identified the premises of the law, which, in my opinion persuasively, he maintained provided us guidance into the state of affairs beyond the limits of the Written Torah (Pentateuch), looking forward but before the Mishnah and cognate compilations, looking backward.[4]

To my knowledge, among accounts of the history of the Halakhah, Halevy was the first to point out that the Halakhah as it is articulated by named sages rests on premises that are not spelled out or subjected to analysis but simply taken for granted as fact. These, he proposes, attest to the state of the Halakhah that is formulated and transmitted in memory, by oral tradition. Upon that solid foundation laid down by Halevy, I constructed my account of the history of the Mishnaic law in the decade from the 1970s into the earliest 1980s, and, then, two decades later, my picture of Scripture and the premises of the Halakhah, now concluded. I have thought about the matter for almost a quarter of a century and still find Halevy's approach compelling.

Clearly, a rather elaborate and intellectually dense process has yielded the detailed results systematized here. Perhaps an easier way would have opened up to the same goal, had I adopted a prevailing rule upon which at that time people insisted. It was stated simply: what is anonymous is "very early" and "goes way back." With that iron rule in hand, one could describe the foundations of the Hala-

---

[4] It is noteworthy that he was framing this speculative, hypothetical conceptualization of matters at the very time the great Harry A. Wolfson was forming his counterpart approach to philosophy! But I doubt that either knew about the other. Halevi focused his powerful critique upon the work of the German Wissenschaft des Judenthums, the work of those whom he called, "Hokhmé Ashkenaz," which work he condemned point by point for hundreds of pages. Wolfson framed his logical-hypothetical method in another context entirely. Outside of the circles of Orthodox Judaism whose viewpoint Halevi advocated, Halevi received no hearing; the scholars of Wissenschaft des Judenthums whom he criticized responded by publishing lists of "errors" they found in his writing, but they did not engage with his basic theses, and I do not think they understood enough of the Halakhic texts to understand them.

khah out of the anonymous statements of the earliest formulations thereof. Why limit my account to the uncertainty of the results of logic: this conception must be prior to that, for that question cannot be raised unless this one has been settled? or why allege only that that principle presupposes this fact and is therefore logically prior to it? Why not accept the frequently-asserted but rarely-justified principle, what is anonymous—disputed or not, whether in the logical position of a premise or in the logical position of a proposition—by definition must be "old"?

Halevy identified undisputed propositions that found a position as the premise of all discourse on a given topic, and I followed him in my two major exercises. But the position that anonymity on its own guarantees antiquity represents a different position from Halevy's and mine. And it is not without foundations in the sources themselves. The documents' own account—e.g., at the commencement of Tosefta-tractate Eduyyot—of the origin of disputes attributes the use of attributions, signaling mooted points, to insufficient learning on the part of the latter-day sages. So the notion that undisputed sayings antedate disputed ones is hardly without its august sponsorship. But I explicitly reject the approach to the same question that identifies as "very old" all unassigned sayings of the Mishnah and subsequent documents. That approach, characteristic of the intellectually vulgar work of Ephraim E. Urbach (who, in the one meeting I had with him, which took place in June, 1976, laid down for me the iron law of the antiquity of anonymous sayings), but not his alone, insists that what is anonymous in the Halakhic documents must go "way back"—whether to Sinai or to Ezra is not then specified.[5]

Three considerations, two of reason, the other of the very character of the textual evidence, including manuscript variants, as distinct from the allegations found therein, suggest otherwise.

That is, first, for a simple reason of interior logic, the governing convictions of the documents' own character and those of the named participants therein, concerning the traditionality of established law. Most unassigned sayings in the Mishnah occur in the context of disputes, in which an attributed saying and an unattributed one appear side by side. When unassigned and assigned sayings intersect

---

[5] In that memorable hour, he also instructed me that we have to believe everything we find in the Rabbinic literature unless there is overwhelming reason not to believe. I did not then have the wit to ask him how we might know we were wrong.

and conflict, the conflict attests to not the antiquity of one of the sayings but the contemporaneity of both sayings, not only the assigned one. That is because, in a system that insists upon its own traditionality and imposes upon disciples the task of exactly memorizing the opinions in the masters in their own wording, it is highly unlikely that a named master would reject a received opinion. The system's own traditionality points to the opposite position, namely, that the named master differs from a contemporary unnamed one. The entire character of the documents tells us that innovation not on the foundations of tradition elicited immediate objection, and named persons rarely are represented as standing against the weight of established views.

Not only so, but, second, when we lay out sequences of ideas, primary, then secondary, simple and primitive, then complex and articulated, we very commonly find an interesting correlation. Assigned sayings given to authorities assumed to have flourished earlier take the primary, the simple, and the primitive position in the unfolding of the Halakhah, while those given to authorities assumed to have flourished later on take the secondary, derivative, and complex one. That persistent trait again argues against the notion that a later authority would dispute an established view but favors the notion that issues settled in one generation, principles established then, rarely would be treated as subject to renewed dispute later on. Once a principle is accepted at the beginnings of a Halakhic sequence, authorities who flourished later on in the sequence do not dispute with the established rule, though they commonly dispute about its implications. The upshot of both facts is, when we have an anonymous and an assigned saying on the same problem, they are likely to represent contemporaneous positions.

But there is a third and quite substantive, because textual, consideration as well. Sayings anonymous in one document are assigned in another to a named sage. That is a routine process. The Tosefta will supply an assigned statement of a Halakhic position that is opposed to an anonymous one in the Mishnah. Or the Tosefta will construct a dispute, the resolution of which is shown to be represented, on its own, in the Mishnah's anonymous formulation. The Talmuds, particularly the Bavli, routinely identify the unnamed authority of an anonymous statement of the Mishnah or the Tosefta, using the standard rhetoric, *man tanna hadetani*, and the like. So the governing premises, as distinct from the mere allegations, of the Rabbinic cor-

pus itself argues against the theory that anonymity on its own signifies antiquity. Hence any working hypothesis that "what is anonymous must be very old" cannot play a role in rigorous inquiry.

So much for what I mean by "Second Temple times" and how I
claim to know anything about Rabbinic Judaism at that time.

III. *Rabbinic Judaism in Second Temple Times?*

But that formulation begs the obvious question: What can we possibly mean when we speak of *Rabbinic* Judaism before 70—even in the
qualifying formulation, "pre-Rabbinic"? I certainly do not claim that
the fully-articulated Rabbinic category-formation—structure and system—had manifested itself before 70. No one has found evidence for
the existence, before 70, of the emblematic marks of Rabbinic
Judaism, whether institutional, political, or mythic. I do not even
imagine that that structure and system in its full realization could
have come about before the crisis of the mid-second century. But
what I aim to show is, when we compare the system viewed whole
and with the elements of the system that can have originated in
Second Temple times, we see more than bits and pieces but an
adumbration of the whole. That result, framed in our historicistic
framework, will not have surprised the sages themselves, who could
and did accommodate, within the myth of the dual Torah, a variety
of accounts of what, in fact, the Oral Torah comprised and how it
defines itself.

But, as everyone knows, while taking over and making its own a
substantial corpus of data deriving from remote antiquity onward
and from various sources. that Judaism began to take shape in the
decades just before and just after 70. That Judaism emerged from the
union of Pharisaism and scribism, the one a sectarian body and
doctrine, the other a profession. The initial Halakhic statement of
Rabbinic Judaism comes to us in the Mishnah, and its aggadic system in fully-realized form in the Talmud of the Land of Israel, ca.
400 C.E. If by Rabbinic Judaism we mean a cogent system, with its
symbolic structure and theological system set forth in Halakhah, with
its paramount symbol and myth embodied by the aggadah of the
dual Torah, with its rabbi as sage and saint, and with its Israel
occupied with sanctification in the here and now in the hope of
salvation then and there—if that is what we mean by Rabbinic

Judaism, then, with nearly the entire world of academic learning,[6] I must say, we cannot speak of *Rabbinic* Judaism much before 70. If the Pharisees formed a coherent social group within the politics of pre-70 Israel, and they did, and if the scribes a profession, and they did, then where we find "rabbis" in particular—other than those bearing a generic title of honor—I do not know. Nor do I conceive that any extant evidence would suggest otherwise.

What we do have are important conceptions that coalesced before the processes of sustained development that yielded the Halakhic construction set forth in the Mishnah and the Tosefta got underway. We also have in hand components of that same system that is richly portrayed in the Halakhic compilations. Certainly we may find some of the elements that later coalesced in that system and structure. The scribes contributed Torah-learning and the Halakhic medium. The Pharisees made their own huge contribution, their way of life and world view focused on sanctification of the here and now in the model of the Temple. The scribes' Torah-learning, the Pharisees practical piety—these in detail, not only in general, formed principal

---

[6] I do not take account of the opinions of the yeshiva-, rabbinical-seminary-, and Israeli-university world, which rest on premises incompatible with those of the academy, being uncritical and yielding paraphrase. Those opinions begin with the affirmation of nearly all attributions, so that if a saying is assigned to a named sage, whatever the date of closure of the document containing the attribution, the man really said it in the time, in the Second Temple period, in which he is supposed to have lived. Again, I do not conceive of a single Judaism, the one we now know in the Rabbinic Judaism, to which all sources, Rabbinic or otherwise, attest (except when they do not). Nor do I treat as a single coherent legal system all rules and laws assigned to Jewish-ethnic origin or provenience, whatever the character of the group in which they originate—a system with a linear history backward to the Torah and forward to the Talmud. None of these convictions has proven tenable, and all scholarship built upon them has to be set aside as, while learned, simply beside the point of critical learning. Until critical premises govern, the theory of a unitary, linear "Jewish law" covering all periods and encompassing all data has simply to be dismissed. The rule of thumb, if a rule is early, it cannot be Rabbinic, and if it is Rabbinic, it cannot be early, familiar among scholars of the library found at Qumran, is equally untenable. Laws can be early and can have entered into the circles that produced Rabbinic Judaism and been adopted by them, for their purpose and in the proportion dictated by them. Laws can surface in the later Rabbinic writings that can be shown, also, to have pertained five hundred years earlier, so they can be both Rabbinic and early. The issue is, at that early point, what would have marked them as Rabbinic, and within what system will they have found their position and made their point? That is a different question from the one implicit in the cited rule of thumb. Finally, efforts at constructing a continuous and linear account of The Halakhah, including the claim to have found "the missing link" between this and that seem to me to evince more enthusiasm than critical judgment. By none of these ephemera are we going to be preoccupied in our inquiry, for reasons fully exposed.

parts of the earliest phases of Rabbinic Judaism and all the subsequent ones. Not only so, but many, many components given place and proportion in the Rabbinic system can be identified as ideas that circulated in Second Temple times, if not in their place and proportion in a system we may call Rabbinic in any terms. These include the Messiah-theme, but then out of phase with sanctification, in the Gospels, for instance. And, it goes without saying, numerous facts of the Halakhah can be shown to have circulated in Second Temple times, if not in any group that we can identify, and if not in any circumstance we can associate with the social components of Rabbinic Judaism in pre- or even post-70 times. The Halakhic systems that we can locate in Temple times—the ones documented in the Qumran library, in Philo's writings, and in the Elephantine papyri, for the main examples—share with the Rabbinic system of Halakhah a vast corpus of facts, beginning with but not limited to those of Scripture. *But these do not form a single, coherent Halakhic system, put forth in the governance of a cogent community, whether all Israel or part thereof, only diverse systems, each representative of its own community.*

So if, as is established fact, in Second Temple times we cannot identify a community of Rabbinic Judaism in the way in which we can identify and document a community of Pharisaic Judaism or a community of Judaism at Elephantine or a community of Judaism represented by the library at Qumran or even that massive community of Jews with a distinctive Judaism attested by Philo's writings to Alexandria, what can we mean by pre-*Rabbinic* Judaism in Second Temple times?

What we cannot mean is, a social group embodying a religious structure and realizing a religious system—that Rabbinic Judaism realized by the Halakhah, embodied by the circles of masters and disciples and the sector of Israel that accepted their authority, and conveyed in the myth of the dual Torah and the symbol of Moses as "our rabbi." That we do not find, and I do not think the fully-developed system of Rabbinic Judaism existed outside of, and before, the category-formation that comes to initial statement in the decades before and after 70. Nor, in any reasonable framework, can we speak of Rabbinic Judaism before the social world constituted by the sages, the Patriarchate, the master-disciple-circles, and the entire panoply of Halakhah and its formulation and systematization.

What we can mean, and what I do mean, is, a body of ideas that, I shall show, not only circulated in a long age of ferment, but—more to the point—*coalesced into a coherent statement by the end of that period.* By "pre-Rabbinic Judaism" in Second Temple times, therefore, I mean, very simply, some of the basic principles and conceptions that we can demonstrate not only form the foundations of the Halakhah of the Mishnah and the Tosefta and of the Talmuds, but also constitute a single, coherent construction, a structure and a system of ideas that in time would come to full articulation and realization in Rabbinic Judaism. I do not know where it all began, though sages insist, it began at Sinai, in Scripture and in oral tradition, and that conviction serves as well as any to account for what is there. Now to clarify the critical points, the starting and ending limits of the work.

IV. *The Phenomenological Reading:* A quo

Everything depends upon the phenomenology, the analysis of the whole that identifies the critical components. These, then, we seek in the data of the Halakhah that surface in Temple times. And to analyze the whole, the answer to a single question defines everything: What does Scripture contribute to the dual Torah? For so far as the Oral Torah particular to Rabbinic Judaism carries out more than a recapitulation of the category-formations of the Written Torah and the amplification of the data of those formations, we find the particularity in the Oral Torah's *own* category-formations and their data, how these hold together and how the two wholes, Scripture and the Halakhah, relate and correlate. So let me now spell out the relationship(s) between Scripture and the Halakhah at its earliest phases, even in its initial categorical formation. We must stress the category-formations, for these are the emblematic traits of Rabbinic Judaism. How do the Halakhic category-formations relate to Scripture to begin with?

If a corpus of Halakhah builds upon a topic defined by the Pentateuch and provides a secondary clarification and refinement of the rules implicit in that topic, then we may say, that body of Halakhah begins in Scripture. Its development from Scripture to the earliest phases of the Mishnah then forms the story of that category-formation in Temple times. If a corpus of Halakhah defines a topic that the Pentateuch does not introduce and formulates Halakhah for that topic, then we may say that that body of Halakhah does not begin in Scripture. As it reaches us, that body of Halakhah commences after

Scripture. If a corpus of Halakhah takes up a topic defined by Scripture but formulates the matter in terms not dictated by Scripture's treatment of the same matter, then we may say, that body of Halakhah begins in Scripture but takes shape altogether outside the limits of Scripture. These distinctions are made explicit by the sages themselves:

A. The absolution of vows hovers in the air, for it has nothing [in the Torah] upon which to depend.
B. The laws of the Sabbath, festal offerings, and sacrilege—lo, they are like mountains hanging by a string,
C. for they have little Scripture for many laws.
D. Laws concerning civil litigation's, the sacrificial cult, things to be kept cultically clean, sources of cultic uncleanness, and prohibited consanguineous marriages have much on which to depend.
E. And both these and those [equally] are the essentials of the Torah.
                                            Mishnah-tractate Hagigah 1:9

A. *The absolution of vows hovers in the air, for it has nothing upon which to depend in the Torah* [M. Hag. 1:8A].
B. But a sage loosens a vow in accord with his wisdom.
C. *The laws of the Sabbath, festal-offerings, and sacrilege are like mountains hanging by a string, for they have little Scripture for many laws* [M. Hag. I :8B].
D. They have nothing upon which to depend.
F. *Laws concerning civil litigation, the sacrificial cult, things to be kept cultically clean, sources of cultic uncleanness, and prohibited consanguineous marriages* [M. Hag. 1:8D],
G. and added to them are laws concerning valuations, things declared *herem*, and things declared sacred—
H. for them there is abundant Scripture, exegesis, and many laws.
I. *They have much on which to depend* [M. Hag. 1:8D].
J. Abba Yosé b. Hanan says, "These eight topics of the Torah constitute *the essentials of the laws* [thereof] [T. Er. 8:24]" [M. Hag. 1:8D-E].
                                            Tosefta Hagigah 1:9

In this context, when we examine the Halakhah from the perspective of the starting point, the *a quo*, we address the relationship between two cognate religious documents, the Pentateuch and the corpus of Halakhah set forth by the Mishnah-Tosefta-Yerushalmi-Bavli. Both contain normative rules or Halakhah. As is already implicit, by "Halakhah" I mean not random rulings on this or that, wherever they surface. Rather, I speak of the entire corpus of law laid out by its native categories as defined by the Halakhah set forth in the Oral part of the Torah and ultimately committed to verbal permanence ("writing") in the primary legal documents of Rabbinic Judaism. We have already reviewed a systematic analysis that yields with great precision answers to these questions concerning the Halakhah of the Oral Torah:

[1] What Halakhah set forth by Moses in Scripture, the Written Torah, pertains to the Halakhah of the Oral Torah?[7]

[2] What are the main points of the Halakhah, the topics of systematic exposition, the principal concerns, the paramount questions, systematically set forth in well-constructed category-formations by the Mishnah-Tosefta-Yerushalmi-Bavli?

[3] What does Scripture contribute to the formation of the Halakhah as finally defined by the definitive documents, and what main points rest on other-than-explicit statements of Moses in the Pentateuch?

The question that governs is simply stated. In relationship to the premises that dictate the problematics of Scripture's law, is the category-formation

[1] dependent upon Scripture, merely developing points already set forth there; here we deal with Halakhah that is symmetrical with Scripture's laws, going over the same ground and saying pretty much the same thing;

[2] autonomous of Scripture, going its own way to explore issues of its own invention, here we address Halakhah that is essentially autonomous of Scripture, which has not contributed the category or even a corpus of rules on the category;

[3] in-between but derivative, that is, Halakhah deriving a topic and perhaps a corpus of facts from Scripture and fabricating a program of problems that Scripture has provoked? or

[4] in-between but fundamentally original, that is, deriving a topic and even some facts from Scripture but formulating a program of problems that Scripture has in no way suggested, invoking conceptions Scripture has not provided? The issue in the fourth classification, then, is, does Scripture define the provocative issues of a given

---

[7] Upon the study of Judaism and its history, the analytical pre-history of the Written Torah, set forth from the nineteenth century forward, has no bearing. That is because Judaism begins with the Pentateuch; all Judaic religious systems from the Pentateuch forward read the Pentateuch as a single, unitary statement set forth by Moses (designated by the sages of the Oral Torah, "our rabbi"). Hence I refer to Moses as author of the Written Torah, since, in the present context, that is the given of all discourse. The interplay of diverse "law codes," e.g., the Priestly Code and the Deuteronomic code, is simply irrelevant to the study of Judaism.

topic, or do those generative problems take shape elsewhere than in the written part of the Mosaic revelation?

So I compare and contrast two bodies of Halakhah, Scripture's and the Oral Torah's and ask how the latter relates to the former.[8] I ask how the former relates to the latter, that is, beginning from the Mishnah and working backward. That yields the systematic and informed characterization of the contribution to the formation of the Halakhah of authorities who flourished (in temporal, historical terms)[9] after the closure of the Pentateuch but before the commence-

[8] I hasten to clarify, at issue is not the exegetical process by which a given verse can have yielded a given Halakhic datum, let alone the systematic examination of the exegetical rules attributed to the sages and the results yielded by those rules. What requires characterization here are the substantive results, the comparison of one corpus of Halakhah, Scripture's, with another corpus, that of the Oral Torah. I make no judgments on how the former corpus can have yielded, and perhaps did yield, some or even all of the Halakhah of the other. I take for granted that at an indeterminate number of points I am dealing with the result of an exegetical process. But my focus is on the large-scale description of that result, or, rather, the starting-out and the outcome thereof. By "the Halakhah" I mean, the principal category-formations seen in large aggregates, inclusive of secondary and tertiary amplifications of details. This becomes clear when, in each of my categories, I describe precisely what I conceive those main traits of the Halakhah in question to have been, the law seen whole for a given category-formation. This "macro-approach" leaves ample space for a "micro-approach," and indeed the approach worked out in this project can be fully realized only when each and every detail of each and every category-formation has been absorbed within the articulated composition of the whole seen whole.

[9] I do not regard temporal, historical terms as the sole possible way of framing the issue, let alone the best way. We could as well speak of characterizing the layer of thought that intervenes between the Pentateuch and the Mishnah and the Tosefta, without making a claim that we know exactly when that layer of thought took shape. The Judaism of the dual Torah contains two theories of the status of the Oral Torah. In the one, it is free-standing and autonomous, a tradition wholly framed in its own terms; in the other, it is secondary and dependent upon the written Torah. The former formulation of matters sustains a different framing of the results of this study. One may argue, and in other contexts some have argued, that the Oral Torah is required to complete the Written One, the logic of the former is fulfilled in that of the latter. The latter framing of matters works best if we invoke temporal and historical categories, treating the autonomous premises of the Oral Torah, and the laws generated thereby, as essentially a later formation of the Torah, one resting perhaps on exegesis, perhaps on a perception of the inner logic of the Written Torah, perhaps on yet other bases. Which of the two formulations works best within the context of the Rabbinic literature and the data it sets forth will be best decided when the characterizations of the dual Torah that are implicit (not only explicit) in the Rabbinic literature from the Mishnah to the Letter of Sherira Gaon have been fully examined; I plan to undertake that exercise in *What, Exactly, Did Our Sages Mean by "the Oral Torah"? An Inductive Answer to the Question of Rabbinic Judaism*. But for the work, *The Four Stages in the Formation of Judaism. From Scripture to the Talmud* (London, 1999: Routledge), I utilize a historical model of formulation, not an essentially mythic-philosophical one such as the complementary relationship of the two components of the Torah would require.

ment of the Mishnah-Tosefta-Yerushalmi-Bavli. That is to say, the
results of this analysis will reveal the character of Halakhic reflection
that took place between the two corpora of literary formulation of the
law, the Pentateuch and the Mishnah along with the Tosefta.

Sages raise the issue investigated in this project when they identify
three types of relationship between Halakhah and the Written Torah. In the results that are set forth and systematized I follow their
taxonomy of relationships between the Written Torah or Pentateuchal Law and the Oral Torah or the Halakhah of the Mishnah-
Tosefta-Yerushalmi-Bavli. As we see, they frame matters in this way:
[I] abundant verses of Scripture supporting many laws; [II] many
laws, little Scripture; [III] laws but no Scripture. Yet all form part of
the revealed Torah of Sinai. My language for my categories is [I]
native categories of the Halakhah that prove nearly wholly concentric with those in the Written Torah; [II] native categories entirely
autonomous of Scripture, e.g., principal topics not treated in the
Pentateuch at all and [III] native categories that occur in Scripture
and that are accorded complex secondary development by the
Halakhah, [IV] native categories that occur in Scripture but that are
developed in ways not precipitated by Scripture.

When we ask Scripture to tell us what it has contributed, and what
derives from some other source, in the answer we may differentiate
the component of the Written Torah from that deriving from that
other source. In the framework of the history of religion and its
appreciation for myth, we may call that other source, "the Oral
Torah"—but only in that framework. But if we wish to know what
the sages themselves can have meant by "the Oral Torah," that other
source presents itself as a prime candidate to supply the contents
thereof.

V. *The Historical Reading:* Ad quem

Working from Scripture forward leads us to an indeterminate end.
The stopping point emerges when we encounter the nascent stages of
the system and structure ultimately set forth in the Halakhah of the
Mishnah and the Tosefta. On what basis do I claim to know Halakhic ideas that were held in particular at, or even before, 70? Upon
the answer to that question rests my picture of the state at 70 C.E. of
the Halakhah ultimately set forth in the Mishnah and Tosefta. Stated

simply: attributions of sayings tend to correlate with the logical status of what is said, so that a saying assigned to an early authority may be shown to be prior in logic and conception to a saying assigned to a later authority; that is ordinarily secondary to, and contingent upon, that which is given in the name of the earlier authority. On that basis—whether we can correlate the status of the attribution with the logic of what is attributed—we are able to falsify or verify the sequence of attributions, and that makes possible a historical reading of the Halakhah. Let me spell out exactly how this works, since the historical reading of the phenomenological results rests upon this method, which has been fully executed for the Mishnah and the Tosefta, the main media of the Halakhah.

One conventional response to the historical question is, sayings are attributed to authorities who lived in the first centuries B.C.E. and C.E., so that is how we identify ideas and facts at the foundations of the development of the Mishnah. Simply put: if a saying is attributed to Hillel or the House of Hillel, Shammai or the House of Shammai, assumed to have lived before 70, then we know the shape of Halakhic opinion before 70. But now that most people in the academic world no longer take as historical fact the attribution of a saying to a named authority, we are left on less certain grounds. We cannot demonstrate that a single saying in the entire Rabbinic literature actually was said by the person to whom it was attributed, and solid obstacles to such a demonstration suffice to require a new approach to the history of ideas. What we cannot show we do not know. Then how do we know anything at all about the sequence in the unfolding of the Halakhah that ultimately comes to closure in the formulation of the Mishnah, ca. 200 C.E., and, specifically, what allows us to describe the state of the Halakhah at the end of Second Temple times, somewhat before and after 70?

Literary data, like the attributions themselves, do not settle any questions of a historical nature. That is because the Mishnah's formulation derives from the work of redaction. So we cannot show that sizable components of the Mishnah were written down, pretty much as we have them, long before the closure of the document as a whole. On formal and literary grounds, the opposite is the fact: most of the Mishnah conforms to a single program of formulation within a few iron rules of rhetoric, and that set of rules on formulation derives from encompassing decisions concerning redaction. We can, however, demonstrate that legal issues or principles in the Mishnah, if not the original wording of those ideas, did derive from periods prior to the age of redaction and formulation.

That demonstration rests on two facts. The first is the corpus of attributions themselves. These on their own do not suffice, but in relationship to other evidence they can be tested and utilized in a limited way. While we cannot show that the sages to whom sayings are attributed actually said what is assigned to them, a second fact makes possible a test of falsification and verification. It is based on two facts, both of them readily established as facts.

First, groups of names appear always with one another and never with names found in other distinct groups. Sages A, B, C, D, commonly believed to have lived at one time, occur in dispute with one another. But rarely, if ever, does sage A, B, C, or D, appear with sages W, X, Y, and Z. Those latter sages likewise stay together and rarely intersect with other groups of names. It follows that The system of attributions works itself out by groups, or generations. To begin with we may collect sayings assigned to sages A, B, C, and D, and treat them as distinct from sayings assigned to W, X, Y, and Z. But what difference does that distinction make?

That leads to a second fact. Problems debated in the Mishnah may be classified as primary and derivative, simple and complex. The former have to have been settled before the latter can be addressed. If we do not know the answer to the former, we cannot begin to investigate the question raised by the latter. It follows that a logical relationship, one of priority of one issue, posteriority of a second, dependant and secondary one, can be demonstrated between and among Halakhic rulings. In the consideration of a problem we may readily isolate the stages in the argument, identify the components of a theme. We may further show, on grounds of logic, that a given element of a problem or component of a theme takes precedence over some other element or component.

Now these two facts, readily discerned in the Mishnah's and the Tosefta's sustained exposition of any of their native categories, intersect and make possible the division of the Halakhic corpus into earlier and later stages—without relying upon attributions except as neutral and abstract data, no different from symbols: A, B, C, instead of Aqiba, Eliezer, Joshua, for one group, X, Y, Z for Meir, Judah, and Simeon, for another.

The division of sages into groups of names, with clear evidence in the documents themselves that one group of names is prior in time to another, joined to the fact, that two or more groups of sayings, each set drawn together on the basis of the appearance of groups of names may intersect in the treatment of a common theme or even problem, opens the way to the testing of the ordering of Halakhic rulings and principles, primary and prior, secondary and posterior. How so? In the two facts just now listed, we have two sequences, the one logical, the other temporal-personal. A given position is assigned to a given sage (or set of sages, two contradictory positions on the same issue being subject to dispute). We cannot show the sages said what is assigned to them. *But we can show that the temporal sequence of attributions and the logical sequence of what is attributed match*—or we can find cases in which they do not match. What is attributed to the earlier set of sages is prior in logic or even in topic, and what is assigned to the later set of sages is posterior in logic, or addresses a subordinate and second-ary topic. That exercise in matching one set of facts against the other permits us to order the unfolding of the law—in detail.

Hence a test of verification or falsification is entirely feasible. Thus, if we observe a sequence of correspondences between the order in which groups of sages engage in a discussion of a problem and the logic by which the problem itself unfolds, we have reason to assign the logically prior position to the time in which the logically prior group of sages flourished. The matter is a bit abstract, so let me give a concrete case to show the simplicity of what I allege. A case suffices, drawn from the Halakhah of Gittin, writs of divorce.

[1] If we do not know that a woman requires a writ of divorce, we shall not ask about how the writ is supposed to be written.

Again, [2] if we do not know that rules dictate the correct compo-sition of the writ of divorce, we are not likely to ask about the conse-quences of a scribal error in the writing of the document. So we see sequential stages in the simple problem before us:

(1) we must know that if a husband wishes to divorce a wife, he must supply her with written evidence that the marriage is severed, and *then*

(2) we must know that such written evidence conforms to a given formula, *before* we may ask

(3) whether, if the document does not conform, the woman is deemed properly divorced. Yet a further stage in the unfolding of the issue will bring us to the question,

(4) how we dispose of the offspring of the woman who, on the basis of a divorce accomplished through an improper document, has remarried and become pregnant.

Now recognizing the obvious stages in the unfolding of an issue, we cannot conclude that these stages in logic correspond to sequences of determinate temporal periods. Why not? Because no one would claim that the logical stages outlined just now mark off fifty-year periods in the history of the law. In a single morning, someone can have thought the whole thing through.

For example, to revert to the case at hand, we can show that

[1] sages A, B, C, and D appear in units of discourse, or pericopes, concerning stage (1) of the issue,

[2] sages G, H, I, and J participate in units of discourse on the matter of stage (2),

[3] M, N, O, and P at stage (3),

[4] and W, X, Y, and Z at stage (4).

Then we may propose the thesis that the issue unfolded in the sequence of historical periods in which the groups of sages lived. Why so? Because the order of logical steps not only corresponds to, but also correlates with, the order of the groups of sages to whom pertinent sayings are attributed. Can that thesis undergo a test of falsification? Of course it can, because we may ask whether to a later group of sages, e.g., M, N, O, and P, are attributed sayings that concern an issue, principle, or premise already supposedly settled among an earlier group of sages, e.g., A, B, C, and D.

Now to state the point relevant to the present study of beginnings of Halakhic discourse: the earliest-named authorities in the sequence of discussions in the Halakhah of Gittin all know as fact that, to severe a marriage, a writ of divorce is required. No one doubts it, and everyone builds on that fact. From that point forward, the complexities of the matter commence, e.g., the formula of the writ of divorce, the way in which it is delivered to her (Gamaliel, Eliezer), the consequences of improperly writing out a writ of divorce (Meir and his generation), including the disposition of offspring of the marriage. The sequence of groups of sages matches the logical order, prior, posterior, of what is attributed. To repeat: before we have established one fact, we cannot take up the second. If Gamaliel and Eliezer, of the first century, were to dispute about how we dispose of the offspring of a divorced woman who remarried on the strength of a faulty writ of divorce, and Meir and Judah, of the second century, were to dispute about what constitutes a disqualifying flaw in a writ of divorce and its delivery, then the sequence of attributions (by generation) would contradict the sequence of what is attributed (by logical order, simple/complex, primitive/refined, and the like). The test of verification contains within itself a test of falsification.

But does it necessarily follow that what is assigned to the generations just before or just after 70, respectively, tells us about questions settled among those generations, thus by 70? No, it does not necessarily follow. First, the facts at hand do not demand a historical explanation. One may account in other ways for the correlation of logical stages with sequences of groups, or generations, of sages. Literary or scholastic conventions can have intervened. The groupings need not be held to represent distinct generations. Second, people can hold three consecutive, logical thoughts, one building on the former, in a single morning. Nothing in the match of earlier authorities to primary principles, later to secondary, places us in the period in which those authorities are assumed to have lived.

All I claim—and all anyone can claim—is that the method of correlating logical and generational sequences allows the proposed historical results—the picture of the history of the Halakhah of the Mishnah's larger system—to undergo tests of falsification and verification. It does not rest on total credulousness in accepting as fact all attributions. In identifying the starting point in the formulation of any given category-formation with the period before and after 70, I stand on an infirm basis. I do not have much evidence outside of the documents themselves—the first of them, the Mishnah, reaching closure more than a century after the starting point I allege to locate therein—that the earlier group of authorities flourished from 70, the later from about a half-century later. But a more critical approach in time to come will improve upon the method outlined here. So my account of the starting point of Halakhic development from 70, with its consequent implications for the character of Halakhic thought in the period from Scripture's closure to the Mishnah's and the Halakhah's documented commencement must be deemed provisional, if I hope, serviceable.

In the account of the situation that prevailed at the *terminus ad quem*, however, we start with systematic results, for I have applied this procedure in a study of the second through the sixth divisions of the Mishnah and the Tosefta, each tractate and every unit of discourse of each tractate. Professor Avery-Peck has done the same for the first division. The results of this rather protracted labor proved not entirely uniform for two reasons. The first and the more important, the

character of the materials did not invariably permit the test of falsification at hand. Some issues arise for the first time in the names of the
final group of authorities, the one that would correspond, in my
example above, to W, X, Y, and Z. That meant I had no basis other
than the attributions on which to assign to the period of those sages
the rules attributed to them. But since the sages at hand flourished
one generation prior to the closure of the Mishnah, it did not appear
an act of mere credulity in assigning what was attributed to that last
stage in the formation of the Mishnah's system of Halakhah.

The second, and less important matter was that, on rare occasion,
it did appear that what was assumed as settled fact in discourse
among an earlier group of sages, e.g., A, B, C, and D, in fact produced substantial dispute among a later group, e.g., W, X, Y, and Z.
These few exceptions often centered on the figure of a critical figure
in the attributions, namely, Aqiba, an early second century authority,
who is believed to have flourished prior to the Bar Kokhba War and
to have trained the principal authorities of the period after the War.
In any event where the test of falsification or verification could be
met, an item had to be set aside and not included in an account of
the history of the law.

To state the general upshot of the procedure, on the basis just now
outlined we may work out the history of the Halakhah of the
Mishnah through three principal periods: before 70, from 70 to 130,
from 140 to 170, that is, before the first war with Rome, between the
two wars, and after the Bar Kokhba War. Obviously, we want to
know how far before 70 the Mishnah's laws extend their roots. If we
rely on the attributions at hand and make use only of those units of
discourse in which we can verify or falsify the attributions, the answer
is simple. The earliest layers of the laws ultimately joined together in
the system of the Mishnah rest upon foundations laid forth somewhat
before or at the beginning of the Common Era. No unit of discourse
in the entire Mishnah can be shown to contain ideas or facts originating in the Mishnah's system prior to the turn of the first century C.E.
To be sure numerous facts and ideas extend back to Scripture; some
go back to Sumerian or Akkadian times. But so far as facts or ideas
serve a purpose distinctive to the Mishnah's system and so may be
represented as systematic and so called systemic, not merely episodic
and routine, all facts and ideas begin at the designated period. To
state the matter simply: the system of the Mishnah's Halakhah begins
at the turn of the first century C.E., though details, commonly rou-

tine facts of a common law, may originate as much as two thousand years earlier than that.

VI. *Constructing Categories for Comparison and Contrast: The Systemic Approach*

What, exactly, defines the field of analysis, the smallest whole unit of description, analysis, and interpretation? It is not the isolated fact but the category-formation that defines the context, therefore, the meaning, of that fact along with others, deemed cognate. Here we seek to see whole and complete the two correlative compilations, the Written Torah, with special reference to its presentation of the law for Israel, and the Oral Torah, which everyone agrees is the counterpart. In both cases we work on the coherent legal statements of the pertinent parts of the Torah, and these, I hasten to insist, in the main, though not always, come to us in sizable composites of rules that cohere. It is common, in Scripture, to find a topic that holds together in a coherent composition a variety of cognate, pertinent rules, all of them clarifying, giving details that realize, that topic. It is uncommon in Scripture to come across diverse sentences, each a rule unto itself, none of them forming with others coherent paragraphs of topical exposition. A simple survey of the organization of the law set forth in Exodus, Leviticus, Numbers, and portions (though only portions!) of Deuteronomy makes that point clear. And the Oral Torah, as is self-evident, is organized in large-scale, coherent, systematic topical expositions, by subject-matter. These topical expositions, called in English tractates and in Hebrew *massekhtot*, commonly, though not always, pursue a single program of questions, expounding a given topic in line with a coherent problematic that dictates the information about said topic that the law proposes to reveal.

Now, if we work with the coherent building blocks of fully-articulated category-formations—for Scripture, exemplified by Numbers 5 and 6, for the Halakhah, exemplified by tractates Sotah and Nazir—we deal with cogent statements, comprised by detailed rules that coalesce. These define our field of inquiry. I describe the category-formations, analyze how they make a cogent statement and specify what I think that statement is, and I interpret the composite seen whole. The work of interpretation involves comparison of counterpart category-formations of Scripture and the Halakhah commencing with the Mishnah, then the contrast of those same category-formations to highlight what is distinctive to, characteristic of, the Halakhic category-formation set forth by the Mishnah-Tosefta-Yerushalmi-Bavli. Treating the details as autonomous units for inquiry, I have no way of establishing the context in which discrete statements find their place and bear meaning. There is no comparison and contrast out of context. The category-formations establish that context: the building blocks of which the two structures, the Written and the Oral Torah, are build.

It follows that I try to show the relationship of the category-formations of the Halakhah with their counterparts in Scripture. I am not concerned here with how a given component of a category-formation—a particular rule—of the Halakhah relates to, is generated by, or even contradicts, a counterpart, particular rule of the Pentateuch. That work has been fully carried out in the Tosefta, Yerushalmi, Bavli, and Tannaite Midrash-compilations, and I do not think anyone is going to improve upon that formidable corpus of learning. Nor would the results contribute to the attainment of our goal here. Since I wish to characterize the Oral Torah, its qualities of mind and its distinctive approach to category-formation within the Halakhah, I am required to focus upon the intermediate building-blocks of the two Torahs, written and oral, and to compare and contrast those of the one with those of the other. On a smaller scale, all I can find out is how a verse of Scripture provoked the formulation of a statement of the Oral Torah (in our case, its law), and that will not yield systemic comparison. On a larger scale, all that can be anticipated is generalizations of slight heuristic interest: the one complements the other, for instance, and other unsurprising, even uncomprehending, propositions.

VII. *The Formative History of the Halakhic Category-Formations*

We cannot show the presence within the documents of the Oral Torah of a huge pre-70 stratum of Halakhah, nor can we excavate a dense corpus of examples of the three principal category-formations particular to the Oral Torah that have been identified earlier. The main result is, we can show how points critical to the Halakhah as it is fully worked out are represented in one detail or another in pre-70 opinion. These then I allege to adumbrate the category-formations that encompass them in the fully-realized system particular to the Oral Torah. So we work from shards and remnants to the shape and proportions of the Oral Torah's structure. Then the issue cannot be, the category-formation of the Halakhah before 70. It can only be, can we identify powerful themes of the Halakhah that defined distinctive foci of the Oral Torah before 70, even though the category-formations that now frame matters did not, at that time, emerge and extend and impose structure and order on the laws? Indeed we can, and let us now proceed to do so.

The Halakhah of the Mishnah-Tosefta-Yerushalmi-Bavli takes shape in three stages through a twofold process. The first stage is Temple times, the second, the period from 70 to 135, and the third, the mid-second century, from 135 forward. The process is in two parts, first, the identification of a category-formation by the definitive logic in play, second and consequently, the expansion and full actualization in the details of law of said category-formation. In the second century formulation of the Halakhic structure, at numerous points, first comes the choice of a category-formation, then, and only then, the collection and organization of data pertinent to the category-formation, whether or not a generative problematic animates the category-formation or a mere interest in collecting and arranging information accounts for its character. Thus once a theme is introduced early in the history of law, it will be taken up and refined later on. So in the second and third stages in the formation of the Halakhah set forth in the Mishnah-Tosefta-Yerushalmi-Bavli, many new themes with their problems will emerge. These then are without precedent in the antecedent thematic heritage.

How are we to understand the successive stages in the repertoire of the category-formations that would ultimately impart structure and order to the Halakhah, and that do just that in the Mishnah-Tosefta-Yerushalmi-Bavli? The common foundations for the whole are Scripture, whole or in variable proportion, much to very little. To envisage the completed composition I may present a simple architectural simile: a house on a hill in San Francisco. The Halakhah organized in the category-formations before us is like a completed construction of scaffolding, a construction built on the side of a hill and creating a level plane at the top by means of supports and buttresses down the side of the hill. The foundation is a single variable, descending surface, the Scriptures. The top platform is a single plane, the Halakhah itself. But the infrastructure by reason of the topography is differentiated. So what do we see? Underneath one part of the upper platform will be several lower platforms, so that the supporting poles and pillars reach down to intervening platforms; only the bottom platform rests upon pillars set in the foundation. Yet another part of the upper platform rests upon pillars and poles stretching straight down to the foundation, without intervening platforms at all. And here and there jut out little balconies, integral to the house but not resting on the ground, directly or through pillars, at all. So viewed from above, the uppermost platform of the scaffolding forms a single, uniform, and even plane. That is the category-formation defined by the Mishnah and the Tosefta as we have it, six Divisions, sixty-three tractates, five hundred thirty-one chapters (for the Mishnah in particular). But viewed from the side, that is, from the perspective of analysis, there is much differentiation, so that, from one side, the upper platform rises from a second, intermediate one, and, in places, from even a third, lowest one. And yet some of the pillars reach directly down to the bedrock foundations. And, as I say, here and there jut out balconies and porches, integral, to the whole but resting on no more than the architect's calculations of stresses. But houses in San Francisco survive earthquakes, and so has the Halakhic structure and system.

To reveal the result at the outset: the category-formations of the Halakhah as we know the Halakhah took shape only in the mid-second century. Then what is new in the period beyond the wars is that part of the ultimate plane—the Halakhic category-formation as a whole—which in fact rests upon the foundations not of antecedent thought but of Scripture alone. What is basic in the period before 70 C.E. is the formation of that part of the Halakhic category-formation that sustains yet a second and even a third layer of platform construction. What emerges between the two wars will both form a plane with what comes before, that platform at the second level, and yet will also lay foundations for a level above itself. But this intermediate platform also will come to an end, yielding that space filled only by the pillars stretching from Scripture on upward to the ultimate plane of the Mishnah's completed and whole system. Lowest down the hill, resting on the most complex scaffolding, are the category-formations adumbrated by sayings of Temple times; higher are those formed by sayings reliably assigned to the period between the wars, and at the top, the main corpus of the structure, which defines the character of the whole endows it with proportion, is the category-formation devised after the period of war, 67-135, had concluded and the reconstruction of the Torah begun.

VIII. *The Halakhah before 70*

Viewed from the perspective of the large category-formations of which it is comprised, the Mishnah—therefore the Halakhah as a whole—as we know it originated in its Division of Purities.[10] There we find the most fully realized category-formation, though from the perspective of the Halakhah, still a partial one. The striking fact is that the Sixth Division is the only one that yields a complete and whole statement of a topic dating from Temple times, before the wars. Its principal parts are (1) what imparts uncleanness; (2) which kinds of objects and substances may be unclean; and (3) how these objects or substances may regain the status of cleanness. Joined to episodic rulings elsewhere, the principal parts of the Sixth Division speak, in particular, of cleanness of meals, food and drink, pots and pans. It then would appear that the ideas ultimately expressed in the Mishnah began among people who had a special interest in observing cultic cleanness, as dictated by the Priestly Code. There can be no doubt, moreover, that the context for such cleanness is the home, not solely the Temple, about which Leviticus speaks. The issues of the law leave no doubt on that score. Since priests ate heave offering at home, and did so in a state of cultic cleanness, it was a small step to apply the same taboos to food which was not a consecrated gift to the priests.

What is said through the keeping of these laws is that the food eaten at home, not deriving from the altar and its provision for the priesthood of meat not burned up in the fire, was as holy as the meal offerings, meat offerings, and drink offerings, consecrated by being set aside for the altar and then, in due course, partly given to the priests and partly tossed on the altar and burned up. If food not

---

[10] That qualification is critical: "from the perspective of the large category-formations." I do not think that episodic laws, even ad hoc rulings, commence only with their entry into the Mishnah's corpus of the Halakhah. On the contrary, we can demonstrate the antiquity, even to remote times, of much of what becomes the Halakhah set forth by the Mishnah-Tosefta-Yerushalmi-Bavli. Nor do I maintain that the Halakhah we find in the Mishnah-corpus belongs uniquely to the sages who bear responsibility therefor. There too it is easy to demonstrate the opposite. I am asking only one question: at what stage do the category-formations of the Mishnah-Tosefta-Yerushalmi-Bavli and their principal components appear to have taken shape? The antiquity of some, even much, of the corpus of data, the Halakhic facts, that those category-formations utilize is not at issue. It is how the whole coalesces into a single closed system that I propose to work out along the historico-phenomenological lines spelled out here.

consecrated for the altar, not protected in a state of cleanness (in the case of wheat), or carefully inspected for blemishes (in the case of beasts), and not eaten by priests in the Temple, was deemed subject to the same purity-restrictions as food consecrated for the altar, this carries implications about the character of that food, those who were to eat it, and the conditions in which it was grown and eaten. First, all food, not only that for the altar, was to be protected in a state of levitical cleanness, thus holiness, that is, separateness. Second, the place in the Land, in which the food was grown and kept was to be kept cultically clean, holy, just like the Temple. Third, the people, Israel, who were to eat that food were holy, just like the priesthood, in rank behind the Temple's chief caste. Fourth, the act of eating food anywhere in the Holy Land was analogous to the act of eating food in the Temple, by the altar.

All of these obvious inferences point to a profound conviction about the Land, people, produce, condition, and context of nourishment. The setting was holy. The actors were holy. And what, specifically, they did which had to be protected in holiness was eating. For when they ate their food at home, they ate it the way priests did in the Temple. And the way priests ate their food in the Temple, that is, the cultic rules and conditions observed in that setting, was like the way God ate his food in the Temple. That is to say, God's food and locus of nourishment were to be protected from the same sources of danger and contamination, preserved in the same exalted condition of sanctification. So by acting, that is, eating like God, Israel became like God: a pure and perfect incarnation, on earth in the Land which was holy, of the model of heaven. Eating food was the critical act and occasion, just as the priestly authors of Leviticus and Numbers had maintained when they made laws governing slaughtering beasts and burning up their flesh, baking pancakes and cookies with and without olive oil and burning them on the altar, pressing grapes and making wine and pouring it out onto the altar. The nourishment of the Land—meat, grain, oil, and wine—was set before God and burned ("offered up") in conditions of perfect cultic antisepsis.

In context this antisepsis provided protection against things deemed the opposite of nourishment, the quintessence of death: corpse matter, people who looked like corpses (Lev. 13), dead creeping things, blood when not flowing in the veins of the living, such as menstrual blood (Lev. 15), other sorts of flux (semen in men, non-menstrual blood in women) which yield not life but then its opposite, so death. What these excrescencies have in common, of course, is that they are ambivalent. Why? Because they may be one thing or the other. Blood in the living is the soul; blood not in the living is the soul of contamination. The corpse was once a living person, like God; the person with skin like a corpse's and who looks dead was once a person who looked alive; the flux of the zab (Lev. 15) comes from the flaccid penis which under the right circumstances, that is, properly erect, produces semen and makes life. What is at the margin between life and death and can go either way is what is the source of uncleanness. But that is insufficient. For the opposite, in the priestly code, of unclean is not only clean, but also holy. The antonym is not to be missed: death or life, unclean or holy.

So the cult is the point of struggle between the forces of life and nourishment and the forces of death and extinction: meat, grain, oil, and wine, against corpse matter, dead creeping things, blood in the wrong setting, semen in the wrong context, and the like. Then, on the occasions when meat was eaten, mainly, at the time of festivals or other moments at which sin offerings and peace offerings were made, people who wished to live ate their meat, and at all times ate the staples of wine, oil, and bread, in a state of life and so generated life. They kept their food and themselves away from the state of death as much as possible. And this heightened reality pertained at home, as much as in the Temple, where most rarely went on ordinary days. The Temple was the font of life, the bulwark against death.[11]

Once the meal became a focus of attention, the other two categories of the law which yield principles or laws deriving from the period before the wars present precisely the same sorts of rules. Laws on growing and preparing food will attract attention as soon as people wish to speak, to begin with, about how meals are to be eaten. That accounts for the obviously lively interest in the biblical taboos of agriculture.[12] Since, further, meals are acts of society, they call together a group. Outside of the family, the natural unit, such a group will be special and cultic. If a group is going to get together, it will be on a Sabbath or festival, not on a workday. So laws governing the making of meals on those appointed times will inevitably receive attention.[13] Nor is it surprising that, in so far as there are any rules pertinent to the cult, they will involve those aspects of the cult which

---

[11] Cf. my *History of the Mishnaic Law of Purities*. Leiden, 1974-1977. I-XXII.

[12] Cf. Alan J. Avery-Peck, *History of the Mishnaic Law of Agriculture*. Chico, 1985.

[13] Cf. my *History of the Mishnaic Law of Appointed Times*. Leiden, 1981-1983. I-V.

apply also outside of the cult, that is, how a beast is slaughtered, rules governing the disposition of animals of a special status (e.g., firstborn), and the like.[14]

That the rules for meals pertain not to isolated families but to a larger group is strongly suggested by the other area which evidently was subjected to sustained attention before the wars, laws governing who may marry whom. The context in which the sayings assigned to the authorities before the wars are shaped is the life of a small group of people, defining its life apart from the larger Israelite society while maintaining itself wholly within that society. Three points of ordinary life formed the focus for concrete, social differentiation: food, sex, and marriage. What people ate, how they conducted their sexual lives, and whom they married or to whom they gave their children in marriage would define the social parameters of their group. These facts indicate who was kept within the bounds, and who was excluded and systematically maintained at a distance. For these are the things—the only things—subject to the independent control of the small group. The people behind the laws, after all, could not tell other people than their associates what to eat or whom to marry. But they could make their own decisions on these important, but humble, matters. By making those decisions in one way and not in some other, they moreover could keep outsiders at a distance and those who to begin with adhered to the group within bounds. Without political control, they could not govern the transfer of property or other matters of public interest. But without political power, they could and did govern the transfer of their women. It was in that intimate aspect of life that they firmly established the outer boundary of their collective existence. The very existence of the group and the concrete expression of its life, therefore, comes under discussion in the transfer of women. It therefore seems no accident at all that those strata of Mishnaic law which appear to go back to the period before the wars, well before 70, deal specifically with the special laws of marriage (in Yebamot), distinctive rule on when sexual relations may and may not take place (in Niddah), and the laws covering the definition of sources of uncleanness and the attainment of cleanness, with specific reference to domestic meals (in certain parts of Ohalot, Zabim, Kelim, and Miqvaot). Nor is it surprising that for the conduct of the cult and the sacrificial system, about which the group may

---

[14] Cf. my *History of the Mishnaic Law of Holy Things*. Leiden, 1979. I-VI.

have had its own doctrines but over which it neither exercised control nor even aspired to, there appears to be no systemic content or development whatsoever.

Once the group take shape around some distinctive, public issue or doctrine, as in odd taboos about eating, it also must take up the modes of social differentiation which will ensure the group's continued existence. For the group, once it comes into being, has to aspire to define and shape the ordinary lives of its adherents and to form a community expressive of its larger world view. The foundations of an enduring community will then be laid down through rules governing what food may be eaten, under what circumstances, and with what sort of people; whom one may marry and what families may be joined in marriage; and how sexual relationships are timed. Indeed, to the measure that these rules not only differ from those observed by others but in some aspect or other render the people who keep them unacceptable to those who do not, as much as, to the sect, those who do not keep them are unacceptable to those who do, the lines of difference and distinctive structure will be all the more inviolable.

IX. *The Interim-Category-Formation:*
The Halakhah between the Wars of 66-70 and 132-135

The period between the wars marks a transition in the unfolding of the Mishnaic law and system. The law moved out of its narrow, sectarian framework. But it did not yet attain the full definition, serviceable for the governance of a whole society and the formation of a government for the nation as a whole, which would be realized in the aftermath of the wars. The marks of the former state remained. But those of the later character of the Mishnaic system began to make their appearance. Still, the systemic fulfillment of the law would be some time in coming. For, as I shall point out in the next section, the system as a whole in its ultimate shape would totally reframe the inherited vision. In the end the Mishnah's final framers would accomplish what was not done before or between the wars: make provision for the ordinary condition of Israelite men and women, living everyday lives under their own government. The laws suitable for a sect would remain, to be joined by others which, in the aggregate, would wholly revise the character of the whole. The shift after the Bar Kokhba War would be from a perspective formed upon

the Temple mount to a vision framed within the plane of Israel, from
a cultic to a communal conception, and from a center at the locative
pivot of the altar, to a system resting upon the utopian character of
the nation as a whole.[15]

When we take up the changes in this transitional period, we notice, first of all, continuity with the immediate past. What was taking
place after 70 is encapsulated in the expansion, along predictable and
familiar lines, of the laws of uncleanness, so to these we turn first.

If the destruction of Jerusalem and the Temple in 70 marks a
watershed in the history of Judaism, the development of the system of
uncleanness does not indicate it. The destruction of the Temple in no
way interrupted the unfolding of those laws, consideration of which is
well attested when the Temple was standing and the cult maintained.
Development is continuous in a second aspect as well. We find that,
in addition to carrying forward antecedent themes and supplying
secondary and even tertiary conceptions, the authorities between the
wars develop new areas and motifs of legislation. These turn out to
be both wholly consonant with the familiar ones, and, while fresh,
generated by logical tensions in what had gone before. If, therefore,
the destruction of the Temple raised in some minds the question of
whether the system of cleanness at home would collapse along with
the cult, the rules and system before us in no way suggest so. To be
sure, the destruction of the Temple does mark a new phase in the
growth of the law. What now happens is an evidently rapid extension
of the range of legislation, on the one side, and provision of specific
and concrete rules for what matters of purity were apt to have been
taken for granted but not given definition before 70, on the other. So
the crisis of 70 in the system of uncleanness gives new impetus to
movement along lines laid forth long before.

Let us first dwell upon the points of continuity, which are many
and impressive. The development of the rules on the uncleanness of
menstrual blood, the zab, and corpse uncleanness is wholly predictable on the basis of what has gone before. The principal conceptual
traits carry forward established themes. For example, if we have in
hand an interest in resolving matters of doubt, then, in the present
age, further types of doubts will be investigated. Once we know that
a valid birth is not accompanied by unclean blood, we ask about the
definition of valid births. The present thought on the zab (Lev. 15)

---

[15] Cf. my *History of the Mishnaic Law of Women.* Leiden, 1979-1980. I-VI.

depends entirely on the materials assigned to the Houses, which, moreover, appear to be prior to, and independent of, what is attributed to the authorities after 70. The transfer of the zab's uncleanness through pressure, forming so large and important a part of the tractate of Zabim, begins not with a reference to the zab at all, but to the menstruating woman. The fresh point in this regard is to be seen as a step beyond Scripture's own rule, a shift based on analogical thinking. Rulings on corpse contamination dwell upon secondary and derivative issues. One new idea is the interest in projections from a house and how they too overshadow and so bring corpse uncleanness. It is from this point that an important development begins. Once we treat the tent as in some way functional, it is natural to focus upon the process or function of overshadowing in general. A major innovation in regard to transfer of the contamination of corpse matter through the tent is the notion that the tent takes an active role, combining the diverse bits and pieces and corpse uncleanness into a volume sufficient to impart corpse uncleanness. What is done is to treat the overshadowing as a function, rather than the tent as a thing. Here the mode of thought is both contrastive and analogical.

What is new now requires attention. The comparison of the table in the home to the cult in the Temple is an old theme in the Mishnaic system. What is done at just this time appears to have been the recognition of two complementary sequences, the removes of uncleanness, the degrees of holiness. The former involves several steps of contamination from the original source of uncleanness. The latter speaks of several degrees of sanctification, ordinary food, heave offering, food deriving from the altar (holy things), and things involved in the preparation of purification water. Each of the latter is subject to the effects of contamination produced by each of the former, in an ascending ladder of sensitivity to uncleanness.

An essentially new topic for intense analysis was Holy Things. At issue now is the formation, between the wars, of laws governing the cult. The principal statement of this new system is as follows: the Temple is holy. Its priests therefore are indispensable. But the governance of the Temple now is to be in accord with Torah, and it is the sage who knows Torah and therefore applies it. Since a literal reading of Scripture prevented anyone's maintaining that someone apart from the priest could be like a priest and do the things priests do, it was the next best thing to impose the pretense that priests must obey laymen in the conduct even of the priestly liturgies and services.

This is a natural step in the development of the law. A second paramount trait of the version of the system between the wars is its rationalization of those uncontrolled powers inherent in the sacred cult as laid forth by Leviticus. The lessons of Nadab and Abihu and numerous other accounts of the cult's or altar's intrinsic mana (inclusive of the herem) are quietly set aside. The altar sanctifies only what is appropriate to it, not whatever comes into contact with its power. In that principle, the sacred is forced to conform to simple conceptions of logic and sense, its power uncontrollably to strike out dramatically reduced. This same rationality extends to the definition of the effective range of intention. If one intends to do improperly what is not in any event done at all, one's intention is null. Third, attention is paid to defining the sorts of offerings required in various situations of sin or guilt. Here too the message is not to be missed. Sin still is to be expiated, when circumstances permit, through the sacrificial system. Nothing has changed. There is no surrogate for sacrifice, an exceedingly important affirmation of the cult's continuing validity among people burdened with sin and aching for a mode of atonement. Finally, we observe that the established habit of thinking about gifts to be paid to the priest accounts for the choices of topics on fees paid to maintain the cult. All pertain to priestly gifts analogous to tithes and heave offerings. Tithe of cattle is an important subject, and the rules of firstlings and other gifts to the priests are subject to considerable development. The upshot is that the principal concerns of the Division of Holy Things are defined by the end of the age between the wars.[16]

Systematic work on the formation of a Division of Appointed Times did not get under way in the aftermath of the destruction of the Temple. The established interest in rules governing meals, however, was carried forward in laws reliably assigned to the time between the wars. There is some small tendency to develop laws pertinent to the observance of the Sabbath; a few of these laws were important and generated later developments. But the age between the wars may be characterized as a period between important developments. Work on legislation for meals on Sabbaths and festivals had begun earlier. The effort systematically and thoroughly to legislate for the generality of festivals, with special attention to conduct in the Temple cult, would begin later on. In the intervening generations only a little work was done, and this was episodic and random.

---

[16] Cf. M. Tohorot 2:2-7, for instance.

When fully worked out, the Mishnah's Division of Women would pay close attention to exchanges of property and documents attendant upon the transfer of a woman from her father's to her husband's house. Authorities between the wars provided only a little guidance for such matters. For a very long time before 70 the national, prevailing law must have defined and governed them. What is significant is that broader and nonsectarian matters, surely subject to a long history of accepted procedure, should have been raised at all. It means that, after the destruction, attention turned to matters which sectarians had not regarded as part of their realm of concern. This may have meant that others who had carried responsibility for the administration of public affairs, such as scribes, now made an appearance. And it also may have meant that the vision of the sectarians themselves had begun to broaden and to encompass the administration of the life of ordinary folk, not within the sect. Both meanings are to be imputed to the fact of interest in issues of public administration of property transfers along with the transfer of women to and from the father's home. Concern for definition of personal status devolves upon genealogical questions urgent to the priesthood, and, it follows, in the present stratum are contained matters of deep concern to yet a third constituency. But these matters of interest to scribes and priests do not predominate. It is their appearance, rather than their complete expression and articulation, which is of special interest. Whoever before 70 had settled those disputes about real estate, working conditions, debts and loans, torts and damages, and other sorts of conflicts which naturally came up in a vital and stable society, the group represented in the Mishnah did not.[17] That is why the Division of Damages, dealing with civil law and government, contains virtually nothing assigned to authorities before the wars. Scribes in Temple times served as judges and courts within the Temple government, holding positions in such system of administration of the Israelite part of Palestine as the Romans left within Jewish control. The Division of Damages is remarkably reticent on what after the destruction they might have contributed out of the heritage of their earlier traditions and established practices. Materials of this period yield little evidence of access to any tradition prior to 70, except (predictably) for Scripture. When people at this time did take up topics relevant to the larger system of Damages, they directed

---

[17] Cf. My *History of the Mishnaic Law of Damages*. Leiden, 1983-1985. I-V.

their attention to the exegesis of Scriptures and produced results which clarify what Moses laid down, or which carry forward problems or topics suggested by the Torah. That is not evidence that thinkers of this period had access (or wished to gain access) to any source of information other than that one, long since available to the country as a whole, provided by Moses. It follows that, in so far as any materials at all relevant to the later Mishnaic system of Damages did come forth between the wars, the work appears to have begun from scratch. And not much work can have been done to begin with. There is no evidence of sustained and systematic thought about the topics assembled in the Division of Damages. We find some effort devoted to the exegesis of Scriptures relevant to the Division. But whether or not those particular passages were selected because of a large-scale inquiry into the requirements of civil law and government, or because of an overriding interest in a given set of Scriptures provoked by some other set of questions entirely, we cannot say.

The net result of the stage in the law's unfolding demarcated by the two wars is that history—the world-shattering events of the day— is kept at a distance from the center of life. The system of sustaining life shaped essentially within an ahistorical view of reality, goes forward in its own path, a way above history. Yet the facts of history are otherwise. The people as a whole can hardly be said to have accepted the ahistorical ontology framed by the sages and in part expressed by the systems of Purities, Agriculture, and Holy Things. The people followed the path of Bar Kokhba and took the road to war once more. When the three generations had passed after the destruction and the historical occasion for restoration through historical—political and military—action came to fulfillment, the great war of 132 to 135 broke forth. A view of being in which people were seen to be moving toward some point within time, the fulfillment and the end of history as it was known, clearly shaped the consciousness of Israel after 70 just as had been the case in the decades before 70. So if to the sages of our legal system, history and the end of history were essentially beside the point and pivot, the construction of a world of cyclical eternities being the purpose and center, and the conduct of humble things like eating and drinking the paramount and decisive focus of the sacred, others saw things differently. To those who hoped and therefore fought, Israel's life had other meanings entirely.

The Second War proved still more calamitous than the First. In 70 the Temple was lost, in 135, even access to the city. In 70 the people, though suffering grievous losses, endured more or less intact. In 135 the land of Judah—surely the holiest part of the holy Land—evidently lost the bulk of its Jewish population. Temple, Land, people—all were gone in the forms in which they had been known. In the generation following the calamity of Bar Kokhba, what would be the effect upon the formation of the system of Halakhah of the Mishnah? It is to that question that we now turn.

X. *The Halakhah of the Mid-Second Century:*
The Halakhah's Fully-Realized Category-Formation in Structure and System

The Halakhah reached its full and complete statement, as the Mishnah would present it, after the Bar Kokhba War. Over the next sixty years, from ca. 140 to ca. 200, the system as a whole took shape. If I am correct that the initial category-formation encompasses the large themes of Eden and the Land, intentionality, and sanctification and uncleanness, then it was after the Bar Kokhba War that the second and vastly augmented construction came to full articulation. What was implicit in the original category-formation, the imperative of restoration of Israel to the Land as of Adam and Eve to Eden and the concomitant victory of life over death now was realized in the Halakhic construction of Israel's social order, structure and system alike. But that is hardly surprising. The Oral Torah's own category-formation represents a reading of the Pentateuchal narrative of exile and return and a translation of that narrative into social norms. The Halakhic category-formation as we know it in the Mishnah-Tosefta-Yerushalmi-Bavli took shape in response to an event understood (rightly, in my view) within the precedent of Scripture: the destruction of another Temple and its closure for no one knew how long. And here too, I should claim, sages read from Scripture forward to their own day, transforming into an account of the Israelite social order and its character the story of Israel from creation through the first destruction into a paradigm to account for the contemporary recapitulation. The whole then was intended to restore Eden: life with God, life over death, all in the hands of Israel by reason of its own will, intentionality, and attitude.

To describe the fully realized category-formation of the Halakhah, we survey the six divisions and their tractates and the main points covered in each.

The Division of Agriculture treats two topics, first, producing crops in accord with the Scriptural rules on the subject, second, paying the required offerings and tithes to the priests, Levites, and poor. The principal point of the Division is that the Land is holy, because God has a claim both on it and upon what it produces. God's claim must be honored by setting aside a portion of the produce for those for whom God has designated it. God's ownership must be acknowledged by observing the rules God has laid down for use of the Land. In sum, the Division is divided along these lines: (1) Rules for producing crops in a state of holiness—tractates Kilayim, Shebi'it, Orlah; (2) Rules for disposing of crops in accord with the rules of holiness—tractates Peah, Demai, Terumot, Maaserot, Maaser Sheni, Hallah, Bikkurim, Berakhot.

The Mishnaic Division of Appointed Times forms a system in which the advent of a holy day, like the Sabbath of creation, sanctifies the life of the Israelite village through imposing on the village rules on the model of those of the Temple. The purpose of the system, therefore, is to bring into alignment the moment of sanctification of the village and the life of the home with the moment of sanctification of the Temple on those same occasions of appointed times. The underlying and generative theory of the system is that the village is the mirror image of the Temple. If things are done in one way in the Temple, they will be done in the opposite way in the village. Together the village and the Temple on the occasion of the holy day therefore form a single continuum, a completed creation, thus awaiting sanctification.

The village is made like the Temple in that on appointed times one may not freely cross the lines distinguishing the village from the rest of the world, just as one may not freely cross the lines distinguishing the Temple from the world. But the village is a mirror image of the Temple. The boundary lines prevent free entry into the Temple, so they restrict free egress from the village. On the holy day what one may do in the Temple is precisely what one may not do in the village. So the advent of the holy day affects the village by bringing it into sacred symmetry in such wise as to effect a system of opposites; each is holy, in a way precisely the opposite of the other. Because of the underlying conception of perfection attained through the union of opposites, the village is not represented as conforming to the model of the cult, but of constituting its antithesis.

The world thus regains perfection when on the holy day heaven and earth are united, the whole completed and done: the heaven, the earth, and all their hosts. This moment of perfection renders the events of ordinary time, of "history," essentially irrelevant. For what really matters in time is that moment in which sacred time intervenes and effects the perfection formed of the union of heaven and earth, of Temple, in the model of the former, and Israel, its complement. It is not a return to a perfect time but a recovery of perfect being, a fulfillment of creation, which explains the essentially ahistorical character of the Mishnah's Division on Appointed Times. Sanctification constitutes an ontological category and is effected by the creator.

This explains why the Division in its rich detail is composed of two quite distinct sets of materials. First, it addresses what one does in the sacred space of the Temple on the occasion of sacred time, as distinct from what one does in that same sacred space on ordinary, undifferentiated days, which is a subject worked out in Holy Things. Second, the Division defines how for the occasion of the holy day one creates a corresponding space in one's own circumstance, and what one does, within that space, during sacred time. The issue of the Temple and cult on the special occasion of festivals is treated in tractates Pesahim, Sheqalim, Yoma, Sukkah, and Hagigah. Three further tractates, Rosh Hashshanah, Taanit, and Megillah, are necessary to complete the discussion. The matter of the rigid definition of the outlines in the village, of a sacred space, delineated by the limits within which one may move on the Sabbath and festival, and of the specification of those things which one may not do within that space in sacred time, is in Shabbat, Erubin, Besah, and Moed Qatan.

While the twelve tractates of the Division appear to fall into two distinct groups, joined merely by a common theme, in fact they relate through a shared, generative metaphor. It is the comparison, in the context of sacred time, of the spatial life of the Temple to the spatial life of the village, with activities and restrictions to be specified for each, upon the common occasion of the Sabbath or festival. The Mishnah's purpose therefore is to correlate the sanctity of the Temple, as defined by the holy day, with the restrictions of space and of action which make the life of the village different and holy, as defined by the holy day.

The Mishnaic system of Women defines the position of women in the social economy of Israel's supernatural and natural reality. That position acquires definition wholly in relationship to men, who impart form to the Israelite social economy. It is effected through both supernatural and natural, this-worldly action. What man and woman do on earth provokes a response in heaven, and the correspondences are perfect. So the position of women is defined and secured both in heaven and here on earth, and that position is always and invariably relative to men.

The principal interest for the Mishnah is the point at which a woman becomes, and ceases to be, holy to a particular man, that is, enters and leaves the marital union. These transfers of women are the dangerous and disorderly points in the relationship of woman to man, therefore, to society as well. Five of the seven tractates of the Division of Women are devoted to the formation and dissolution of the marital bond. Of them, three treat what is done by man here on earth, that is, formation of a marital bond through betrothal and marriage contract and dissolution through divorce and its consequences: Qiddushin, Ketubot, and Gittin. One of them is devoted to what is done by woman here on earth: Sotah. And Yebamot, greatest of the seven in size and in formal and substantive brilliance, deals with the corresponding heavenly intervention into the formation and end of a marriage: the effect of death upon both forming the marital bond and dissolving it through death. The other two tractates, Nedarim and Nazir, draw into one the two realms of reality, heaven and earth, as they work out the effects of vows, perhaps because vows taken by women and subject to the confirmation or abrogation of the father or husband make a deep impact upon the marital life of the woman who has taken them. So, in sum, the Division and its system delineate the natural and supernatural character of the woman's role in the social economy framed by man: the beginning, end, and middle of the relationship.

The Mishnaic system of Women thus focuses upon the two crucial stages in the transfer of women and of property from one domain to another, the leaving of the father's house in the formation of a marriage, and the return to the father's house at its dissolution through divorce or the husband's death. There is yet a third point of interest, though, as is clear, it is much less important than these first two stages: the duration of the marriage. Finally, included within the Division and at a few points relevant to women in particular are rules of vows and of the special vow to be a Nazir. The former is included because, in the Scriptural treatment of the theme, the rights of the father or husband to annul the vows of a daughter or wife form the central problematic. The latter is included for no very clear reason except that it is a species of which the vow is the genus.

There is in the Division of Women a clearly defined and neatly conceived system of laws, not about women in general, but concerning what is important about women to the framers of the Mishnah. This is the transfer of woman and property associated with that same transfer from one domain, the father's, to another, the husband's, and back. The whole constitutes a significant part of the Mishnah's encompassing system of sanctification, for the reason that heaven confirms what men do on earth. A correctly prepared writ of divorce on earth changes the status of the woman to whom it is given, so that in heaven she is available for sanctification to some other man, while, without that same writ, in heaven's view, should she go to some other man, she would be liable to be put to death. The earthly deed and the heavenly perspective correlate. That is indeed very much part of larger system, which says the same thing over and over again.

The formation of the marriage comes under discussion in Qiddushin and Ketubot, as well as in Yebamot. The rules for the duration of the marriage are scattered throughout, but derive especially from parts of Ketubot, Nedarim, and Nazir, on the one side, and the paramount unit of Sotah, on the other. The dissolution of the marriage is dealt with in Gittin, as well as in Yebamot. We see very clearly, therefore, that important overall are issues of the transfer of property, along with women, covered in Ketubot and to some measure in Qiddushin, and the proper documentation of the transfer of women and property, treated in Ketubot and Gittin. The critical issues therefore turn upon legal documents—writs of divorce, for example—and legal recognition of changes in the ownership of property, e.g., through the collection of the settlement of a marriage contract by a widow, through the provision of a dowry, or through the disposition of the property of a woman during the period in which she is married. Within this orderly world of documentary and procedural concerns a place is made for the disorderly conception of the marriage not formed by human volition but decreed in heaven, the levirate connection. Yebamot states that supernature sanctifies a woman to a man (under the conditions of the levirate connection). What it says by indirection is that man sanctifies too: man, like God, can sanctify that relationship between a man and a woman, and can also effect the cessation of the sanctity of that same relationship.

The Division of Damages comprises two subsystems, which fit

together in a logical way. One part presents rules for the normal conduct of civil society. These cover commerce, trade, real estate, and other matters of everyday intercourse, as well as mishaps, such as damages by chattels and persons, fraud, overcharge, interest, and the like, in that same context of everyday social life. The other part describes the institutions governing the normal conduct of civil society, that is, courts of administration, and the penalties at the disposal of the government for the enforcement of the law. The two subjects form a single tight and systematic dissertation on the nature of Israelite society and its economic, social, and political relationships, as the Mishnah envisages them.

The main point of the first of the two parts of the Division is expressed in the sustained unfolding of the three Babas, Baba Qamma, Baba Mesia, and Baba Batra. It is that the task of society is to maintain perfect stasis, to preserve the prevailing situation, and to secure the stability of all relationships. To this end, in the interchanges of buying and selling, giving and taking, borrowing and lending, it is important that there be an essential equality of interchange. No party in the end should have more than what he had at the outset, and none should be the victim of a sizable shift in fortune and circumstance. All parties' rights to, and in, this stable and unchanging economy of society are to be preserved. When the condition of a person is violated, so far as possible the law will secure the restoration of the antecedent status.

An appropriate appendix to the Babas is at Abodah Zarah, which deals with the orderly governance of transactions and relationships between Israelite society and the outside world, the realm of idolatry, relationships which are subject to certain special considerations. These are generated by the fact that Israelites may not derive benefit (e.g., through commercial transactions) from anything which has served in the worship of an idol. Consequently, commercial transactions suffer limitations on account of extrinsic considerations of cultic taboos. While these cover both special occasions, e.g., fairs and festivals of idolatry, and general matters, that is, what Israelites may buy and sell, the main practical illustrations of the principles of the matter pertain to wine. The Mishnah supposes that gentiles routinely make use, for a libation, of a drop of any sort of wine to which they have access. It therefore is taken for granted that wine over which gentiles have had control is forbidden for Israelite use, and also that such wine is prohibited for Israelites to buy and sell. This other matter—

ordinary everyday relationships with the gentile world, with special reference to trade and commerce—concludes what the Mishnah has to say about all those matters of civil and criminal law which together define everyday relationships within the Israelite nation and between that nation and all others in the world among whom, in Palestine as abroad, they lived side by side.

The other part of the Division describes the institutions of Israelite government and politics. This is in two main aspects, first, the description of the institutions and their jurisdiction, with reference to courts, conceived as both judicial and administrative agencies, and, second, the extensive discussion of criminal penalties. The penalties are three: death, banishment, and flogging. There are four ways by which a person convicted of a capital crime may be put to death. The Mishnah organizes a vast amount of information on what sorts of capital crimes are punishable by which of the four modes of execution. That information is alleged to derive from Scripture. But the facts are many, and the relevant verses few. What the Mishnah clearly contributes to this exercise is a first-rate piece of organization and elucidation of available facts. Where the facts come from we do not know. The Mishnah tractate Sanhedrin further describes the way in which trials are conducted in both monetary and capital cases and pays attention to the possibilities of perjury. The matter of banishment brings the Mishnah to a rather routine restatement by flogging and application of that mode of punishment conclude the discussion.

These matters, worked out at Sanhedrin-Makkot, are supplemented in two tractates, Shebuot and Horayot, both emerging from Scripture. Lev. 5 and 6 refer to various oaths which apply mainly, though not exclusively, in courts. Lev. 4 deals with errors of judgment inadvertently made and carried out by the high priest, the ruler, and the people; the Mishnah knows that these considerations apply to Israelite courts too. What for Leviticus draws the chapters together is their common interest in the guilt offering, which is owing for violation of the rather diverse matters under discussion. Now in tractates Shebuot and Horayot the materials of Lev. 5-6 and 4, respectively, are worked out. But here is it from the viewpoint of the oath or erroneous instruction, rather than the cultic penalty. In Shebuot the discussion in intellectually imaginative and thorough, in Horayot, routine. The relevance of both to the issues of Sanhedrin and Makkot is obvious. For the matter of oaths in the main enriches the discussion of the conduct of the courts. The possibility of error is principally in the courts and other political institutions. so the four tractates on institutions and their functioning form a remarkable unified and cogent set.

The goal of the system of civil law is the recovery of the prevailing order and balance, the preservation of the established wholeness of the social economy. This idea is powerfully expressed in the organization of the three Babas, which treat first abnormal and then normal transactions. The framers deal with damages done by chattels and by human beings, thefts and other sorts of malfeasance against the property of others. The Babas in both aspects pay closest attention to how the property and person of the injured party so far as possible are restored to their prior condition, that is, a state of normality. So attention to torts focuses upon penalties paid by the malefactor to the victim, rather than upon penalties inflicted by the court on the malefactor for what he has done. When speaking of damages, the Mishnah thus takes as its principal concern the restoration of the fortune of victims of assault or robbery. Then the framers take up the complementary and corresponding set of topics, the regulation of normal transactions. When we rapidly survey the kinds of transactions of special interest, we see from the topics selected for discussion what we have already uncovered in the deepest structure of organization and articulation of the basic theme.

The other half of this same unit of three tractates presents laws governing normal and routine transactions, many of them of the same sort as those dealt with in the first half. Bailments, for example, occur in both wings of the triple tractate, first, bailments subjected to misappropriation, or accusation thereof, by the bailiff, then, bailments transacted under normal circumstances. Under the rubric of routine transactions are those of workers and householders, that is, the purchase and sale of labor; rentals and bailments; real estate transactions; and inheritances and estates. Of the lot, the one involving real estate transactions is the most fully articulated and covers the widest range of problems and topics. The Babas all together thus provide a complete account of the orderly governance of balanced transactions and unchanging civil relationships within Israelite society under ordinary conditions.

The character and interests of the Division of Damages present probative evidence of the larger program of the philosophers of the Mishnah. Their intention is to create nothing less than a full-scale Israelite government, subject to the administration of sages. This government is fully supplied with a constitution and bylaws (Sanhedrin, Makkot). It makes provision for a court system and procedures (Shebuot, Sanhedrin, Makkot), as well as a full set of laws governing civil society (Baba Qamma, Baba Mesia, Baba Batra) and criminal justice (Sanhedrin, Makkot). This government, moreover, mediates between its own community and the outside ("pagan") world. Through its system of laws it expresses its judgment of the others and at the same time defines, protects, and defends its own society and social frontiers (Abodah Zarah). It even makes provision for procedures of remission, to expiate its own errors (Horayot).

The (then non-existent) Israelite government imagined by the second-century philosophers centers upon the (then non-existent) Temple, and the (then forbidden) city, Jerusalem. For the Temple is one principal focus. There the highest court is in session; there the high priest reigns. The penalties for law infringement are of three kinds, one of which involves sacrifice in the Temple. (The others are compensation, physical punishment, and death.) The basic conception of punishment, moreover, is that unintentional infringement of the rules of society, whether "religious" or otherwise, is not penalized but rather expiated through an offering in the Temple. If a member of the people of Israel intentionally infringes against the law, to be sure, that one must be removed from society and is put to death. And if there is a claim of one member of the people against another, that must be righted, so that the prior, prevailing status may be restored. So offerings in the Temple are given up to appease heaven and restore a whole bond between heaven and Israel, specifically on those occasions on which without malice or ill will an Israelite has disturbed the relationship. Israelite civil society without a Temple is not stable or normal, and not to be imagined. And the Mishnah is above all an act of imagination in defiance of reality.

The plan for the government involves a clear-cut philosophy of society, a philosophy which defines the purpose of the government and ensures that its task is not merely to perpetuate its own power. What the Israelite government, within the Mishnaic fantasy, is supposed to do is to preserve that state of perfection which, within the same fantasy, the society to begin everywhere attains and expresses. This is in at least five aspects. First of all, one of the ongoing principles of the law, expressed in one tractate after another, is that people are to follow and maintain the prevailing practice of their locale. Second, the purpose of civil penalties, as we have noted, is to restore the injured party to his prior condition, so far as this is possible, rather than merely to penalize the aggressor. Third, there is the conception of true value, meaning that a given object has an intrinsic worth, which, in the course of a transaction, must be paid. In this way the seller does not leave the transaction any richer than when he entered it, or the buyer any poorer (parallel to penalties for damages). Fourth, there can be no usury, a biblical prohibition adopted and vastly enriched in the Mishnaic thought, for money ("coins") is what it is. Any pretense that it has become more than what it was violates, in its way, the conception of true value. Fifth, when real estate is divided, it must be done with full attention to the rights of all concerned, so that, once more, one party does not gain at the expense of the other. In these and many other aspects the law expresses its obsession with the perfect stasis of Israelite society. Its paramount purpose is in preserving and ensuring that that perfection of the division of this world is kept inviolate or restored to its true status when violated.

The Division of Holy Things presents a system of sacrifice and sanctuary: Matters concerning the praxis of the altar and maintenance of the sanctuary. The praxis of the altar, specifically, involves sacrifice and things set aside for sacrifice and so deemed consecrated. The topic covers these among the eleven tractates of the present Division: Zebahim and part of Hullin, Menahot, Temurah, Keritot, part of Meilah, Tamid, and Qinnim. The maintenance of the sanctuary (inclusive of the personnel) in dealt with in Bekhorot, Arakhin, part of Meilah, Middot, and part of Hullin.

Viewed from a distance, therefore, the Mishnah's tractates divide themselves up into the following groups (in parentheses are tractates containing relevant materials): (1) Rules for the altar and the praxis of the cult—Zebahim Menahot, Hullin, Keritot, Tamid, Qinnim (Bekhorot, Meilah); (2) Rules for the altar and the animals set aside for the cult—Arakhin, Temurah, Meilah (Bekhorot); and (3) Rules for the altar and support of the Temple staff and buildings—Bekhorot, Middot (Hullin, Arakhin, Meilah, Tamid). In a word, this Division speaks of the sacrificial cult and the sanctuary in which the cult is conducted. The law pays special attention to the matter of the status of the property of the altar and of the sanctuary, both materials to be utilized in the actual sacrificial rites, and property the value of which supports the cult and sanctuary in general. Both are deemed to be sanctified, that is: *qodoshim*, "holy things."

The system of Holy Things centers upon the everyday and rules always applicable to the cult: the daily whole offering, the sin offering and guilt offering which one may bring any time under ordinary circumstances; the right sequence of diverse offerings; the way in which the rites of the whole, sin, and guilt offerings are carried out; what sorts of animals are acceptable; the accompanying cereal offerings; the support and provision of animals for the cult and of meat for the priesthood; the support and material maintenance of the cult and its building. We have a system before us: the system of the cult of the Jerusalem Temple, seen as an ordinary and everyday affair, a continuing and routine operation. That is why special rules for the cult, both in respect to the altar and in regard to the maintenance of the buildings, personnel, and even the hold city, will be elsewhere—in Appointed Times and Agriculture. But from the perspective of Holy Things, those Divisions intersect by supplying special rules and raising extraordinary (Agriculture: land-bound; Appointed Times: time-bound) considerations for that theme which Holy Things claims to set forth in its most general and unexceptional way: the cult as something permanent and everyday.

The order of Holy Things thus in a concrete way maps out the cosmology of the sanctuary and its sacrificial system, that is, the world of the Temple, which had been the cosmic center of Israelite life. A later saying states matters as follows: "Just as the navel is found at the center of a human being, so the land of Israel is found at the center of the world ... and it is the foundation of the world. Jerusalem is at the center of the land of Israel, the Temple is at the center of Jerusalem, the Holy of Holies is at the center of the Temple, the Ark is at the center of the Holy of Holies, and the Foundation Stone is in front of the Ark, which spot is the foundation of the world." (Tanhuma Qedoshim 10).

The Division of Purities presents a very simple system of three principal parts: sources of uncleanness, objects and substances susceptible to uncleanness, and modes of purification from uncleanness. So it tells the story of what makes a given sort of object unclean and what makes it clean. The tractates on these several topics are as follows: (1) sources of uncleanness—Ohalot, Negaim, Niddah, Makhshirin, Zabim, Tebul Yom; (2) objects and substances susceptible to uncleanness—Kelim, Tohorot, Uqsin; and (3) modes of purification —Parah, Miqvaot, Yadayim.

Viewed as a whole, the Division of Purities treats the interplay of persons, food, and liquids. Dry inanimate objects or food are not susceptible to uncleanness. What is wet is susceptible. So liquids activate the system. What is unclean, moreover, emerges from uncleanness through the operation of liquids, specifically, through immersion in fit water of requisite volume and in natural condition. Liquids thus deactivate the system. Thus, water in its natural condition is what concludes the process by removing uncleanness. Water in its unnatural condition, that is, deliberately affected by human agency, is what imparts susceptibility to uncleanness to begin with. The uncleanness of persons, furthermore, is signified by body liquids or flux in the case of the menstruating woman (Niddah) and the zab (Zabim). Corpse uncleanness is conceived to be a kind of effluent, a viscous gas, which flows like liquid. Utensils for their part receive uncleanness when they form receptacles able to contain liquid. In sum, we have a system in which the invisible flow of fluid-like substances or powers serve to put food, drink, and receptacles into the status of uncleanness and to remove those things from that status. Whether or not we call the system "metaphysical," it certainly has no material base but is conditioned upon highly abstract notions. Thus in material terms, the effect of liquid is upon food, drink, utensils, and man. The consequence has to do with who may eat and drink what food and liquid, and what food and drink may be consumed in which pots and pans. These loci are specified by tractates on utensils (Kelim) and on food and drink (Tohorot and Uqsin).

The human being is ambivalent. Persons fall in the middle, between sources and loci of uncleanness, because they are both. They serve as sources of uncleanness. They also become unclean. The zab, the menstruating woman, the woman after childbirth, the Tebul Yom, and the person afflicted with *nega* (Scripture: leprosy)—all are sources of uncleanness. But being unclean, they fall within the system's loci, its program of consequences. So they make other things unclean and are subject to penalties because they are unclean. Unambiguous sources of uncleanness never also constitute loci affected by uncleanness. They always are unclean and never can become clean: the corpse, the dead creeping thing, and things like them. Inanimate sources of uncleanness and inanimate objects are affected by uncleanness. Systemically unique, man and liquids have the capacity to inaugurate the processes of uncleanness (as sources) and also are subject to those same processes (as objects of uncleanness). The Division of Purities, which presents the basically simple system just now described, is not only the oldest in the Mishnah. It also is the largest and contains by far the most complex laws and ideas.

XI. *The Oral Torah Seen Whole:*
The Restoration of Eden through the Reconstruction of Israel's Social Order

Seen whole and in its fully realized formulation in the Mishnah-Tosefta-Yerushalmi-Bavli, the Halakhah of the Oral Torah translates the Pentateuch's cases into rules, the rules into governing, abstract principles—exemplary of the success of the Oral Torah throughout. The formulation as abstractions of rules of cases turns the entire Halakhic structure, a composite of inert information, into a working system, able to absorb and reconstitute a nearly-unlimited variety of discrete and incongruous cases. These the system forms into a single set of coherent principles, an account of the social order and its metaphysical foundations seen whole. The category-formation of the Halakhah, critical elements of which surfaced in Temple times, came to fulfillment only when all of Scripture's category-formations had been taken over and recapitulated in the Halakhah of the Oral Torah, its rules and cases reframed as principles within the large construction we have now surveyed.

It must follow that the Halakhah states in its way, through the formation of social norms, what Scripture sets forth in its manner, through narratives and case-laws. Just as sages found in the Pentateuch, and in the Authorized History from the Pentateuch through Kings, a theological hermeneutics expressed through history, so in the Oral Torah they realized that same theology, now framed as the norms of the social order. The theological system that is built upon the Halakhah set forth in the Mishnah, Tosefta, and baraita-corpus, rests on four propositions, all of them variations on the authorized history of Scripture from Genesis through Kings, that are articulated in the Aggadah contained within the Talmuds and the Midrash-compilations:

1. God formed creation in accord with a plan, which the Torah reveals. World order can be shown by the facts of nature and society set forth in that plan to conform to a pattern of reason based upon justice. Those who possess the Torah—Israel—know God and those who do not—the gentiles—reject him in favor of idols. What happens to each of the two sectors of humanity, respectively, responds to

their relationship with God. Israel in the present age is subordinate
to the nations, because God has designated the gentiles as the medium for penalizing Israel's rebellion, meaning through Israel's subordination and exile to provoke Israel to repent. Private life as much
as the public order conforms to the principle that God rules justly in
a creation of perfection and stasis .

2. The perfection of creation, realized in the rule of exact justice, is
signified by the timelessness of the world of human affairs, their
conformity to a few enduring paradigms that transcend change. Involved here is a theology of history, an account of how God works
through what happens to man. No present, past, or future marks
time, but only the recapitulation of those patterns. Perfection is further embodied in the unchanging relationships of the social com-
monwealth. What is required here is a theology of political
economy, which assures that scarce resources, once allocated, remain in stasis. In that way the politics and economics of the social
order will correspond to that perfection that was attained at Eden. A
further indication of perfection lies in the complementarity of the
components of creation, on the one side, and, finally, the correspondence between God and man, in God's image (theological an-
thropology), on the other. At stake here is an account of God's view
of man, a systematic investigation of how God intended man to be.

3. Israel's condition, public and personal, marks flaws in creation.
What disrupts perfection is the sole power capable of standing on its
own against God's power, and that is man's will. What man controls
and God cannot coerce is man's capacity to form intention and
therefore choose either arrogantly to defy, or humbly to love, God.
Because man defies God, the sin that results from man's rebellion
flaws creation and disrupts world order. The paradigm of the rebellion of Adam in Eden governs, the act of arrogant rebellion leading
to exile from Eden thus accounting for the condition of humanity.
But, as in the original transaction of alienation and consequent exile,
God retains the power to encourage repentance through punishing
man's arrogance. In mercy, moreover, God exercises the power to
respond to repentance with forgiveness, that is, a change of attitude
evoking a counterpart change. Since, commanding his own will,
man also has the power to initiate the process of reconciliation with
God, through repentance, an act of humility, man may restore the
perfection of that order that through arrogance he has marred.

4. God ultimately will restore that perfection that embodied his plan
for creation. In the work of restoration death that comes about by
reason of sin will die, the dead will be raised and judged for their
deeds in this life, and most of them, having been justified, will go on
to eternal life in the world to come. In the paradigm of man restored
to Eden is realized in Israel's return to the Land of Israel. In that
world or age to come, however, that sector of humanity that through
the Torah knows God will encompass all of humanity. Idolaters will

perish, and humanity that comprises Israel at the end will know the one, true God and spend eternity in his light.[18]

Now, recorded in this way, the story told by the Halakhah set forth in the Mishnah-Tosefta-Yerushalmi-Bavli proves remarkably familiar, with its stress on God's justice (to which his mercy is integral), man's correspondence with God in his possession of the power of will, man's sin and God's response. But the Mishnah and the other Halakhic compilations do not tell their story through narrative but through law. The story that the law means to translate into normative rules of conduct turns out to account for the condition of the world and also to adumbrate the restoration of humanity to Eden through the embodiment of Israel in the Land of Israel. That is what I mean when I say that the Oral Torah systematizes the anecdotal rules of the Pentateuch into the design for the social order, the actualization of which restores Eden.

XII. *One Whole Torah, Oral and Written?*

Sages in later generations would call the Mishnah "the oral Torah,"[19] and it is therefore correct to ask, is the purpose of the literature congruent with the message of the Hebrew Scriptures, a.k.a., the Written Torah? If we translate into the narrative of Israel, from the beginning to the calamity of the destruction of the (first) Temple, what is set forth in both abstract and concrete ways in the Oral Torah, we turn out to state a reprise of the story laid out in Genesis through Kings and amplified by the principal prophets. Recorded in this way, the story told through law by the Mishnah and related writings proves remarkably familiar, with its stress on God's justice (to which his mercy is integral), man's correspondence with God in his possession of the power of will, man's sin and God's response.

---

[18] I have shown that these four propositions encompass the entire system of Rabbinic Judaism in my *Theology of the Oral Torah: Revealing the Justice of God* (Kingston, 1999: McGill-Queens University Press).

[19] I refer to my *What, Exactly, Did the Rabbinic Sages Mean by "the Oral Torah"? An Inductive Answer to the Question of Rabbinic Judaism*. Atlanta, 1998: Scholars Press for South Florida Studies in the History of Judaism. This is not the place to ask the historical question, when did the conception of "the dual Torah, oral and written," take shape, and at what point in its development did the "oral Torah" find its definition in the Mishnah and related documents? These questions are answered in that monograph.

Are the Halakhah's sages right about the written part of the Torah, meaning, is what they say the Written Torah says actually what
the ancient Israelite Scriptures say? Will those who put forth the
books of Genesis through Kings as a sustained narrative and those
who in that same context selected and organized the writings of the
prophets, Isaiah, Jeremiah, Ezekiel, and the twelve, in the aggregate
have concurred in sages' structure and system? Certainly others who
lay claim to these same Scriptures from the Gospels forward could
not and did not concur. At the time the sages did their greatest
theological work, in the fourth and fifth century C.E., their Christian
counterparts, in the Latin, Greek and Syriac speaking sectors of
Christianity alike, not only read Scripture in a very different way but
also accused the rabbis of falsifying the Torah. How would the sages
have responded to the charge? They would point to the fact that
nearly every proposition they set forth, the main beams of the structure of faith they construct, all sets securely and symmetrically upon
the written Torah. Proof-texts constantly reinforce the structure by
showing its scriptural foundations. That is why sages speak of the one
whole Torah, in two media, correlative and complementary. Second,
sages' formulation of the Torah, the one whole Torah of Moses, our
rabbi, defines holy Israel's relationship with God for all time to come.
Accordingly—that is now sages' view—if we take up the Oral Torah
and explore its theological structure and system, we meet Judaism,
pure and simple. There we find its learning and its piety, what it
knows about and hears from God, what it has to say to God. So
much for the claim of theological apologetics.

The facts support that claim. Sages have hermeneutics on their
side. In their reading of the written Torah whole, in canonical context, as a record of life with God, they are right to say their story goes
over the written Torah's story. But in the Halakhah of the Mishnah
and its continuator-compilations, they design the story of the restoration of Israel to the Land, of Adam to Eden. Start to finish, creation
through Sinai to the fall of Jerusalem, all perceived in the light of the
prophets' rebuke, consolation, and hope for restoration, Scripture's
account is rehearsed in the Oral Torah. All is in proportion and
balance. Viewed as a systematic hermeneutics, the sages' theology
accurately sets forth the principal possibility of the theology that is
implicit in the written part of the Torah—to be sure, in a more
systematic and cogent manner than does Scripture. And that is with
greater emphasis on the theme that the fulfillment of Scripture's

promise can only be restoration. So it is entirely within the imaginative capacity of the Oral Torah to raise the question: what came before in relationship to what we have in hand? To state the matter more directly, are the rabbis of the Oral Torah right in maintaining that they have provided the originally oral part of the one whole Torah of Moses our rabbi? To answer that question in the affirmative, sages would have only to point to their theology in the setting of Scripture's as they grasped it. The theology of the Oral Torah embodied in the Halakhah of the Mishnah and associated compilations tells a simple, sublime story.

[1] God created a perfect, just world and in it made man in his image, equal to God in the power of will.

[2] Man in his arrogance sinned and was expelled from the perfect world and given over to death. God gave man the Torah to purify his heart of sin.

[3] Man educated by the Torah in humility can repent, accepting God's will of his own free will. When he does, man will be restored to Eden and eternal life.

In our terms, we should call it a story with a beginning, middle, and end. In sages' framework, we realize, the story embodies an enduring and timeless paradigm of humanity in the encounter with God: man's powerful will, God's powerful word, in conflict, and the resolution thereof. The task of the law of the Mishnah and related writings was to spell out the requirements of that community that would restore Adam and Eve to Eden through Israel to the Land of Israel. That is the upshot of the category-formation in three large composites that I found particular to the Oral Torah.

But if about the written Torah I claim sages were right, then what about the hermeneutics of others? If the sages claimed fully to spell out the message of the written Torah, as they do explicitly in nearly every document and on nearly every page of the Oral Torah, so too did others. And those others, who, like the sages, added to the received Scripture other writings of a (to-them) authoritative character, set forth not only the story of the fall from grace that occupied sages but, in addition, different stories from those the sages told. They drew different consequences from the heritage of ancient Israel. Sages' critics will find their account not implausible but incomplete, a truncated reading of Scripture. They will wonder about leaving out nearly the whole of the apocalyptic tradition. But, in the balance, sages' critics err. For no one can reasonably doubt that sages' restorationist reading of Scripture recovers, in proportion and accurate stress and balance, the main lines of Scripture's principal story, the one about creation, the fall of man and God's salvation of man through Israel and the Torah. Adumbrated in Temple times, if not embodied in the category-formations that would frame the structure and the system as a whole, the fully-realized Halakhic system came to fruition in the mid-second century, when the Pentateuchal pattern of exile and return and return reached its recapitulation with the closure of Jerusalem, but the story of the return was yet to commence. It would be a long time in coming to realization.

CHAPTER THREE

FORM AND MEANING IN THE MISHNAH

I. *Formulation and Transmission of the Mishnah: By Whom, For What?*

The dominant stylistic trait of the Mishnah is the acute formalization of its syntactical structure, specifically, its intermediate divisions, so organized that the limits of them correspond to those of formulary pattern.[1] The balance and order of the Mishnah are particular to. Tosefta does not sustainedly reveal equivalent traits. Since the Mishnah is so very distinctive a document, we now investigate the intentions of the people who made it. About whom does it speak? And why, in particular, have its authorities distinctively shaped language, which in Tosefta does not speak in rhymes and balanced, matched declarative sentences, imposing, upon the conceptual, factual prose of the law, a peculiar kind of poetry? Why do they create rhythmic order, grammatically balanced sentences containing discrete laws, laid out in what seem to be carefully enumerated sequences, and the like? Language not only contains culture, which could not exist without it. Language—in our case, linguistic and syntactical style and stylization—expresses a worldview and ethos. Whose worldview is contained and expressed in the Mishnah's formalized rhetoric?[2]

---

[1] This essay makes reference in particular to the Mishnah's Division of Purities and derives from my *History of the Mishnaic Law of Purities* (Leiden, 1977), XXI:298-330. But the same analysis serves for the other five divisions of the Mishnah, which is rhetorically uniform. But anyone who has conducted form-analysis of the Tosefta will know that the generalizations offered here are particular to the document under study; the rhetoric of the Tosefta, viewed as a coherent document (as people these days argue it should be), bears its own distinctive and indicative traits, all the more so, the modes of construction and redaction. If the Mishnah is formalized to facilitate memorization, then the Tosefta does not exhibit the same mnemonic devices and is not meant for memorization (or at least: memorization in the same manner as the Mishnah); that is the fact, all the more so, of the two Talmuds, which as we have them presuppose formulation and transmission in writing, not in memory. But how materials now collected and preserved in the Talmud were originally formulated and transmitted presents another set of problems, to which much more thought must be devoted.

[2] In the discussion that follows I make no reference whatsoever to the similarly stylized and formalized modes of expression in other documents of law or religion, in

There is no reason to doubt that if we asked the tradental-redactional authorities behind the Mishnah the immediate purpose of their formalization, their answer would be, to facilitate memorization. For that is the proximate effect of the acute formalization of their document. Much in its character can be seen as mnemonic. The Mishnah was not published in writing, Lieberman (*Publication*, p. 87) maintains: "Since in the entire Talmudic literature we do not find that a book of the Mishnah was ever consulted in the case of controversies or doubt concerning a particular reading, we may safely conclude that the compilation was not published in writing;, that a written ekdosis [edition] of the Mishnah did not exist." The Mishnah was published in a different way:

> "A regular oral ekdosis, edition, of was in existence, a fixed text recited by the Tannaim of the college. The Tanna ("repeater", reciter) committed to memory the text of certain portions of the Mishnah which he

---

ancient times and later on. Self-evidently, the traits of stylization to which I allude are not distinctive to Mishnah, except in its own context. David Mellinkoff, *The Language of Law* (Boston, 1963) points to many traits of legal language which will be familiar to readers of this work e.g., distinctive use of a common language for a particular purpose, the presence of mannerisms of various kinds, formal words and expressions, and the like. Literary traits of documents much closer to the Mishnah in time upon examination appear to be not distant from the Mishnah's. Remarkably reminiscent of Sifra, the Pahlavi Nirangestan, for example, presents citations of Avesta followed by something very like pericope in dispute-form, a statement of a problem, with diverse opinions, in the names of authorities + guft (= 'omer) + balanced and matched opinions. (I have published some preliminary observations on the correspondence of forms and *Gattungen* in Rabbinic and Zoroastrian texts in *Judaism and Zoroastrianism at the Dusk of Late Antiquity. How Two Ancient Faiths Wrote Down Their Great Traditions.* Atlanta, 1993: Scholars Press for South Florida Studies in the History of Judaism. But the work has scarcely begun.) By interpretation of the relationship between Mishnaic rhetorical patterns and the reality contained and expressed therein and of the larger meaning of that rhetoric is directed wholly and completely to the document at hand and to the system of which it is a principal expression. It is by no means meant to exclude them possibility that similar literary preferences in other systems and their literature generate exactly the same approach to the interpretation of the meaning of those preferences, or the possibility that exactly the same literary traits bear wholly other meanings in other systems. The claim in all that follows is that Mishnaic redactional and formal traits are to be interpreted, in this context, as expressions of the Mishnaic world and testimonies to its conceptions of reality. Systemic interpretation is all that is attempted here. A more wide-ranging and comparative approach certainly is of interest. But since exactly the same phenomenon may, in diverse systems, bear quite various meanings, the comparative approach must be to systems, not to matters of detail. The problem of undertaking the requisite comparison for me is that I known work equivalent to mine in the systematic exposition of the laws, system, and language of rules of uncleanness, e.g., of the Pahlavi code.

subsequently recited in the college in the presence of the great masters of the Law. Those Tannaim were pupils chosen for their extraordinary memory, although they were not always endowed with due intelligence... When the Mishnah was committed to memory and the Tannaim recited it in the college, it was thereby published and possessed all the traits and features of a written ekdosis... Once the Mishnah was accepted among the college Tannaim (reciters) it was difficult to cancel it."

While he speaks with certainty, in fact, Lieberman's evidence for these conclusions is drawn from two sources, first, his own faith in the historicity of sayings within the Rabbinical corpus and stories about how diverse problems of transmission of materials were worked out, second, parallels, only some of them germane but none of them probative, drawn from Graeco-Roman procedures of literary transmission. Nonetheless, that view is broadly acknowledged and should be noted.

Lieberman missed the main point, which is this: the traits of the document itself, which he never subjected to systematic analysis. Considerably more compelling evidence of the same proposition derives from the internal character of the Mishnah itself. But if stylization and formalization testify to a mnemonic program, then absence of the same traits must mean that some materials were not intended to be memorized; or that they were, at least, not so formulated and transmitted as to facilitate memorization; it comes down to the same thing. The Mishnah, and the Mishnah alone, was the corpus to be formulated for memorization and transmitted through 'living books', Tannaim, to the coming generations. Internal traits demonstrate beyond doubt that the Tosefta cannot have been formulated along the same lines. Accordingly, the Mishnah is given a special place and role by those who stand behind it.

In whose worldview is memorization of the principal corpus a major component? The Rabbinic compilations, beginning with Tosefta, claim that the Mishnah as we know it is the product of many generations of formalization and stylization of law. T. Zab. 1:5 speaks of Aqiba's systematizing laws for his pupils. But the evidence before us hardly permits the specification of what was formally and stylistically old, as distinct from the work of the ultimate tradental-redactional generation. On the contrary, what we know strongly suggests, and in my judgment proves, that the work of organization, formulation, and redaction is accomplished in one and the same process by a single generation. There are no substantial traces of many, very extensive earlier collections that have been inserted whole and used as the framework for the organization of tractates or even large intermediate divisions therein.[3] Lieberman (p. 91) translates the pericope in Zabim, "When R. Aqiba systematized Mishnayoth for his pupils." The text refers to Halakhot, laws or legal pericopae. Further (p. 95), he reaffirms, "R. 'Aqiba is explicitly credited with an edition of the Mishnah . . ." This of course is not the substance of the cited saying. And again, "At any rate the part played by R. 'Aqiba as a systemizer of the Mishnah is quite evident from the tradition reported in Aboth deR. Nathan," which says that 'Aqiba "converted the whole Torah into rings" (!). This generates the further notion (p. 96):

> The disciples of R. 'Aqiba continued their teacher's work; they added the comments of R. 'Aqiba and his contemporaries to the body of the new Mishnah . A large number of different versions of the Mishnah was created by R. 'Aqiba's disciples around the middle of the second century. The various Tannaim in the different colleges memorized divergent superpositions on R. 'Aqiba's Mishnah . The multiplication of such different versions of the latter would eventually result in multiplying and deepening controversies in Israel. For this reason R. Judah the Prince undertook a new edition of the Mishnah around the end of the second or the beginning of the third century C.E. His Mishnah was virtually canonized; the rest of the Mishnayoth were declared 'external,' Baraithoth, which had only a secondary authority in comparison with the Mishnah of R. Judah the Prince.

The Order of Purities contains no hint of this long process of re

---

[3] It is true that there clearly are earlier collections, e.g., the apophthegmatic constructions of M. Par. 8: 27 and M. Nid. 6: 2-10. These in fact form intermediate units, in accord with the discussion above. But the claim that various authorities, e.g., Aqiba or some of his students, created whole "the Mishnah s", that is to say, complete and systematic accounts of the halakhic system covering the whole range of the law, certainly is false for our Order. Sometimes a conception of a Yavnean, e.g., Aqiba, Eliezer, or Joshua, or the opposite of such a conception, forms the generative problematic of a (later) tractate. But there is no evidence known to us after our survey of the Order of Purities which justifies the widespread conception that before the Mishnah as we know it were prior, comparable Mishnahs. That is not to suggest that there were not the mishnahs—that is, pericopes, fairly formally fixed cognitive units—or that the language of some of the cognitive units in a general way derives from the period before Rabbi. I think there were. It seems to me that the intermediate units formed around apophthegm or around the names of authorities supports that notion. But the only the Mishnah, the existence of which is indicated by the Mishnah as we know it, is the Mishnah attributed to Judah the Patriarch. I suppose that it is conceptual unclarity that has led to the contrary, and, unfortunately, widespread conception.

vision and complication. Its stylistic economy testifies to formalization and redaction within a single limited circle. The imposition from
the outset (let us say, from the time of Aqiba) of a small handful of
strictly enforced formulaic and redactional conventions is not alleged
in the sources. The claim of the sources (and scholars) summarized
by Lieberman is that there was divergence, that the Mishnah as we
know it was necessitated not merely by the growth of the tradition's
size but the diversity of its character: "the multiplication of different
versions . . ."

We see throughout the Mishnah, when it is properly analyzed as
to its rhetorical traits,[4] the marks of a remarkably coherent, cogent,
and exceedingly limited corpus of literary-formulaic devices and
redactional conventions. We have been wholly unable to point to
significant divergence from a single norm of agglutination: reliance
upon distinctive formulary traits that are imposed on a sequence of
sentences, and upon distinctive thematic substance, expressed by
these same patterned sentences. That is how intermediate units were
put together and accounts also for the formalization of small ones—
without reference to the diversity of authorities cited tlerein. Four
distinctive syntactical patterns characterize all, with the "simple declarative sentence" itself so shaped as to yield its own distinctive
traits. If there are traces of diverse theories of formulation and
redaction of materials in our Order, which would reflect the individual preferences and styles of diverse circles over two hundred
years, we have not found them. Those who maintain that the Mishnah as we know it not merely contains ideas from successive generations but also preserves the language and whole sequences of pericopae made up by these successive generations will want to specify
the criteria for the recognition o the diverse literary results of those
divergent groups.

The unified and cogent formal character of the Mishnah testifies
in particular to that of its ultimate tradent-redactors. We learn in the
Mishnah about the intention of that last generation of Palestinian
authorities, who gave us the document as we have it. It is their way
of saying things that we know for certain. From this we hope to learn
some thing about them and their worldview. One certain fact is that
they choose to hand on important materials in such a form as facili-

---

[4] That work is carried out in my *History of the Mishnaic Law* series, and then
recapitulated in the comparative study of the rhetoric of the various Rabbinic documents in *The Documentary Form-History* project.

tated memorization. The second, which follows closely, is that the document is meant to be memorized. Whether or not it also was copied and transmitted in writing, and whether or not such copies were deemed authoritative, are not questions we can answer on the basis of the Mishnah's internal evidence. Tosefta certainly suggests that the Mishnah pericopae were copied and glossed, but its evidence does not pertain to these larger issues.

II. *Rhetoric and Reality*

It follows that the system of grammar and syntax distinctive to the Mishnah expresses rules and conventions intelligible to members of a particular community, that which stands behind the Mishnah. It certainly is a peculiar kind of formalized language. It is formed to facilitate a principal function, memorization and transmission of special rules. The language of the Mishnah therefore does not relate those who made and used it to one another or to the world in which they lived. It is not a functional instrument of neutral communication. Rather, it distinguishes its users from that ordinary world, and sets apart one aspect of their interrelationships, the one defined in the Mishnah, from such other aspects as do not require speech in a few patterns and in a kind of poetry. Accordingly, while the language represented in part by the Mishnah may or may not have been used for other purposes than those defined by the Mishnah, the way in which that language is used in the Mishnah bespeaks a limited and circumscribed circumstance. How things were said can have been grasped primarily by the people instructed in saying and hearing things in just that way. In this sense formalized language sets the Mishnah apart from its larger linguistic context, for Middle Hebrew was a language utilized outside of Rabbinical circles.

The Mishnah's is language for an occasion. The occasion is particular: formation and transmission of special sorts of conceptions in a special way. The predominant, referential function of language, which is to give verbal structure to the message itself, is secondary in our document. The expressive function, to convey the speaker's attitude toward what he is talking about, the connative function, to focus upon who is being addressed, and other ritualized functions of language come to the fore. The Mishnah's language therefore is special, meant as an expression of a non-referential function (Farb, *Wordplay*, pp. 23-4). So far as the Mishnah was meant to be memorized by a particular group of people for a distinctive purpose, it is language that includes few and excludes many, unites those who use it and sets them apart from others who do not.

The formal rhetoric of the Mishnah is empty of content, which is proved by the fact that pretty much all themes and conceptions can be reduced to these same few formal patterns. These patterns, I have shown, are established by syntactical recurrences, as distinct from repetition of sounds.[5] The same words do not recur, except in the case of the few forms we have specified, or keywords in a few con texts. These forms have to be excised from the formulary patterns in which they occur, e.g., 'WMR, M'SH, the dispute, so that we may discern the operative and expressive patterns themselves. On the other hand, long sequences of sentences fail to repeat the same words —that is, syllabic balance, rhythm, or sound—yet the do establish a powerful claim to order and formulary sophistication and perfection. That is why we could name a pattern, *he who . . . it is . . . apocopation*: the arrangement of the words, as a grammatical pattern, not their substance, is indicative of pattern. Accordingly, while we have a document composed along what clearly are mnemonic lines, *the document s susceptibility to memorization rests principally upon the utter abstraction of recurrent .syntactical patterns rather than on the concrete repetition of particular words rhythms syllabic counts or sounds.*

A sense for the deep, inner logic of word-patterns, of grammar and syntax, rather than for their external similarities, governs the Mishnaic mnemonic. Even though the Mishnah is to be memorized and handed on orally, it expresses a mode of thought attuned to abstract

---

[5] I have not alluded to the high probability that the Mishnah was intended to be chanted. The musical line evidently was meant to serve any sequence of words, determined rather by the structure and position of phrases. Bathja Bayer (*Encyclopaedia Judaica* 15, p. 753) states, "The transmission of an unwritten text depends on constant repetition ..., and the more formal such a text becomes, the more its rendition will tend to develop into a formal—and soon also formulaic—sequence of quasi-melodic phrases." T. Oh. 16:8 has Aqiba tell his students to sing, and b. Meg. 32b is more explicit still, "He who repeats [the Mishnah traditions] without a tune ..." Accordingly, we have every reason to suppose there was some sort of "melodic (or rather melodized) rendition," but we do not know the nature or structure of these melodies for the Mishnah . In any event the repetition of a melodic line for diverse materials will have constituted still one more formal pattern. Everyone knows that in ancient times the classical texts were sung and declaimed, and in the case of philosophical dialogues, some hold they also were performed. So the Mishnah's blatantly formalized character, its rhythms and its matched repetitions, invite just the kind of singing performance that we see, today, in the authentic yeshivas.

relationships, rather than concrete and substantive forms. The formulaic, not the formal, character of Mishnaic rhetoric yields a picture of a subculture that speaks of immaterial and not material things. In this subculture the relationship, rather than the thing or person that is related, is primary and constitutes the principle of reality. The thing in itself is less than the thing in cathexis with other things, so too the person. The repetition of form creates form. But what here is repeated is not form, but formulary pattern, a pattern effected through persistent grammatical or syntactical relationships and affecting an infinite range of diverse objects and topics. Form and structure emerge not from concrete, formal things but from abstract and unstated, but ubiquitous and powerful relationships.

This fact—the creation of pattern through grammatical relation ship of syntactical elements, more than through concrete sounds[6]— tells us that the people who memorized conceptions reduced to these particular forms were capable of extraordinarily abstract perception. Hearing peculiarities of word-order in quite diverse cognitive con texts, their ears and minds perceived regularities of grammatical arrangement, repeated functional variations of utilization of diverse words, grasping from such subtleties syntactical patterns not imposed or expressed by recurrent external phenomena and autonomous of particular meanings. What they heard, it is clear, not only were abstract relationships, but also principles conveyed along with and through these relationships. For what was memorized, as I have said, was a fundamental notion, expressed in diverse examples but in recurrent rhetorical-syntactical patterns. Accordingly, what they could and did hear was what lay far beneath the surface of the rule: both the unstated principle and the unsounded pattern. This means, I stress, that their mode of thought was attuned to what lay beneath the surface, their mind and their ears perceived what was not said behind what was said, and how it was said. Social interrelationships within the community of Israel are left behind in the ritual speech of the Mishnah, just as, within the laws, natural realities are made to give form and expression to supernatural or metaphysical regularities. The Mishnah speaks of Israel, but the speakers are a group

---

[6] To be sure, mnemonic patterns make use of keywords. Furthermore, we do find repetition of whole phrases and large-scale clauses, e.g., a fixed apodosis will serve diverse protases, or a uniform predicate, a range of subjects. But I think these external mnemonic devices are secondary to what is ubiquitous, which is the patterning of grammar and syntax, autonomous of what actually is said and sounded.

apart. The Mishnah talks of this-worldly things, but the things stand for and evoke another world entirely.

Who is the persona, serving as the Mishnah's voice? The Mishnah is remarkably indifferent to the identification and establishment of the character of the person who speaks. It not only is formally anonymous, in that it does not bear a signature or a single first person identification. It also is substantively anonymous, in that it does not permit variation of patterns of formulation to accord with the traits of individuals or even to suggest that individuals who do occur have distinctive traits of speech, word choice, or, in the final analysis, even generative conception. This absence of individuation should not suggest that our Order is essentially neutral as to the imposition of a highly distinctive mode of discourse. The contrary is the case. William Scott Green (*Biography*) states this matter as follows:

> These documents appear to be not accidental, inchoate collections, but carefully and deliberately constructed compilations. Each document has its own ideological or theological agendum, and it is axiomatic that the agendum of any document, though shaped to a degree by inherited materials, ultimately is the creation of the authorities, most of whom are anonymous, who produced the document itself. They have determined the focus, selected the materials, and provided the framework that unites the discrete pericopae and gives the document its internal consistency and coherence. The features of these documents suggest that their agenda transcend the teaching of any single master.
>
> First, rabbinic documents contain a substantial amount of unattributed material. This gives them an atemporal quality, and creates the sense that the document, or the tradition, is speaking for itself, independent of an individual mind.
>
> Second, rabbinic documents are not constructed around the sayings of any individual, but follow either a thematic, formal, topical, or scriptural arrangement in which the teachings of opinions of various masters are gathered together to address a single issue or to interpret a particular verse of scripture. This sort of arrangement points to a process of selection in which the teachings of individuals have been made subservient to the goals of the documents. Indeed, within the documents the comments of the masters and their disagreements with each other almost always focus on matters of detail. The larger conceptions which inform the documents themselves are never called into question . . .
>
> Third, although every teaching in rabbinic literature originated in the mind of an individual, the continued vitality of those teachings depended on the rabbinic circles and communities who preserved and transmitted them. The chain of tradents, only occasionally mentioned by name, the redactors and the editors who stand behind the present form of both discrete pericopae and entire documents substantively

revised, embellished and refined received materials, and sometimes invented new ones, to suit their various agenda.

All of this means that we know about early rabbinic is what the
various authorities behind the documents want us to know, and we
know it in the way they wanted us to know it. Consequently, the historical context, the primary locus of interpretation for any saying attributed
to a given master or story about him is the document in which the
passage appears, not the period in which he is alleged to have lived.

What does the rhetoric of the Mishnah leave unstated? The first
thing we never are told is who is speaking, where we are, and the
purpose for which discourse is undertaken. These may be taken for
granted, but nothing in The Mishnah of our Order and little enough
in Tosefta (T. Zab. 1: 5 at best is a suggestive exception) cares to tell
us about the societal or concrete context of rhetoric. If this is a mode
of communication, then to whom is communication addressed?
Who, we ask again, is the speaker, and who the listener?

The sole evidence of the speaker is the use of the invariable attributive, 'WMR, a particle that bears no meaning particular to a
saying and homogenizes all sayings into a common form. 'WMR
states only that what follows bears the name of an authority and
therefore is claimed to be authoritative. 'WMR is all we are told
about the setting of a saying, where it was said, for what purpose,
and, in all, in what social, spatial, temporal, and intellectual context.
To put matters simply, 'WMR obscures all data of particularity and
human circumstance. Yet 'WMR generally, though not always, is
intellectually partitive. That is, once we have the presence of 'WMR,
we know that a private authority, not the anonymous and unanimous
consensus of the corpus represented by the speaker—the document
—is at hand. The use of 'WMR establishes that the conception now
to be stated is private. No claim is to be made for the consensus of
the community for what is to be said. It follows that the silence of the
Mishnah on the authority behind a saying means to claim the consensus of the community (to speak in solely secular terms) for the
stated proposition.

But is what is stated to be interpreted as transactional, in that
relationships between speaker, listener, and topic are presupposed?
The Mishnah is remarkably reticent on that very matter. Its language
invariably is descriptive, in the continuous participle. Its claim,
through formal rhetoric, is that is the way things are, describes and
establishes the norms and forms of being. There is no speaker nor
person-spoken-to, in the sense that a single individual to some other

gives private expression to what is said (whether it reflects consensus or private opinion) or private context to what is heard. The acute formalization of all things detaches from the private person any claim that he alone says, in his own way, a particular opinion. It imposes upon all sayings the authority of the document as a whole (again, to use secular and descriptive language). The absence of differentiation among, and description of, the audience to what is said bears the same implication. This is how things are, without regard to the situation to which they are addressed, the condition, let alone opinion, of the people by whom they are heard. The abstraction of thought is carried over into the indifference to the nuanced situation of the people by whom and to whom thought is conveyed (see above, p. 18).

In this sense, therefore, the language of the Mishnah and its grammatically formalized rhetoric create a world of discourse quite separate from the concrete realities of a given time, place, or society. The exceedingly limited repertoire of grammatical patterns by which all things on all matters are said gives symbolic expression to the notion that beneath the accidents of life are a few, comprehensive relationships: *unchanging and enduring patterns lie deep in the inner structure of reality and impose structure upon the accidents of the world.* This means, as I have implied, that reality for Mishnaic rhetoric consists in the grammar and syntax of language, consistent and enduring patterns of relationship among diverse and changing concrete things or persons. What lasts is not the concrete thing but the abstract interplay governing an and all sorts of concrete things. There is, therefore a congruence between rhetorical patterns of speech, on the one side, and the framework of discourse established by these same patterns, on the other. Just as we accomplish memorization by perceiving not what is said but how what is said is persistently arranged, so we speak to, undertake to address and describe, a world in which what is concrete and material is secondary. The mode of expression in all contexts is principal.

The Mishnah's ideas are shaped, in particular, as gnomic expressions. They deal with basic truths, make use of devices to create a pattern (if not one of sound). The vocabulary is invariably impersonal, they do or one does or he who. And the verb nearly always is in the present tense, and always is in the present tense for descriptive rules. This too enhances the aura of universal application. So too, "Constructions such as parallelism, symmetry, and reversal of the elements in the expression are common" (Farb, Word Play, p. 118).

Farb states, "These characteristics combine to produce a strategy of language manipulation for the particular purposes of teaching, conveying wisdom, and expressing a philosophy." (Farb, p. 118). But all of this is attained, as we have seen, through formalization of language.

The skill of the formulators of the Mishnah is to manipulate the raw materials of everyday speech.[7] What they have done is so to structure language as to make it strange and alien, to impose a fresh perception upon what to others—and what in Tosefta—are merely unpatterned and ordinary ways of saying things. What is said in the Mishnah is simple. How it is said is arcane. Ordinary folk cannot have had much difficulty understanding the words, which refer to ordinary actions and objects. How long it must have taken to grasp the meaning of the patterns into which the words are arranged, how hard it was and is to do so, is suggested by the necessity for the creation of Tosefta, the Gemarot, and the commentaries in the long centuries since the Mishnah came into being. In this sense the Mishnah speaks openly about public matters, yet its deep substructure of syntax and grammatical forms shapes what is said into an essentially ritualistic language. It takes many years to master the difficult argot, though only a few minutes to memorize the simple patterns. That paradox reflects the situation of the creators of the Mishnah .

Up to now we have said only a little about tense structure. The reason is that the Mishnah exhibits remarkable indifference to the potentialities of meaning inherent therein. Its persistent preference for the plural participle, thus the descriptive present tense, is matched by its capacity to accept the mixture of past, present, and future tenses, which can be jumbled together in a single sentence and, even more commonly, in a single pericope. It follows that the Mishnah is remarkably uninterested in differentiation of times-sequences. This fact is most clearly shown by the *Gemisch* of the extreme-apocopated sentence, with its capacity to support something like the following: "He who does so and so . . . the rain came and wet it down . . . if he was happy . . . it [is] Under the law, If water be put." Clearly, the matter of tense, past, present, future, is simply not relevant to the purpose of the speaker. If tense is irrelevant, however, then we find ourselves in the undifferentiated present. What is said is meant to

---

[7] A reliable statement of the complex linguistic situation is Joseph A. Fitzmyer, "The Languages of Palestine in the First Century A.D.," *Catholic Biblical Quarterly* 32, 1970, pp. 501-531.

bear no relationship whatever to the circumstance or particular time or context in which what is said applies. The absence of a powerful and recur rent system of tense-differentiation is strong evidence in favor of our conception that the Mishnah describes a world detached from time.

The temporal and worldly authority of the Mishnah's unspecified "speaker" likewise is curiously unspecified. What is omitted is any reference to a system of institutional enforcement, political or supernatural. At no point in our Order is there an effort to give nuance to language to be used for one setting, as against some other, in the home as distinct from the Temple, the court, the school, or the street. The homogenization of thought and its expression in a limited and uniform rhetorical pattern impose the conception that the norms are axiomatic for, and expose the logic of, all situations in general, but pertain to none in particular. This once again brings to the surface the notion, implicit in the way the Mishnah says things, that the Mishnah describes how things are, whether or not material-reality conforms. The absence of descriptive reference to a speaker and his role reinforces the conception that this-worldly details of identified authorities, with circumscribed and concrete authority, are not pertinent. The reason is that what comes under description does not depend upon the details of this-worldly institutions. That is why the document is so strikingly indifferent to the differentiation of rhetoric. Diverse ideational materials are reduced to a single rhetoric. The various contexts to which what is said is applicable are never given specific definition in the choice of words or rhetorical patterns. In the profoundly conventional discourse of the Mishnah, the one thing left untouched by the affect of convention is the concrete world which is to conform, whether in fact it does or does not conform.

It scarcely needs saying that this sameness of rhetoric hardly is functional to the situation of ordinary people. If the language of the Mishnah serves a small group, its intent is quite the opposite: to encompass and describe all things. We have therefore to distinguish between the effects of formalization of thought, which produce a private framework of discourse among specialists, and the function thereof, which is to make discourse among individuals public and general and abstract it from the ordinary life. The Mishnah lacks abundant ways to speak in grammatical utterances, reducing to its handful of possibilities all truths about all things pertinent to Purities. A level of address has been chosen, and, it is clear, is severely imposed upon all themes and all contexts. It is not possible for that aesthetic_ mnemonic sameness to express the diverse things which need saying in ordinary circumstances.

In this sense Mishnaic rhetoric, while anti-contextual, creates its own context of meaning. Its indifference to any other setting of discourse but its own is suggested by its partitive attributional formula, the same for all sayings of one genre, and also by its single honorific. The Mishnah is remarkably uninterested in diverse honorifics, using the single title, Rabbi, in all circumstances and for nearly all named authorities. The sole differentiation effected by the title is to omit from consideration the teachings of people who do not have that title, and this is effected solely in Tosefta. The absence of all reference to who is listening imposes an equivalent sameness upon the audience. What is said is said to whom it may concern, and the important parts of what is said are stated by people who are permitted neither individuation nor identification, who talk, as I have emphasized, in the same syntactical patterns about all subjects and in all contexts. In context it is trivial to notice that sexual differences play no role, except as demanded by the setting of a case or rule. Since women do the cooking, cases and examples of rules which deal with kneading dough will use the feminine form. In general, though, in the Mishnah there is neither male nor female, nor is there the slightest suggestion that women speak differently from men. Where a woman is quoted, what she is made to say, hardly surprisingly, is in the familiar rhetoric. The reason is that differences of sex are as irrelevant to the Mishnah's speech-world as differences of context, social status, or institutional circumstance.

Outside of the precedents (ma'asim), the formal characteristics of which are difficult to discern and which in any case occur seldom in the Mishnah, our Order presents remarkably little living dialogue. (X says is not dialogue, nor are disputes and debates dialogical in any natural sense.) Mishnaic syntax is based upon the monologue. Occasionally, as in disputes, two or more monologues are juxtaposed, but scarcely constitute dialogues. The reciter recites. No response is suggested within our document. In this sense, dialogue, a basic form of human speech, is noteworthy for its absence. Tosefta makes up for the matter, with its citation of the Mishnah, as if to assume one side of a conversation, and its even more pronounced effort at inter change, its reference to something mentioned by the Mishnah in the form, "What are . . . ?" or "Under what circumstances . . . ?" But in the main the document's highly formal character precludes the possibility of dialogue, there being only a few ways of possibly uttering a thought, and these, as we have seen, not only formal but also gnomic.

The extraordinary lack of a context of communication—specification of speaker, hearer—of our document furthermore suggests that for the Mishnah, language is a self-contained formal system used more or less incidentally for communication. It is a system for description of a reality, the reality of which is created and contained by, and exhausted within, the description. The saying of the words, whether heard meaningfully by another or not, is the creation of the world. Speech is action and creation. The speech-community represented by the Mishnah stands strongly not only against nuance but also against change. The imposition of conventional and highly patterned syntax clearly is meant to preserve what is said without change (even though, we know, changes in the wording of traditions were effected for many centuries thereafter). The language is meant to be unshakeable, and its strict rules of rhetoric are meant not only to convey, but also to preserve, equally strict rules of logic, or, more really, equally permanent patterns of relationship. What was at stake in this formation of language in the service of permanence? Clearly, how things were said was intended to secure eternal preservation of what was said. Change affects the accidents and details. It cannot reshape enduring principles, and language will be used to effect their very endurance. What is said, moreover, is not to be subjected to pragmatic experimentation. The unstated but carefully considered principles shape reality and are not shaped and tested by and against reality. Use of pat phrases and syntactical cliches divorced from different thoughts to be said and different ways of thinking testifies to the prevailing notion of unstated, but secure and unchanging, reality behind and beneath the accidents of context and circumstance.

Clearly, so far as Middle Hebrew serves as a secular language, the Mishnah has transformed a common speech to sacred language and has done so through peculiar formalization of syntactical structures in particular. Yet we cannot point to anything intrinsically sacred even in those structures and patterns. For example, there is no use of the divine name, no tendency either to cite, let alone to model sentences after those of, Sacred Scripture. Indeed, Scripture is treated with remarkable disinterest. The treatment of leprosy in Leviticus Chapters Thirteen and Fourteen follows an illogical thematic scheme. Negaim revises that theme and introduces the appropriate correc-

tion. Our Order is remarkably uninterested in Scriptural proofs for
its propositions, a matter on which we have dwelt at some length.
Accordingly, what serves as the vehicle of sanctification is the imposition upon common speech of fixed, secular patterns of syntax,
which functionally transform talk about common things into sacred
language through the employment of certain stereotype patterns.
What is regular is sacred. These patterns themselves on the surface,
are routine and secular, yet in function accomplish the sanctification
of language, its transformation into something other than, and different from, ordinary speech. We should expect distinctive word-
choices, but I discern none. (By contrast, a story at b. Qiddushin 70a-
b states that rabbis have their own language, different from that of
ordinary folk (italics=Aramaic):

V.5 A. *There was a man from Nehardea who went into a butcher shop in
Pumbedita. He said to them, "Give me meat."*

B. *They said to him, "Wait until the servant of R. Judah bar Ezekiel gets
his, and then we'll give to you."*

C. *He said, "So who is this Judah bar Sheviskel who comes before me to get
served before me?"*

D. *They went and told R. Judah.*

E. *He excommunicated him.*

F. *They said, "He is in the habit of calling people slaves."*

G. *He proclaimed concerning him, "He is a slave."*

H. *The other party went and sued him in court before R. Nahman.*

I. *When the summons came, R. Judah went to R. Huna, he said to him,
"Should I go, or shouldn't I go?"*

J. *He said to him, "In point of fact, you really don't have to go, because
you are an eminent authority. But on account of the honor owing to the
household of the patriarch [of the Babylonian Jews], get up and go."*

K. *He came. He found him making a parapet.*

L. *He said to him, "Doesn't the master concur with what R. Huna bar Idi
said Samuel said,* 'Once a man is appointed administrator of
the community, it is forbidden for him to do servile labor
before three persons'?"

M. *He said to him, "I'm just making a little piece of the balustrade."*

N. *He said to him, "So what's so bad about the word, 'parapet,' that the
Torah uses, or the word 'partition,' that rabbis use?"*

O. *He said to him, "Will the master sit down on a seat?"*

P. *He said to him, "So what's so bad about 'chair,' which rabbis use, or
the word 'stool,' which people generally use?"*

Q. *He said to him, "Will the master eat a piece of citron-fruit?"*

R. *He said to him, "This is what Samuel said,* 'Whoever uses the
word "citron-fruit" is a third puffed up with pride.' *It should be
called either etrog, as the rabbis do, or 'lemony-thing,' as people do."*

S. *He said to him, "Would the master like to drink a goblet of wine?"*

T. *He said to him, "So what's so bad about the word 'wineglass,' as rabbis say, or 'a drink,' as people say?"*

The story proceeds in its own direction; what is important is now self-evident. Clearly, linguistic usages signified social differentiation. But at no point does our Order of the Mishnah contain an equivalent suggestion. Who used the Mishnah's language? Clearly, people who memorized the Mishnah used it. To them was accorded significant status in the later schools. But that does not answer the question, Who first used this language and for what purpose? The answer by now is familiar. It was a group which proposed to create a document which would be transmitted by memory and therefore required formulation which would facilitate the mnemonic process.

Two facts have been established. First, the formalization of Mishnaic thought-units is separate from the utilization of sound and other extrinsic characteristics of word-choice. It depends, rather, upon recurrent grammatical patterns independent of the choices of words set forth in strings. The listener or reader has to grasp relations of words, in a given sequence of sentences, quite separate from the substantive character of the words themselves.

Accordingly, second, the natural language of Middle Hebrew is not apt to be represented by the highly formal language of the Mishnah. Mishnaic language constitutes something more than a random sequence of words used routinely to say things. It is meant as a highly formulaic way of expressing a particular set of distinctive conceptions. It is, therefore, erroneous to refer to Mishnah-language; rather, we deal with the Mishnaic revision of the natural language of Middle Hebrew. And, it is clear, what the Mishnah does to revise that natural language is ultimately settled in the character of the grammar, inclusive of syntax, of the language. Middle Hebrew has a great many more grammatical sequences than does Mishnaic Hebrew, and, it follows, Mishnaic Hebrew declares ungrammatical—that is, refuses to make use of—constructions which Middle Hebrew will regard as wholly grammatical and entirely acceptable.

The single striking trait of the formalization of Mishnaic language therefore is that it depends upon grammar. And just as, by definition, "Grammar is autonomous and independent of meaning" (Chomsky, p. 17), so in the Mishnah, the formalization of thought into recurrent patterns is beneath the surface and independent of discrete meanings. Yet the Mishnah imposes its own discipline, therefore its own deeper level of unitary meaning, upon everything and anything which actually is said.

To summarize our discussion of Mishnaic rhetoric, let us now ask about the ecology of Mishnaic modes of speech (Haugen, pp. 336-7). What is its classification in relationship to other languages? A variety of Middle Hebrew, it is used in particular by people engaged in the memorization and transmission of teachings on behalf of which is claimed divine revelation. Accordingly, its users are religious specialists. What are the domains of use? So far as we know, the Mishnah's distinctive modes of speech are particular to the Mishnah . But this judgment must be qualified. Even in Tosefta the same modes do not consistently occur and scarcely serve to characterize inter mediate divisions. Accordingly, what is particular to the Mishnah is not the remarkably distinctive sentence-structures we have discerned, but recurrent use of such sentence-structures to give expression)n to sizable groups of cognitive units. That indeed is a limited domain of use. What concurrent languages are employed by the users of this mode of speech? Clearly, we may assume, Middle Hebrew in non-Mishnaic patterns was available to them. Whether in addition they spoke Aramaic or Greek is not equivalently clear, nor do we know that they spoke Middle Hebrew as a language of ordinary use. Accordingly, we do not know the dialinguistical data necessary to answer this question. Does the Mishnah yield evidence of dialect?

The answer is clearly that it does not. On the contrary, the speech is decidedly uniform and unnuanced. To what degree has the Mishnaic variety of Middle Hebrew been standardized, united and codified? Here the answer is clear. We have the highest degree of standardization. What kind of institutional support stands behind the Mishnah ? The answer is not wholly clear from the data we have examined. I am inclined to think that, if we take seriously the claim in behalf of the Mishnah that it is Oral Torah, then we have to assign to the Mishnah the claim of an extraordinary sort of Heavenly support for its variety of patterns of speech. The Mishnah probably also is supported through the activities of those who memorized the language and those who supported them, a wide circle of savants. What are the attitudes of the users toward the language? It certainly is public and ritualistic, not a language of intimacy. Its use assuredly confers upon the user a defined status, leading to personal identification as a Tanna in the schools and a rabbi outside of them. (But the evidence in behalf of these claims is not within the Mishnah itself.)

Finally, how does the Mishnaic variety of Hebrew relate to other languages? The answer is, of course, that it is not a language at all, but, rather, a variety of a language, limited and formalized for special purposes. Its ecology will then share the profile of cultic languages in general, with the qualification that, if Middle Hebrew was widely used, it is a revision of a common language into a cultic language. Its relatedness to, and difference from, unpatterned Middle Hebrew serves to shape and express the ethos and worldview of a particular speech-community.

III. *Form and Meaning*

How and for what purpose was the Mishnah edited into final form, and what is the nature of the sources used for the final product? The consideration of the Mishnah's external traits, of its limited repertoire of patterns of language and of its single and uniform procedure for the conglomeration of materials into intelligible patterns—principal divisions, intermediate divisions, cognitive units—helps to secure the redefinition of these questions. We shall now take up a fresh agendum of questions, but revert time and again to the discussion, just concluded, of Mishnaic rhetoric and its relationship to the social realities of its linguistic world. This results in a measure of repetition, necessitated by the reconsideration, from a different perspective, of virtually identical data.

We turn first to the nature of the sources used in the formulation of the Mishnah. We cannot define or describe these sources—though we must take for granted there were sources of some kind, in which antecedent sayings were preserved—because the Mishnah appears so completely to have reformulated whatever sorts of materials in whatever kinds of collections that were in hand, as to obliterate their former literary-formulary character and distinctive traits. Accordingly, one fact about those who framed and formed the Mishnah as we know it is that, while they drew upon diverse and ancient corpora of ideas, and while at their disposal were not simply ideas but ideas given particular and concrete form in words, sentences, paragraphs, and the like, the formal character of the antecedent heritage has been radically revised. We cannot specify extensive collections of antecedent materials preserved in the Mishnah but revised therein. But we do know that Scripture—a collection of particularly authoritative character—assuredly did exist and was available. Yet its literary character produced no impact whatsoever on that of the Mishnah.[8]

Perhaps, along these same lines, there were catanae of sayings assigned to a given authority. Episodically, the existence of collections organized around a single name has come before us. Likewise, there were constructions of diverse sayings on a wide range of topics organized in terms of a single powerful syntactic and grammatical structure. These too are known. But we have too few of either sort of construction to propose that behind the Mishnah are extensive collections of sayings in the name of a single authority or of rules on diverse topics in the model of a single grammatical syntactical form. If there were, however, form by the Mishnah is joined to, and revised by, substance and deprived of its antecedent organizing power. Authority is rendered secondary to the paramount confluence of substance and form. Accordingly, if we assume that the shards in our hands testify to older corpora, then two earlier modes of redaction, by form and by authority, have been set aside. The Mishnah therefore has its own theory of how sayings are to be stated and organized, and that is, we have proved beyond doubt, in the union of theme and formulary pattern.

It follows that, in the absence of more than episodic evidence, we must speculate about the purpose of the editing of the Mishnah in final form solely by systematically extrapolating from the facts of its redaction insight into the purpose of its redaction. What we learn from the character of the literature about the circle that produced the

---

[8] This fact suggests that Rabbi and his colleagues were remarkably sure of themselves and certain of their own tastes. It would have been far more 'conservative' to take over and revise existing collections, e.g., sayings of a given authority, apophthegmatic constructions, and the like, than to destroy such collections as had come down and rework the whole in the thematic and formulary structure before us. I am reminded of the tearing down of the medieval foundations of Oxford—then many hundreds of years old—and the substitution for such antiquities by the great then modern Palladian architecture of the English Renaissance. The poorer colleges preserved their medieval buildings into modern times; the richer ones replaced them. Such confidence in one's own taste and judgment in my view is commendable. But then as we know, this most modern document is alleged—contrary to the explicit evidence of its fresh, totally unbiblical rhetoric and of all of its cited authorities—also to have been revealed by God to Moses at Sinai!—the allegation of Abot 1:1 on the face of it is contradicted by every line of Mishnah, yet the Rabbinical sponsors of Mishnah made it. I suppose that, while from one viewpoint, this is a paradox, from another, it is unmitigated gall. Signing Moses's name to the Mishnah without even pretending to imitate his language (as was done by the Essenes of Qumran) is like a forger's signing his own name to someone else's check—and successfully cashing it.

literature, so far as that character speaks of those who created it, is nothing whatsoever. The people who made the Mishnah do not want us to know them, as I said above, because, I should imagine, nothing about them was deemed important in the understanding of what they did. That is why they do not organize materials around given names of authorities, though some such constructions do survive. It is futile to ask whether the redactors were lawyers, philosophers, wonder-workers, teachers, government officials, preachers, soldiers, holy men, priests, anointed messiahs, or any of the other things people who produce a holy document such as this might have been. To ask whether they legislated for themselves or for all Israelites is equally hopeless, because, as we know, silent as they are on themselves, so reticent are they about those to whom they seek to speak.

Yet they do take certain things for granted. In order to make sense of what they do tell us, there are things that we have to know and that are not told to us by them. But from the perspective of form and rhetoric the catalogue hardly is a long one. The Mishnah presupposes the existence of Scripture. It is not possible to make sense of the details of any tractate without knowledge of Scriptural laws. Yet what, in rhetoric and grammar, is it about, and in, Scripture that is presupposed? It is not, I have stressed, the style and language of Scripture. It is necessary to know certain facts of Scripture, e.g., that a corpse contaminates, that there is a dimension of the clean and the unclean. The knowledge even of facts of Scripture by themselves cannot, of course, suffice. The Mishnah has distinctive conceptions even of the meaning of simple facts, data of Scripture themselves. In the present context, what is important is that knowledge of Scripture's forms and style in no important way improves understanding of those of the Mishnah or even is relevant to interpreting them.

Yet there is a side to Scripture that, I think, is at the very bed rock of the Mishnah's linguistic character and explains the Mishnah's self-evident preoccupation with the interplay of theme and form. Scripture speaks of creation through words, and, we know, it is as much through how things are said as through what is said that the Mishnah proposes to effect its own creative purpose. The priestly notion of creation by means of speech is carried through in the Mishnah's most distinctive and ubiquitous attributive, X 'WMR, one says, just as at Genesis 1:3, 6, 9, 11, 14, 20, 24, 29, at each of the stages of creation, God says ('MR) something and it is. The supposition of the Mishnah that Scripture is known is, while not trivial, obvious.

There is a second, less blatant supposition. It is that the language of the Mishnah will be understood, its nuances appreciated, its points of stress and emphasis grasped.[9] Our discussion of the cathectically neutral and indifferent style of the Mishnah, its failure to speak to some distinct audience in behalf of some defined speaker, does not obscure the simple fact that the Mishnah is not gibberish, but a corpus of formed and intensely meaningful statements, the form of which is meant to bear deep meaning. Accordingly, the gnomic sayings of the Mishnah, corresponding in their deep, universal grammar to the subterranean character of 'reality,' permit the inference that the reality so described was to be grasped and understood by people of mind. Given the unarticulated points at which stress occurs, the level of grammar autonomous of discrete statements and concrete rulings, moreover, we must conclude that the framers of the Mishnah expected to be under stood by remarkably keen ears and active minds. Conveying what is fundamental at the level of grammar autonomous of meaning, the manifest confidence that the listener will put many things together and draw the important conclusions for himself or herself. That means that the Mishnah assumes an active intellect, capable of perceiving inferred convention, and a vividly participating audience, capable of following what was said with intense concentration.

This demands, first, memorizing the message, second, perceiving the subtle and unarticulated message of the medium of syntax and, grammar. The hearer, third, is assumed to be capable of putting the two together into the still further insight that the cogent pattern exhibited by diverse statements preserves a substantive cogency among those diverse and delimited statements. Superficially-various

---

[9] And, I think I should add, the Mishnah takes for granted that people will want to understand and study the document, that it will be not only interesting but urgent for generations to come. The measure of success in this regard is complete, down to this, my own last and least testimony to the extraordinary power of the Mishnah to engage minds and command attention. Quite bluntly, I think the authorities of the Mishnah cannot have been surprised by their amazing success, because they so stated matters as to secure it to begin with. It is a triumph of rhetoric no less remarkable than that of Plato or other philosophers who wrote to be read and understood outside of their immediate and concrete context. This side to the anti-contextual character of Mishnaic rhetoric should not be missed. And when we take account of the doggedly concrete and uninspiring matters under discussion—not the meaning of knowledge or the definition of the good but the affects of a dead creeping thing on a loaf of bread set aside for a priest— the full nature of Mishnah's achievement comes into view. testifies

rules, stated in sentences unlike one another on the surface and made up of unlike word-choices, in fact say a single thing in a single way. None of this is possible, it goes without saying, without anticipating that exegesis of the fixed text will be undertaken by the audience. The Mishnah demands commentary. It takes for granted that the audience is capable of exegesis and proposes to undertake the work. The Mishnah commands a sophisticated and engaged socio-intellectual context within the Israelite world. The Mishnah's lack of specificity on this point should not obscure its quite precise expectation: The thing it does not tell us is that the Mishnah will be understood. The process of understanding, the character of the Mishnah's language, is complex and difficult. The Mishnah is a document that compliments its audience.

IV. *Language, Reality, and Power*

Language serves the authorities of the Mishnah as an instrument of power, specifically, power to create reality. Wittgenstein (cited by Farb, p. 192) said, "The limits of my language mean the limits of my world." What are the limitations of the Mishnah's formalized modes of speech? What sort of reality is made possible within them and is constructed by them? To what degree, specifically, does Mishnaic language attain new possibilities for the containment and creation of reality precisely by its tendency to avoid explicit generalizations and its perpetual expression of precise but abstract relationships between things only in concrete terms? And, finally, we return to the central and inescapable question, For what purpose was the Mishnah made?

We begin with the gnomic character of Mishnaic discourse. Clearly, the Mishnah claims to make wise and true statements, statements that, moreover, apply at any time and in any place. It follows, second, that the Mishnah proposes to describe how things truly are. And third, accordingly, the people who made the Mishnah did so in order to put together, in a single document and in encapsulated form, an account of the inner structure of reality, specifically, of that aspect of reality that, in their judgment, is susceptible of encapsulation in formally-patterned words. When, fourth, we recall the exceedingly limited repertoire of ways by which statements are made, we recognize that, to the authorities of the Mishnah, all of the diverse and changing things in the world can be reduced to a few simple,

descriptive equations. These, fifth, are to be expressed in particular b
the inner and deep traits of the interrelationships of words, by persistent patterns of grammar and of syntax, rather than by superficial
traits of sound and repetition of concrete thought. The principle is to
be derived by the listener's reflection upon any set of diverse rules or
statements, his contributed perception of what unites the whole,
which will be left unsaid but everywhere deemed obvious.[10]

Relying entirely on the traits of syntax and grammar that are
before us, what can we say about the deepest convictions concerning
reality characteristic of people who spoke in the ways we have considered? There is a deep sense of balance, of complementarity, of the
appropriateness of opposites in the completion of a whole thought.
many times do we hear: if thus, then so, and if not this, then not so.
Mishnaic rhetoric demands, because Mishnah's creators' sense of
grammar requires, the completion of the positive by the negative,
and of the negative by the positive. The contrastive complex predicate is testimony to the datum that order consists in completion and
wholeness. So, too, the many balanced declarative sentences before
us reveal the same inner conviction that in the completion of a pattern, in the working out of its single potentiality through a sequence
of diverse actualities, lie that besought order and wholeness. The fact
that it is the intermediate division that constitutes the formulary context of the Mishnah needs no further specification. Accidents do
require specification and repetition. The Mishnah is scarcely satisfied
to give a single instance of a rule, from which we may generalize. It

---

[10] Professor Wayne A. Meeks comments: "Is it really true of the Mishnah that 'the
limits of its language ac the limits of its world'? Or do we see in the peculiar language
of the Mishnah only a tip of the iceberg that is its linguistic world? Does the Mishnah
create a world or does it presuppose a world?" This is, of course, an entirely valid
observation. Mishnah surely presupposes a world. But the contention here is that the
world presupposed is the world created. We certainly have only the tip of the iceberg
of a linguistic world, as Meeks says. But the Mishnah stands: it is what its makers
wanted it to be, presenting and preserving those patterns of syntax and of thought
which are, by their inclusion, designated for memorization and preservation. Meeks
further comments, "In group language can also function as a shorthand for a more
discursive language which the group ordinarily uses on other occasions or in different
media (e.g., orally instead of in writing, when meeting together rather than speaking
to outsiders). The laconic style of the Mishnah has always struck me as of that sort.
One can hardly understand what is being said unless he already knows. That is, the
reader who understands is not necessarily one of 'remarkably keen ears and active
mind,' but just one who knows the code." I think these points are wholly correct. But
to know the code, one must have remarkable capacities of oral-aural perception and
powers of rapid synthetic reasoning.

strongly prefers to give us three or six or nine instances, on the basis of which we may then conclude that there is, indeed, an underlying rule. The singleton case is not the rule solely for itself, nor, all by itself, for all things.

I do not perceive an equivalent meaning in the duplicated subject. When, however, we come to apocopation—beside the sequentially balanced sentence, the Mishnah's other remarkable formulary structure— we once more perceive something from the external of expression about the mind, the inner structure of which is subject to articulation. What do we have in apocopation? It is, first of all, a powerful sense of superficial incompleteness and disorder. Apocopated sentences form Sentences are composed of disjoined phrases. The subject of such sentences generally is made up of two or more such phrases, each of them introducing its own actor and acted upon, its subject and predicate. What unites the several clauses and imposes meaning upon all of them is the ultimate predicate. This, by itself, cannot always be asked to refer to any single one of the phrases of the subject. But it encompasses the result of all of them, all together. It is, there fore, a construction, the meaning of which depends upon a context that is inferred from, but not made explicit by, its constituents. In a profound sense, the apocopated sentence, that we found so distinctive to the Mishnah, expresses that deep sense of a wholeness beneath discrete parts that Mishnaic language presupposes.

For it is the mind of the hearer that makes sense of the phrases and clauses of the subject and perceives the relationship, endowing whole meaning upon the clauses of the subject, required by the predicate. The mind of the hearer is central in the process by which apocopation attains meaning. The capacity for perceiving the rational and orderly sense of things exhibited by that mind is the unstated necessity of apocopation. That, as we have seen in the preceding discussion, is characteristic of Mishnaic modes of expression, there fore also of perception. Hearing discrete rules, applicable to cases related in theme and form, but not in detail and concrete actualities, the hearer puts together two things. First is the repetition of grammatical usages. Second is the repetition of the same principle, the presence of which is implied by the repetition of syntactical patterns in diverse cases. These two, stable principle and disciplined grammar autonomous of meaning, are never stated explicitly but invariably present implicitly.

So there are these two striking traits of mind reflected within Mishnaic rhetoric: first, the perception of order and balance, second, the perception of the mind's centrality in the construction of order and balance, the imposition of wholeness upon discrete cases, in the case of the routine declarative sentence, and upon discrete phrases, in the case of the apocopated one. Both order and balance are contained from within and are imposed from without. The relation ships revealed by deep grammatical consistencies internal to a sentence and the implicit regularities revealed by the congruence and cogency of specified cases rarely are stated but always are to be discerned. Accordingly, the one thing that the Mishnah invariably does not make explicit but that always is necessary to know is, I stress, the presence of the active intellect, the participant who is the hearer. It is the hearer who ultimately makes sense of, perceives the sense in, the Mishnah. Once more we are impressed by the Mishnah's expectation of high sophistication and profound sensitivity to order and to form on the part of its impalpable audience.

In this sense the Mishnah serves both as a book of laws and as a book for learners, a law-code and a schoolbook. But it is in this sense alone.

If our Order of the Mishnah is a law-code, it is remarkably reticent about punishments for infractions of its rules. It rarely says what one must do, or must not do, if he or she becomes unclean, and hardly even alludes to punishments or rewards consequent upon disobedience or obedience to its laws. "Clean" and "unclean" rhetorically are the end of the story and generate little beyond themselves.

If our Order serves as a schoolbook, it never informs us about its institutional setting, speaks of its teachers, sets clear-cut perceptible educational goals for its students, and, above all, attempts to stand in relationship to some larger curriculum or educational and social structure. Its lack of context and unselfconsciousness framework of discourse hardly support the view that, in a this-worldly and ordinary sense, we have in our hands a major division of a law-code or of a schoolbook.

Nor is the Mishnah a corpus of traditions that lay claim to authority or to meaning by virtue of the authorities cited therein. That is why the name of an authority rarely serves as a redactional fulcrum. As I have stressed, the tense-structure is ahistorical and anti-historical. Sequences of actions generally are stated in the descriptive present tense. Rules attain authority not because of who says them, but because (it would seem) no specific party at a specific time stands behind them. The reason, I think, that shortly after the promulgation of the Mishnah, the Mishnah gained for itself the place in the revealed Torah of Moses at Sinai, testifies against its capacity to serve as an essentially historical statement of who said what, when, and for which purpose. The Mishnah, as I have emphasized, is descriptive of how things are. It is indifferent to who has said so, uninterested in the cumulative past behind what it has to say. These are not the traits of a corpus of "traditions." I am inclined to think that law-code, school-book, and corpus of traditions all are not quite to the point of the accurate characterization of the Mishnah.

Yet, if not quite to the point, all nonetheless preserve a measure of proximate relevance to the definition of the Mishnah. The Mishnah does contain descriptive laws. These laws require the active participation of the mind of the hearer, thus are meant to be learned, not merely obeyed, and Self-evidently are so shaped as to impart lessons, not merely rules to be kept. The task of the hearer is not solely or primarily to obey, though I think obedience is taken for granted, but to participate in the process of discovering principles and uncovering patterns of meaning. The very form of Mishnaic rhetoric, its formalization and the function of that form testify to the role of the learner and hearer, that is, the student, in the process of definitive and indicative description, not communication, of what is and of what is real. Self-evidently, the Mishnah's citation of authorities makes explicit the claim that some men, now dead, have made their contribution, therefore have given shape and substance to tradition, that which is shaped by one and handed onward by another. So the Mishnah indeed is, and therefore is meant as, a law-code, a school-book, and a corpus of tradition. It follows that the purpose for which the Mishnah was edited into final form was to create such a multi-purpose document, a tri partite goal attained in a single corpus of formed and formal sayings. And yet, it is obvious, the Mishnah is something other than these three things in one. It transcends the three and accomplishes more than the triple goals that on the surface form the constitutive components of its purpose.

To describe that transcendent purpose, we return to Wittgenstein's saying. "The limits of my language mean the limits of my world." The Mishnah's formulaic rhetoric on the one side imposes limits, boundaries, upon the world. What fits into that rhetoric, can be said by it, constitutes world, world given shape and boundary by the Mishnah. The Mishnah implicitly maintains, therefore, that a wide range of things fall within the territory mapped out by a limited number of linguistic conventions, grammatical sentences. What is grammatical can be said and therefore constitutes part of the reality created by Mishnaic word. What cannot be contained within the grammar of the sentence cannot be said and therefore falls outside of the realm of Mishnaic reality. Mishnaic reality consists in those things that can attain order, balance, and principle. Chaos then lies without. Yet, if we may extrapolate from the capacity of the impoverished repertoire of grammar to serve for all sorts of things, for the eleven topics of our Order, for example, then .re must concede that all things can be said by formal revision. Everything can be reformed, reduced to the order and balance and exquisite sense for the just match characteristic of the Mishnaic pericope. Anything of which we wish to speak is susceptible of the ordering and patterning of Mishnaic grammar and syntax. That is a fact that is implicit throughout our Order. Accordingly, the territory mapped out by Mishnaic language encompasses the whole of the pertinent world under discussion. There are no thematic limitations of Mishnaic formalized speech.

Yet reality, the world of clean and unclean in the present context, is forced to surpass itself, to strive for a higher level of order and meaning through its submission to Mishnaic formalization. Implicit in the rhetoric of our document is the notion, now alluded to many times, of deep regularities that in principle unite cases, just as regularities in rhetoric unite cases. What is abstract need not be spelled out and instantiated endlessly because it already is spelled out through recurrent, implicit relationships among words, among cases. In this context we recall Green's statement (cited above), "If the performance of rituals within the Temple exposes the lines of God's revealed reality, then thinking. . . about these rituals out side the Temple, even without the possibility of performing all of them, has the same result. The Mishnaic rabbis express their primary cognitive statements, their judgments upon large matters, through . . . law, not through myth or theology, neither of which is articulated at all. Early Rabbinism took ritual beyond the realm of practice and transformed it into the object of speculation and the substance of thought. Study, learning, and exposition became. . . the basic Rabbinic activity. . ." Restating this view in terms of Mishnaic grammatical rhetoric, we may say that the thinking about matters of detail within a particular pattern of cognitive constructions treats speculation and thought as themselves capable of informing and shaping being, not merely expressing its external traits.

V. *Language Becomes ontology*

Language in the Mishnah replaces cult, formalism of one kind takes the place of formalism of another. The claim that infinitely careful and patterned doing of a particular sort of deeds is ex opere operato an expression of the sacred has its counterpart in the implicit character of the Mishnah's language. Its rhetoric is formed with infinite care, according to a finite pattern for speech, about doing deeds of a particular sort. Language now conforms to cult then. The formal cult, once performed in perfect silence, now is given its counterpart in formal speech. Where once men said nothing, but through gesture and movement, in other circumstances quite secular, performed holy deed, now they do nothing, but through equally patterned revision of secular words about secular things perform holy speech. In the cult it is the very context that makes an intrinsically neutral, therefore secular, act into a holy one. Doing the thing right, with precision and studied care, makes the doing holy. Slaughtering an animal, collecting its blood and butchering it, burning incense and pouring wine— these by themselves are things that can be and are done in the home as much as in the cult. But in the cult they are characterized by formality and precision. In the Mishnah, by contrast, there is no spatial context to sanctify the secular act of saying things. The con text left, once cult is gone, is solely the cultic mode of formalism, the ritualization of speech, that most neutral and commonplace action. the Mishnah transforms speech into ritual and so creates the surrogate of ritual deed. That which was not present in cult, speech, is all that is present now that the silent cult is gone. And, it follows, it is by the formalization of speech, its limitation to a few patterns, and its perfection through the creation of patterns of relationships in particular, that the old nexus of Heaven and earth, the cult, now is to be replicated in the new and complementary nexus, cultic speech about all things.

What the limitation of Mishnaic language to a few implicit relational realities accomplishes, therefore, is the reduction of the world to the limits of language. In ritual-grammar the world therein contained and expressed attains formalization among, and simplification by, the unstated but remarkably few principles contained within, and stated by, the multitudinous cases that correspond to the world. Mishnaic language makes possible the formalization of the whole of the everyday and workaday world. It accomplishes the transformation of all things in accord with that sense for perfect form and unfailing regularity that once were distinctive to the operation of the cult. Mishnaic language explores the possibility of containing and creating a new realm of reality, one that avoids abstractions and expresses all things only through the precision of grammatical patterns, that is, the reality of abstract relationships alone.

Have we come closer to a perception of the purpose for which, according to the internal testimony of our Order, the Mishnah was created? In a concrete sense, of course, we have not. Mishnaic rhetoric says nothing explicit about the purpose of the rhetoric. In the simplest sense, as we noted long ago, the proximate purpose of formalization was to facilitate the mnemonic process. Yet it is to beg the question to say that the purpose of facilitating memorization is to help people remember things. The Mishnah wants to be memorized for a reason. The reason transcends the process, pointing, rather, to its purpose. Nor do we stand closer to the inner intentions of the Mishnah's authorities when we raise the polemical purpose of memorization. This was to act out the claim that there are two components of the one whole Torah that "Moses, our rabbi," received from God at Sinai, one transmitted in writing, the other handed on by tradition, in oral form only. True, the claim for the Mishnah, laid down in Abot, the Mishnah's first and most compelling apologetic, is that the authority of the Mishnah rests upon its status as received tradition of God. It follows that tradition handed on through memory is valid specifically because, while Self-evidently not part of the written Torah, which all Israel has in hand, it is essential to the whole Torah. Its mode of tradition through memory verifies and authenticates its authority as tradition begun by God, despite its absence from the written part of Torah. Both these things—the facilitation of memorization, the authentication of the document through its external form —while correct also are post facto. They testify to the result of Mishnaic rhetoric for both educational-tradental and polemical apologetic purposes. Once we memorize, we accomplish much. But why, to begin with, commit these gnomic sayings to such language as facilitates their memorization?

In a world such as the Mishnah's, in which writing is routine, memorization is special. What happens when we know something by heart that does not happen when we must read it or look for it in a scroll or a book is that when we walk in the street and when we sit at home, when we sleep and when we awake, we carry with us in our everyday perceptions that memorized gnomic saying. The process of formulation through formulization and the coequal process of memorizing patterned cases to sustain the perception of the under lying principle, uniting the cases just as the pattern unites their language, extends the limits of language to the outer boundaries of experience, the accidents of everyday life itself. Gnomic sayings are routine in all cultures. But the reduction of all truth, particularly to gnomic sayings is not.

To impose upon those sayings an underlying and single structure of grammar corresponding to the inner structure of reality is to transform the structure of language into a statement of ontology. Once our minds are trained to perceive principle among cases and pattern within grammatical relationships, we further discern in the concrete events of daily life both principle and underlying autonomous pattern. The form of the Mishnah is meant to correspond to the formalization perceived within, not merely upon imposed upon, the conduct of concrete affairs, principally, the meaning and character of concrete happenings among things, in the workaday life of people. The matter obviously is not solely ethical, but the ethical component is self-evident. It also has to do with the natural world and the things that break its routine, of which our Order speaks so fully and in such exquisite detail. Here all things are a matter of relationship, circumstance, fixed and recurrent interplay. *If X, then Y, if not X, then not Y—* that is the datum by which minds are shaped.

The way to shape and educate minds is to impart into the ear, thence into the mind, perpetual awareness that what happens recurs, and what recurs is pattern and order, and, through them, wholeness. How better than to fill the mind with formalized sentences, generative both of meaning for themselves and of significance beyond themselves, in which meaning rests upon the perception of relation ship? Pattern is to be discovered in alertness, in the multiplicity of events and happenings, none of which states or articulates pattern. Mind, trained to memorize through what is implicit and beneath the surface, is to be accustomed and taught in such a way to discern pattern. Order is because order is discovered, first in language, then in life. As the cult in all its precise and obsessive attention to fixed detail effected the perception that from the orderly center flowed lines of meaning to the periphery, so the very language of the Mishnah, in the particular traits which I have specified, also in its precise and obsessive concentration on innate and fixed relationship, effects the

perception of order deep within the disorderly world of lacunae.
nature, and man.

What we have said about matters of form and language has now
to be set into the appropriate context of our document, which is, the
realm of the sacred. For the memorization and repetition of the
Mishnah from the time of the creation of the Mishnah are perceived
as holy, an intrinsically sacred action, not merely an informative and
functionally useful one. Indeed, given the subject-matter of our Order, it is difficult to see why someone should want the in formation of
the Mishnah, or what function thereby is to be served. Accordingly,
we turn at the end to a discussion o the character of religion, so far as
religion conveys a worldview, as the Mishnah's formal character certainly does. Clifford Geertz (*Ethos*, pp. 421-2) states:

> In recent anthropological discussion, the moral (and aesthetic) aspects
> of a given culture, the evaluative elements, have commonly been
> summed up in the term 'ethos,' while the cognitive, existential aspects
> have been designated by the term 'worldview.' A people's ethos is the
> tone, character, and quality of their life, its moral and aesthetic style
> and mood; it is the underlying attitude toward them selves and their
> world that life reflects. Their worldview is their picture of the way
> things, in sheer actuality, are, their concept of nature, of self, of society.
> It contains their most comprehensive ideas of order. Religious belief
> and ritual confront and mutually confirm one another; the ethos is
> made intellectually reasonable by being shown to represent a way of life
> implied by the actual state of affairs which the worldview describes, and
> the worldview is made emotionally acceptable by being presented as an
> image of the actual state of affairs of which such a way of life is an
> authentic expression.
>
> This demonstration of a meaningful relation between the values a
> people holds and the general order of existence within which it finds
> itself is an essential element in all religions, however those values or that
> order be conceived. Whatever else religion may be, it is in part an
> attempt (of an implicit and directly felt rather than explicit and con-
> sciously thought about sort) to conserve the fund of general meanings in
> terms of which each individual interprets his experience and organizes
> his conduct...Sacred symbols thus relate an ontology and a cosmology
> to an aesthetics and a morality: their peculiar power comes from their
> presumed ability to identify fact with value at the most fundamental
> level, to give to what is otherwise merely actual, a comprehensive, nor-
> mative import. The number of such synthesizing symbols is limited in
> any culture, and though in theory we might think that a people could
> construct a wholly autonomous value system independent of any meta-
> physical referent, an ethics without ontology, we do not in fact seem to
> have found such a people. The tendency to synthesize world view and

ethos at some level, if not logically necessary, is at least empirically
coercive; if it is not philosophically justified, it is at least pragmatically
universal ... It is a cluster of sacred symbols, woven into some sort of
ordered whole, which makes up a religious system . . .

For those who are committed to it, such a religious system seems to
mediate genuine knowledge, knowledge of the essential conditions in
terms of which life must, of necessity, be lived . . . Religion supports
proper conduct by picturing a world in which such conduct is only
common sense.

It is only common sense because between ethos and worldview between the approved style of life and the assumed structure of reality,
there is conceived to be a simple and fundamental congruence such that
they complete one another and lend one another meaning.

I have cited Geertz at length because he serves to complete the
present discussion. What I have tried to show is that intrinsic and
essential to the ethos of that life represented and formed by the
Mishnah is an aesthetic that also is an ontology, an aesthetic that
contains within itself a profound and implicit, but never articulated,
world view.

There is a perfect correspondence between what the Mishnah proposes to say and the way in which it says it. An essential part of the
ethos of Mishnaic culture is its formal and formulaic sentence, the
means by which it makes its cognitive statements and so expresses its
world view. Not only does ethos correspond to worldview, but worldview is expressed in style as much as in substance. In the case of
Mishnaic form, the ethos and worldview come together in the very
elements of grammatical formalization, which, never made articulate,
express the permanence and paramount character of relationship,
the revelatory relativity of context and circumstance. Life attains
form in structure. It is structure that is most vivid in life. The medium
for the expression of the worldview is the ethos. But for the Mishnah,
ethos neither appeals to, nor, so far as I can see, expresses, emotion.
Just as there is no room for nuance in general in the severe and
balanced sentences of the Mishnah, so there is no place for the nuance of emotion or 'commitment' in general. The rhetoric of our
document makes no appeal to emotion or to obedience, describing,
not invoking, the compelling and ineluctable grounds for assent. This
claim that things are such and so, relate in such and such a way,
without regard or appeal to how we want them to be, is unyielding.
Law is law, despite the accidents of workaday life, and facts are facts.
The bearer of facts and the maker of law is the relationship, the
pattern by which diverse things are set into juxtaposition with one

another, whether subject and predicate, or dead creeping thing and loaf of Heave-offering. What is definitive is not the thing but the context and the circumstance, the time, the condition, the intention of the actor. In all, all things are relative to relative things.

The bridge from ethos to worldview is the form and character of the sentence that transforms the one into the other. The declarative sentence through patterned language takes attitude and turns it into cognition. Mishnaic "religion" not only speaks of values. Its mode of speech is testimony to its highest and most enduring, distinctive value. This language does not speak of sacred symbols but of pots and pans, of menstruation and dead creeping things, of ordinary water that, because of the circumstance of its collection and location, possesses extraordinary power, of the commonplace corpse and the ubiquitous diseased person, of genitalia and excrement, toilet-seats and the flux of penises, of stems of pomegranates and stalks of leeks, of rain and earth and clay ovens, wood, metal, lass, and hide. This language is fllled with words for neutral things of humble existence. It does not speak of holy things and is not symbolic in its substance. It speaks of ordinary things, of workaday things that everyone must have known. But because of the peculiar and particular way in which it is formed and formalized, this same language not only adheres to an aesthetic theory but expresses a deeply embedded ontology and methodology of the sacred, specifically of the sacred within the secular, and of the capacity for regulation, therefore for sanctification, within the ordinary.

To conclude: Worldview and ethos are synthesized in language. The synthesis is expressed in grammatical and syntactical regularities. What is woven into some sort of ordered whole is not a cluster of sacred symbols. The religious system is not discerned within symbols at all. Knowledge of the conditions of life is imparted principally through the description of the commonplace facts of life, which symbolize, stand for, nothing beyond themselves and their consequences for the clean and the unclean. That description is effected through the construction of units of meaning, intermediate divisions composed of cognitive elements. The whole is balanced, explicit in detail, but reticent about the whole, balanced in detail but dumb about the character of the balance. What is not said is what is eloquent and compelling as much as what is said. Accordingly, that simple and fundamental congruence between ethos and world view is to begin with, for the Mishnah, the very language by which the one is given cognitive expression in the other. The medium of patterned speech conveys the meaning of what is said.

Abbreviations

Chomsky, *Language* = Noam Chomsky, *Language and Mind* (N.Y., 1972)

Chomsky, *Reflections* = Noam Chomsky, *Reflections on Language* (N.Y., 1975)

Chomsky, *Structures* = Noam Chomsky, *Syntactic Structures* (The Hague, 1957)

Farb, *Word Play* = Peter Farb, *Word Play. What Happens When People Talk* (N.Y., 1974)

Fishman = Joshua A. Fishman, *The Sociology of Language. An Interdisciplinary Social Science Approach to Language in Society* (Rosley, 1972)

Geertz, *Ethos* = Clifford Geertz, "Ethos, World-View, and the Analysis of Sacred Symbols," *The Antioch Review* 1957, 17:421-437

Geertz, *Religion* = Clifford Geertz, "Religion as a Cultural System," *Anthropological Approaches to the Study of Religion.* Edited by Michael Banton (London, 1966), pp. 1-46.

Green, *Biography* = William Scott Green, "What's in a Name? The Problematic of Rabbinic 'Biography,'" in *Approaches to Ancient Judaism* Volume II, ed. By William Scott Green (Missoula, 1977).

Haugen = Einar Haugen, *The Ecology of Language* (Stanford, 1972)

Lieberman, *Publication* = Saul Lieberman, "The Publication of the Mishnah," in his *Hellenism in Jewish Palestine* (N.Y., 1950) pp. 83-99

Mellinkoff, *Law* = David Mellinkoff, *The Language of the Law* (Boston, 1963)

INDEX